The Atlas of Languages

The Tower of Babel. The biblical story tells of how God destroyed the tower to teach men humility. To confound universal language, He scattered men over the earth speaking in strange tongues so that none could understand the other.

The Atlas of Languages

Revised Edition

The Origin and Development of Languages Throughout the World

Consultant Editors

Bernard Comrie, Stephen Matthews, and Maria Polinksy

Foreword by Jean Aitchison

Facts On File, Inc.

Contents

A QUARTO BOOK

Copyright 2003, 1996 by Quarto Inc.

For information contact:
Facts On File, Inc.
132 West 31st Street
New York NY 10001

Library of Congress Cataloging-in-Publication Data

The atlas of languages : the origin and development of languages throughout the world / consultant editors, Bernard Comrie, Stephen Matthews, and Maria Polinsky ; foreword by Jean Aitchison.--Rev. ed.
p. cm.
Includes bibliographical references and index.
ISBN 0-8160-5123-2
I. Language and languages. I. Comrie, Bernard, 1947-
II. Matthews, Stephen, 1963- III. Polinsky, Maria.

P107.A87 2003
400--dc21
2003043458

ISBN: 0-8160-5123-2

Facts On File books are available at special discounts when purchased in bulk quantities for businesses, associations, institutions, or sales promotions. Please call our Special Sales Department in New York at (212) 967-8800 or (800) 322-8755.

You can find Facts On File on the World Wide Web at
http://www.factsonfile.com

This book was designed and produced by
Quarto Publishing plc
The Old Brewery
6 Blundell Street
London N7 9BH

Editor *Paula Regan*
Designer and Art editor *Elizabeth Healey*
Cover design by *Cathy Rincon*
Cartographer *Julian Baker*
Illustrator *Andrew Green*
Proofreader *Gillian Kemp*
Indexer *Pamela Ellis*

Publisher *Piers Spence*
Art Director *Moira Clinch*

Manufactured by Universal Graphics, Singapore
Printed by Star Standard, Singapore

10 9 8 7 6 5 4 3 2 1

Foreword   6
by Jean Aitchison

Introduction   8
by Bernard Comrie

CHAPTER 1
Development and
Spread of Languages   16
by Stephen Matthews

CHAPTER 2
Europe and Eurasia   36
by Stephen Matthews and
Maria Polinsky

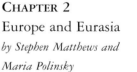

CHAPTER 3
South and
Southeast Asia   56
by Stephen Matthews

CHAPTER 4
Africa and the
Middle East   72
by Owen Nancarrow

CHAPTER 5
Pacific   90
*by Maria Polinsky and
Geoffrey Smith*

CHAPTER 6
Australia   108
by Peter Austin

CHAPTER 7
The Americas   124
by John Stonham

CHAPTER 8
Pidgins and Creoles   142
*by Geoffrey Smith and
Stephen Matthews*

CHAPTER 9
Writing Systems   160
by Roger Woodard

Epilogue   208
*by Stephen Matthews and
Maria Polinsky*

Glossary of terms 218

Bibliography 219

Index 220

Acknowledgments 224

Foreword

Languages are forever changing. Some disappear as traditional ways of life are threatened, others survive but in changed forms. Many of the minority languages in China, for example, such as Miao and Tibetan, are being replaced by Chinese.

Humans, like cows, grasshoppers, woodpeckers, and many other animals, communicate primarily via sounds. Yet language, the human communication system, is the most versatile of all: it can be transferred to writing, or signs, and it can discuss anything, whether it is present, out of sight, or imaginary. Any normal human can produce and comprehend an indefinite number of sentences that have never been said before, even quite bizarre ones, such as "My dodo needs a new toothbrush." And new words are coined daily. Open-endedness is therefore a key characteristic of human language. Consequently, it always has changed, and always will. Yet changes do not cause language to spiral out of control, and become irremediably strange. Any human can potentially learn any language. An English baby adopted by Quechuan or Turkish speaking parents would grow up speaking fluent Quechuan or Turkish with no difficulty. Language, we now realise, is an intrinsic part of being human, and is biologically programed into the species. This powerful communication system emerged around 100,000 years ago, probably in the east of Africa, according to current majority opinion. Humans moved northward into Asia Minor maybe 50,000 years ago, then spread around the world. As humans traveled, languages split and proliferated. There are now around 5,000 languages, according to most counts. They can be grouped into around a dozen major clusters, and a number of minor ones. No languageless community has ever been found. Yet in spite of the importance of language to humans, most people know very little about languages other than their own. Even the names of languages are unfamiliar, and faced with a set of them, say, Abaza,

Dyirbal, Hmong, Hopi, Shona, many English speakers would have a hard time specifying even the continent in which they are spoken. Nor would they know any quick way to find out about them. Even if they found the language listed in an encyclopedia, they would then have to move to a second book, a geographical atlas, to find out the location of the speakers.

One major problem is that languages are spoken by people, and people move around, sometimes in huge groups. The distribution of languages inevitably changes faster than the course of rivers. Views alter on which languages were spoken where in the past: currently, huge controversy surrounds exactly when humans reached America, for example, and how their languages spread. And massive population shifts have occurred throughout history. So publishers have mostly shied away from the task of producing linguistic atlases.

But not now. This Atlas of Languages *is an important and worthwhile project. It maps in a useful, clear and easily consultable way what is spoken where at the beginning of the 21st century. This information may be especially important, because only around one-tenth of today's languages will still be spoken in a hundred years time, according to some current estimates. Hopefully, readers will be inspired to learn more about the splendiferous bouquet of linguistic flowers which exist in the world, and maybe even help to slow down the rate at which languages are dying.*

Jean Aitchison

Oxford 2003

Introduction

Long the subject of myth rather than science, the origins of language are becoming less obscure as clues to the pedigree of humankind are assembled from linguistic, archaeological, and genetic evidence. There remains a huge gulf between the rudimentary linguistic capabilities of apes and the complexity of human communication, which serves to emphasize the uniqueness of human language. Investigation of languages from around the world has revealed deep-seated similarities, as well as surprising differences. However, increasingly, this very diversity is threatened as local languages disappear along with traditional ways of life.

A woman in the traditional dress of one of the ethnic minorities of southern China, the Miao. Miao is one of the main minority languages of China, but speakers are dwindling as a result of the gradual sinicization of ethnic groups.

Above: *Several attempts have been made to teach human-like languages to primates, most successfully with bonobo chimpanzees. Bonobos like Kanzi—a male bonobo trained to use signs by Susan Savage-Rumbaugh at the University of Georgia—have developed linguistic abilities comparable to those of a two-year-old child.*

Language is perhaps the most important single characteristic that distinguishes human beings from other animal species. Certainly, no other animal species has a communication system with the complexity, flexibility, and range of expression of human language. How and when did this remarkable communication system develop? No complete answer can be given to this question, indeed perhaps no complete answer will ever be forthcoming—no linguists were around to observe human origins. But part of the answer can be given by investigating the linguistic abilities of non-human primates, by studying the archeological record of different hominid (human-like) species, and by genetics.

The most successful attempts to teach a human-like language to non-human primates have been with bonobo chimpanzees. Because of the different structure of the vocal apparatus in humans and bonobos, it is not possible for bonobos to imitate the sounds of human language, so they have been taught to use gestures or tokens in place of sounds. The successes that have been achieved over the last few decades by dedicated researchers on bonobos' linguistic abilities have certainly gone beyond what most linguists would have predicted, but bonobos never attain a level of linguistic complexity beyond the approximate level of a two-year-old human child. The further development of language in human children, in particular the development of grammar, appears to be beyond the grasp of bonobos. In this sense language can be seen as a species-specific characteristic of humans. It should also be noted that, in the wild, non-human primates do not spontaneously develop even the linguistic abilities of a two-year-old human child.

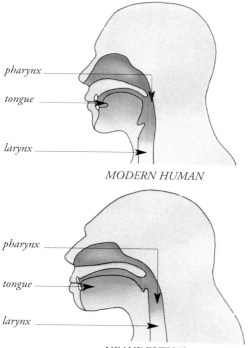

pharynx

tongue

larynx

MODERN HUMAN

pharynx

tongue

larynx

NEANDERTHAL

Turning to the archeological record, it is possible to trace the development of the vocal apparatus of different hominid species from skeletal remains. The comparison of these findings with non-human primates throws light on the range of different articulate sounds that these different species could make; this is important because one of the characteristics of the human vocal apparatus is that the flexibility of the tongue makes a wide range of readily distinguishable sounds possible. The so-called "Language Gene" is also primarily concerned with fine motor articulatory control. There appears to be a significant difference between the vocal apparatus of modern humans (who appear in the archeological record from about 100,000 years ago) and of Neanderthals, who lived from about 230,000 years ago until about 30,000 years ago. In Neanderthals (*see diagram left*), the larynx may have been higher than in modern humans, which means that the tongue would have been much less mobile. If so, the Neanderthals would have been able to produce less differentiated speech than modern humans. The position of the larynx in modern humans represents a marked departure from the larynx position in other hominids and in non-human primates. Interestingly, the human larynx at birth occupies a high position, as with other primates, and only subsequently descends to the position it will occupy in the adult. The lowering of the larynx, though clearly facilitating articulate speech, is in other respects a decided disadvantage; humans, unlike other primates, cannot eat or drink and breathe at the same time without choking.

The archaeological record, unfortunately, tells us nothing significant about brain development. The size of the brain can be deduced from the dimensions of the skull, but brain size tends to be proportional to overall body size, and since the Neanderthals may have been stockier than modern humans it is not surprising that they had, on average, the larger brains, but this tells us nothing about the development of their brains. On the other hand, the archaeological record does provide clear evidence of complex social behavior among Neanderthals, including perhaps care of the old and infirm and burial of the dead. This may indicate the existence of at least a rudimentary form of language as a prerequisite for organizing social behavior.

The evidence thus tends to indicate that, while non-human primates lack linguistic abilities characteristic of modern humans, Neanderthals possessed such abilities in a rudimentary form. Language in its modern form must have appeared no later than about 40,000 years ago, when there was an explosion of complex behavior in areas such as art and technology, and the colonization of harsh environments on a long-term basis became possible. Language may indeed have been present from the appearance of modern humans over 100,000 years ago.

LANGUAGE DIVERSITY

It would seem likely that further light could be thrown on the evolution of human language by studying more and less complex human languages spoken today. However, while it is possible to find parts of one language that are simpler than the corresponding parts of another language, no evidence has ever been produced that would suggest that one particular language as spoken by modern humans is more or less complex than any other. If a language is less complex than another language in one respect, then in some other respect it will be more complex.

A simple example comparing English and Latin illustrates the difficulty in comparing linguistic complexity. In English, regular verbs have only four forms (for example, "walk," "walks," "walked," "walking"), and even the most varied irregular verb has only eight forms ("be," "am," "is," "are," "was," "were," "been," "being"); some verbs have even fewer forms (for example, "cut," "cuts," "cutting"). A Latin verb by contrast has well over a hundred forms, so that whereas English uses the same form in "(I) walk," "(you) walk," "(we) walk," and "(they) walk," Latin distinguishes these as (*ego*) *ambulo*, (*tu*) *ambulas*, (*nos*) *ambulamus*, (*ei*) *ambulant*. In terms of the number of forms that a verb can take, Latin is clearly more complex than English. However, by combining forms of different verbs, English can make a much richer range of distinctions than Latin. To refer to an event in the past, Latin has basically two forms, as with *ambulabam* versus *ambulavi*, both of which can, under appropriate circumstances, be translated as "(I) walked." However, under other circumstances the appropriate English translation of *ambulavi* will be "(I) have walked," while that of *ambulabam* will be "(I) was walking" or "(I) used to walk," not to mention rarer forms like "(I) have been walking" or "(I) used to be walking." These examples show an area where English has six distinct constructions while Latin has only two.

The comparison between different languages is interesting because it reveals how different

Above: *Language in its modern form had probably appeared by about 40,000 years ago when Paleolithic society was transformed by unprecedented developments in both technology and culture. New tools and technology allowed Stone Age hunters to colonize and settle remote and inhospitable regions. At the same time, the extraordinary florescence of cave art, illustrated here by a 14,000-year-old bison drawing from Altamira cave in southern Spain, demonstrates a significant development in both perception and communication.*

languages can be from one another while retaining more or less the same degree of complexity. Much of the material in this book will serve to illustrate this proposition. For now, we will look at just one example, comparing English with the Australian Aboriginal language Dyirbal, spoken near the town of Cairns in Queensland. In an English sentence such as "the man saw the woman and came here," the second clause "came here" lacks overt specification of *who* came here, but we have no difficulty in supplying the missing information, and concluding that *the man* came here. Even though the other interpretation, namely that *the woman* came here, would make perfect sense, English grammar does not allow this sentence to have that meaning.

If we translate the English sentence literally into Dyirbal, the result is *balan jugumbil banggul yaranggu buran, baninyu*, although Dyirbal has relatively free word order, so that *banggul yaranggu balan jugumbil buran, baninyu*, would also be possible. Interestingly, however, this Dyirbal sentence translates as "the man saw the woman and the woman came here." The grammar of Dyirbal is just as strict in requiring this interpretation as the grammar of English is in requiring the opposite interpretation. Both languages have rules of equal complexity; but the particular rule cited above is different in the two languages. We might note in passing that yet other languages, such as Chukchi—spoken on the Chukotka peninsula, the easternmost tip of Asiatic Russia—would

allow both interpretations for the literal translation of this sentence.

It is a mistake to assume that a language will have a simpler structure because it is spoken in a culture that has simpler political structures or a less advanced technology. Linguists are continually surprised by the distinctions that are made in languages outside the mainstream of more familiar languages. In English, for instance, a sentence like "John saw Bill as he was leaving" is ambiguous, depending on whether we take the one who was leaving to be John or Bill. There is no ambiguity in Plains Cree, an Algonquian language of central Canada and adjacent parts of the U.S.A., where different verb forms for "see" mark the difference in meaning: *John Bill-wa waapameew, eesipwehteet* means that John is leaving; *John Bill-wa waapameew, eesipwehteeyit* means that Bill is leaving. To take a different kind of example, most speakers of English have only the one term "salmon," with perhaps a couple of additional terms for varieties of salmon; by contrast in Nuuchahlnuth (a Wakashan language spoken on western Vancouver Island, Canada), there is a rich vocabulary identifying different varieties of salmon (*see page 139*).

LANGUAGES UNDER THREAT

As shown by the few examples given above, and even more so by the many examples scattered throughout this book, human language is extraordinarily diverse, and it is necessary to examine phenomena from a large number of different languages in order to appreciate this diversity. At the beginning of the twenty-first century, it is estimated that over 6,000 languages are spoken in the world. When lay people are asked to guess how many languages are spoken in the world today, they typically underestimate the total by several degrees of magnitude, with answers ranging from a few score to a few hundred. The distribution of languages across the globe is very uneven; this can be seen clearly by comparing the vast area over which Mandarin Chinese is spoken in China with the area of greatest linguistic diversity in the world, the island of New Guinea and surrounding smaller islands, where some 1,000 distinct languages are spoken by a total population of approximately 5 million.

Like the more publicized areas of diversity in the world today such as animals and plants, this diversity of languages is threatened, and it is almost certain that in the not-too-distant future neither professional linguists nor interested lay people will have access to speakers of the range of different languages that are available

today. It is useful to make a three-way distinction among languages with respect to endangerment: a dead language is one that no longer has native speakers (such as Latin or Sumerian); a moribund language is one that still has native speakers but is no longer being acquired by children (such as Dyirbal or many native languages of North America); a living language is one that is still

being acquired by children. A moribund language will normally die out within one or two generations, except in truly extraordinary circumstances—for example, children whose parents did not acquire the language learning it from their grandparents. In an article that appeared in the leading American linguistic journal *Language* in 1992, Michael Krauss of the Alaska Native Language Center estimates that of the languages spoken in the world today, 90 percent will be either dead or moribund a hundred years from now. This represents a far higher rate of endangerment than for animal or plant species. Language death is taking place across the world, ranging from moribund Dyirbal in the Cairns rainforest to Manx, the indigenous Celtic language of the Isle of Man in the Irish Sea, whose last native speaker died in 1974. On the other hand, the successful revival of a dead language, though rare, is not impossible: the clearest example is Hebrew, revived as a spoken language from the late nineteenth century and now a native language for over 3 million people.

Of course, languages have died out throughout recorded history: Sumerian, the language of the first of the great civilizations of Mesopotamia (modern Iraq), died out around 2000BC, while its successor, Akkadian (the language of the Babylonian and Assyrian empires) had in turn died out by around the middle of the first millennium BC. But the extent of language death is undergoing rapid acceleration in the modern world. Until recently, it was perfectly feasible for a small speech community to survive in reasonable isolation, preserving its own language, and perhaps also using a language of wider currency for communication with the outside world where necessary. However, the growing centralization of life at the turn of the millennium

Above: *A wood engraving of the Margarita Philosophica Nova, published by J. Gruninger in 1512, depicts the Institution of Languages, with God distributing the various languages of the world.*

makes this kind of situation increasingly rare. Whether governments are providing health care and education or collecting taxes and recruiting armies, they bring small, isolated communities into the mainstream of their country's life, and this invariably leads to the increased importance of languages of wider currency. It is simply not economically feasible for governments to provide services in every language, including languages spoken by only a few hundred or a few score individuals, even if the will to preserve these languages is present. The growing popularity of the mass media, now spread to the most remote regions by means of satellite communication, also serves to increase the importance of a relatively small number of languages of mass communication, again in part because of the difficulty of justifying the cost of programs in the languages of small speech communities.

The issues involved in this situation are not purely linguistic, but of a more general social and political nature. Certainly, preventing people from gaining access to a language of wider currency, at least as a second language for wider communication alongside the native language used within the community, cannot be justified. If an individual or community has decided to abandon its ancestral language, there is little anyone can (or, perhaps, should) do to stop them: in Tanzania, for instance, younger people are increasingly abandoning their ancestral languages in favor of Swahili, the dominant and official language of the country. In some cases, however, communities have a strong desire to preserve their language, alongside other aspects of their culture, even while acknowledging that they must also be fluent in a language of wider currency. In such cases linguists can provide an invaluable service to the community by assisting in the preservation of the language, for instance by devising a writing

system for the language so that it can be used in a wider range of functions.

But even with the best will in the world on the part of speakers and those with whom they interact, we must accept that a good proportion of the languages currently spoken will no longer be spoken one to four generations from now. Given this situation, it is imperative to salvage as much knowledge of these languages as possible, so that posterity will not lose completely the richness of this aspect of human diversity, of so many solutions to the problem of coming to terms with our environment through language. For linguists, the urgent task is to describe endangered languages by providing a grammar and a dictionary, and to document these languages with annotated audio and video recordings illustrating various uses of the language, from traditional stories to everyday conversation. If you enjoy this book, even more so if you are encouraged to read further about the various languages of the world, please be aware of the fragile ecology on which this description of the world's languages is based.

Below: *The development of satellite technology, which enables television broadcasters to reach remote and hitherto inaccessible regions, such as this town in rural India, means that languages of mass communication, in particular English, are becoming increasingly dominant.*

Development and Spread of Languages

Human languages are far more diverse and numerous than most speakers of major world languages think. There are presently over 6,000 tongues spoken around the world, with distinctions ranging from regional dialects of Chinese to great language families like the Indo-European and Sino-Tibetan. Linguistic histories can be reconstructed by comparison of vocabularies and of grammatical structures, and today the search continues for ever more distant relationships, which may perhaps indicate a single origin of all language.

CHRONOLOGY OF HUMAN LANGUAGE

2000AD	
	SPREAD OF STANDARD LANGUAGES; ACCELERATION OF LANGUAGE LOSS
	COLONIAL PERIOD: RISE OF PIDGINS AND CREOLES
1500	
1000	
	EMERGENCE OF ROMANCE, GERMANIC LANGUAGES
	OLD ENGLISH
500	
0	CLASSICAL LANGUAGES: ANCIENT GREEK, LATIN
	OLDEST RECORDS OF INDO-EUROPEAN LANGUAGES: HITTITE, SANSKRIT
	PROTO-INDO-EUROPEAN
5000	EXPANSION OF AUSTRONESIAN; COLONIZATION OF TAIWAN
	SECOND SETTLEMENT OF NEW WORLD: NA-DENE
10,000	
	FIRST ESTABLISHED SETTLEMENT OF NEW WORLD: AMERIND
	END OF LAST ICE AGE; EXPANSION OF EURASIATIC LANGUAGES
15,000	ESTIMATED PEAK OF LINGUISTIC DIVERSITY: 10–15,000 LANGUAGES
20,000	
25,000	
30,000	EXTINCTION OF NEANDERTHALS: AT MOST PRIMITIVE LANGUAGE
35,000	
40,000	HOMO SAPIENS; EVIDENCE OF COMPLEX BEHAVIOR IMPLIES MODERN LANGUAGE
	COLONIZATION OF AUSTRALIA
45,000	
50,000BC	EMERGENCE FROM AFRICA *(latest estimated date)*

Above: *Dating the origin of a language can only be speculative. The chronology opposite is intended as an approximate guide to the emergence of human language.*

This book aims to give an up-to-date, accessible overview of the languages spoken in each part of the world, of the relationships between them, and of what we know of their origins. A subsidiary goal is to show something of the range of diversity of the world's languages, at a time when concern is mounting over the loss of both cultural and linguistic heritage. Languages are dying out at an accelerating rate which has begun to alarm linguists, anthropologists, and others concerned with the diversity of languages and cultures. Unique languages, such as Ainu and Ubykh, have become extinct in the last few decades of the twentieth century, and it has been estimated that half the world's remaining languages will become extinct over the next hundred years.

Our picture of the world's languages is changing in other ways too. Since the 1960s, substantial advances have been made in our understanding both of language in general, and of particular language groups. Many of these advances have yet to be widely disseminated. Creoles, for example, were once dismissed as degenerate forms of European languages, but they have now become central to our view of the human capacity for language. In another development, recent research has sought to pursue genetic relationships between language families far beyond those currently established. These controversial proposals are now in the forefront of debate and open new perspectives on the history of human language.

LANGUAGE DIVERSITY IN TIME AND SPACE

The diversity of human language may be compared to the diversity of the natural world. Just as the demise of a plant species reduces genetic diversity, and deprives humanity of potential medical and biological resources, so the extinction of a language takes with it a wealth of culture, art, and knowledge. The avoidance registers of Australian aboriginal languages, for example, were used in speaking to "taboo" relatives with whom contact was to be kept to a minimum. The vocabulary of these "mother-in-law languages" is highly restricted, forcing the use of very general, rather than specific, terms and raising some fascinating questions: how do people communicate with such restricted languages, and how do children learn to use them? How do they reflect or reinforce the social relationships involved? We can barely begin to answer these questions because the mother-in-law languages have all but disappeared. Even in the case of those aboriginal languages which are still spoken, the avoidance registers have been lost, together with the traditional lifestyle, and our knowledge of them is based on elderly speakers' memories.

The Indo-European languages, now spoken by half the world's population, dominate both Western countries and their views of language. French, Russian, and Hindi, all Indo-European languages, differ in many respects, yet they

Above: *Ainu, formerly spoken in parts of Hokkaido and Honshu, is the now extinct language of the Ainu, an aboriginal people of Japan.*

THE TOP TWENTY LANGUAGES

In terms of the number of native speakers, 12 of the top 20 languages belong to the Indo-European family, many spread by colonial expansion, as in the case of English, Spanish, and Portuguese.

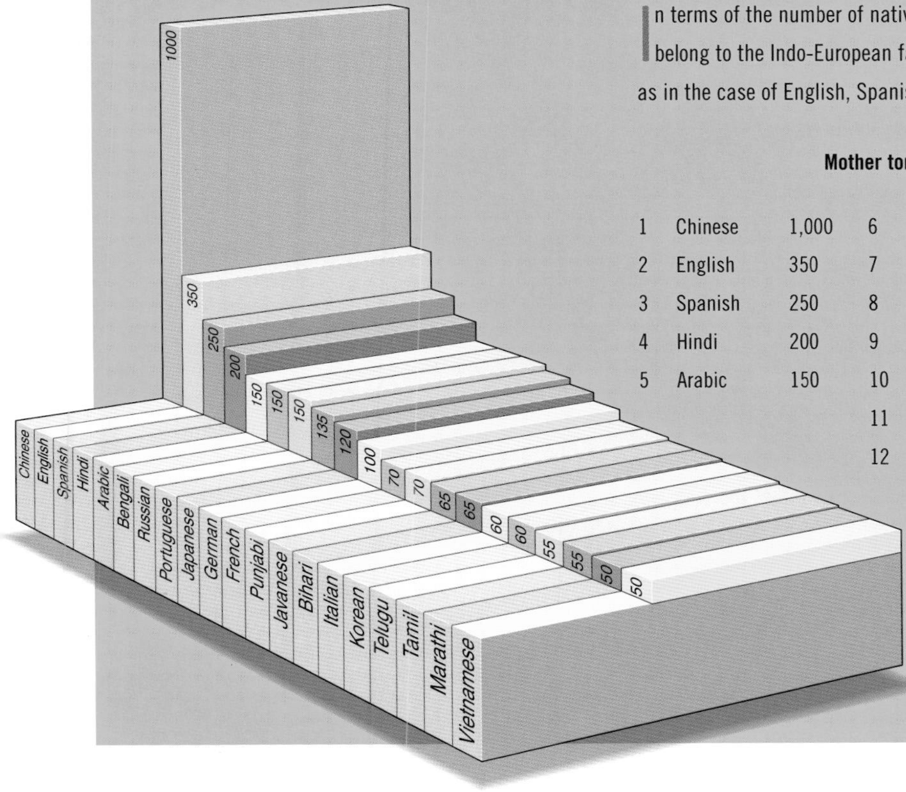

Mother tongue speakers (millions)

1	Chinese	1,000	6	Bengali	150	13	Javanese	65
2	English	350	7	Russian	150	14	Bihari	65
3	Spanish	250	8	Portuguese	135	15	Italian	60
4	Hindi	200	9	Japanese	120	16	Korean	60
5	Arabic	150	10	German	100	17	Telugu	55
			11	French	70	18	Tamil	55
			12	Punjabi	70	19	Marathi	50
						20	Vietnamese	50

represent only a small part of the range of diversity of the world's languages. In terms of the number of native speakers, 12 of the top 20 languages (*see diagram above*) belong to the Indo-European family, many spread by colonial expansion as in the case of English, Spanish, and Portuguese.

Linguistic diversity can be appreciated by any attempt to learn a second or foreign language. A common experience on encountering an unfamiliar language is incredulity that anybody could speak a language so different from one's own. For an English-speaker, this linguistic culture-shock might be provoked by a language where the verb comes at the end of the sentence (such as Japanese), or a tone language which uses pitch to distinguish words (such as Chinese). The scientific study of this range of diversity is called language typology, the study of language types. Some basic typological notions will be used in this book, especially

in describing language families and features common to certain regions. The basic word-order typology, which focuses on the order of subject, verb, and object, is important. It has been found that all six of the logically possible

BASIC WORD ORDER

Word order type		Example languages
SVO	"cows eat grass"	English; Finnish; Chinese; Swahili
SOV	"cows grass eat"	Hindi/Urdu; Turkish; Japanese, Korean
VSO	"eat cows grass"	Classical Arabic; Welsh; Samoan
VOS	"eat grass cows"	Malagasy (an Austronesian language of Madagascar); Tzotzil (a Mayan language of Central America)
OSV	"grass cows eat"	Kabardian (a language of the northern Caucasus)
OVS	"grass eat cows"	Hixkaryana (a Carib language of Brazil)

ARCTIC
OCEAN

FRENCH AND
NATIVE AMERICAN

ENGLISH AND
NA-DENE

NORTH
ATLANTIC
OCEAN

PACIFIC
OCEAN

SPANISH AND
NATIVE AMERICAN

PORTUGUESE AND
NATIVE AMERICAN

SOUTH
ATLANTIC
OCEAN

LANGUAGES OF THE WORLD

The classification of languages into families is still being developed: the Papuan languages of New Guinea may belong to five or more different families, while the Austric and Amerind groupings are recent proposals which remain the subject of debate. Such long-range groupings would reduce the world's languages to as few as 15 super-families. A few languages, such as Basque and Burushaski, which are shown on the detailed maps for each region, still defy classification. As the world map indicates, the Indo-European languages are the most widely represented family, spoken by around half the world's population.

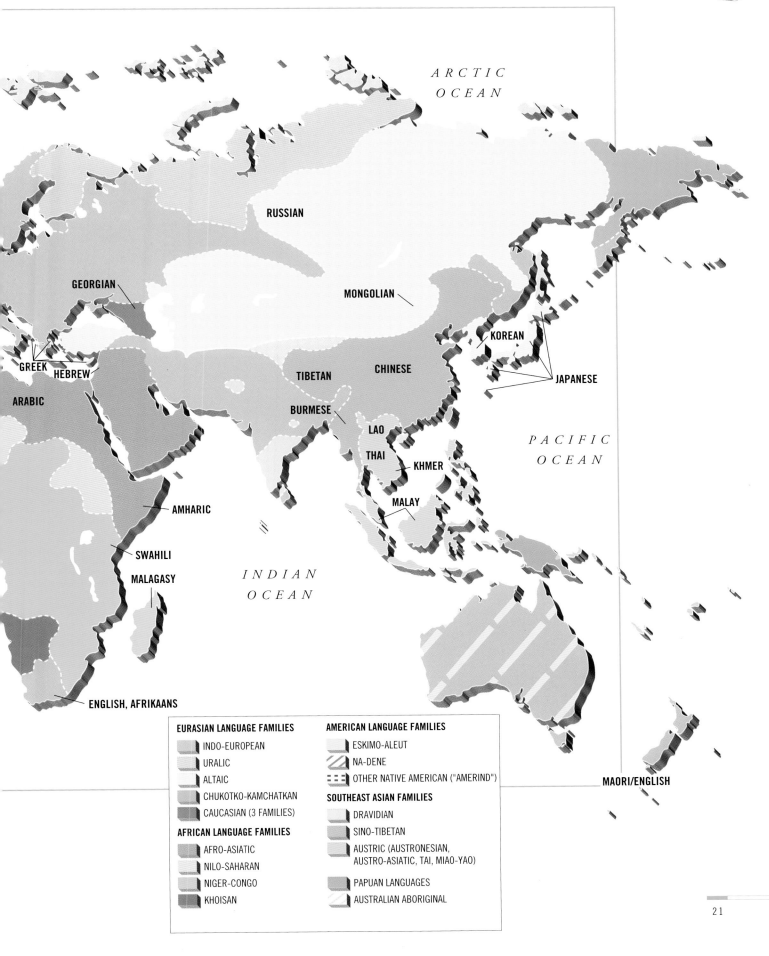

ARCTIC OCEAN

RUSSIAN

GEORGIAN

MONGOLIAN

KOREAN

GREEK

HEBREW

CHINESE

JAPANESE

ARABIC

TIBETAN

BURMESE

LAO

PACIFIC OCEAN

THAI

KHMER

AMHARIC

MALAY

SWAHILI

MALAGASY

INDIAN OCEAN

ENGLISH, AFRIKAANS

MAORI/ENGLISH

EURASIAN LANGUAGE FAMILIES
- INDO-EUROPEAN
- URALIC
- ALTAIC
- CHUKOTKO-KAMCHATKAN
- CAUCASIAN (3 FAMILIES)

AFRICAN LANGUAGE FAMILIES
- AFRO-ASIATIC
- NILO-SAHARAN
- NIGER-CONGO
- KHOISAN

AMERICAN LANGUAGE FAMILIES
- ESKIMO-ALEUT
- NA-DENE
- OTHER NATIVE AMERICAN ("AMERIND")

SOUTHEAST ASIAN FAMILIES
- DRAVIDIAN
- SINO-TIBETAN
- AUSTRIC (AUSTRONESIAN, AUSTRO-ASIATIC, TAI, MIAO-YAO)
- PAPUAN LANGUAGES
- AUSTRALIAN ABORIGINAL

Above: *Chinese is the world's most widely-used language, with some 1,000 million native speakers. Until recently, it was mistakenly thought to be grammatically simple because it lacked the inflections of many European languages.*

word orders occur (*see page 19*). The first three are overwhelmingly more frequent, reflecting the universal tendency for the subject to precede the object.

Although not all languages can be classified in this way (Hungarian has a very free word order and potentially allows all six possibilities), one order predominates in most languages. Word order also tends to be a common feature across geographical regions, shared by neighboring languages which may not be genetically related: for example, both the Indic and the Dravidian languages of India belong to the SOV (subject-object-verb) type.

Alongside the charting of diversity, there is a search for language universals, statements which hold true for all languages. All languages have consonants, for example, and all distinguish between nouns and verbs. Implicational universals identify the properties which go together: one proposed implicational universal is that, if a language places the adjective before the noun (as in "black sheep"), the numeral is also placed before the noun ("five sheep").

Another point of similarity in the midst of diversity is that languages appear to be of approximately equal complexity. There are no simple languages—even pidgins and creoles have their complexities, while sign languages prove to be just as complex as spoken ones. Languages which appear simple in one respect inevitably prove to be complex in others. Chinese, for example, was once thought to be grammatically simple because it lacked the endings (inflections)

of many European languages. The complexity of Chinese sentence structures, however, is just beginning to be appreciated, and the language can express the same concepts, such as time and hypotheticality, as Indo-European verbal inflections do. One feature of Chinese which looks superficially simple is reduplication, the doubling of a word or syllable. This may look like English "baby-talk" (*ma-ma, choo-choo*), but this doubling serves a variety of purposes. It can not only intensify the meaning of a word, but also downplay it: *kàn* ("look"), *kàn-kàn* "take a look." In addition to these two functions, which are very common in the world's languages, Chinese reduplication also has some specific grammatical functions, such as forming adverbs and quantifying words: thus *màn* ("slow") becomes *màn-màn* "slowly"; *rén* ("person") becomes *rén-rén* ("everyone").

Linguists generally believe that languages possess the same expressive power: even if a language lacks the vocabulary for, say, a certain field of science, the necessary words can readily be created or borrowed. Similarly, all languages have literature and poetry, whether written, oral, or signed, and its extent or quality depend on the creativity of the culture and its artists, rather than on the language itself.

Languages and Dialects

How do we distinguish between a language and dialects of a single language? The answer often seems obvious: Dutch, German, Danish, and Norwegian are separate languages, while Cockney and Glaswegian are dialects of English, and Swiss and Bavarian are dialects of German. This obvious answer, however, is based on political rather than on linguistic realities. Many native speakers of English understand as little of Glaswegian as they do of Dutch. German and Dutch are each national languages, yet by linguistic criteria, Dutch and "Low" German would be described as dialects of the same language. Conversely, the many varieties of Chinese are generally referred to as dialects, yet they are as different from each other as Romance languages such as French and Spanish. The defining difference is socio-political rather than linguistic: the Chinese "dialects" are spoken within a single nation, with a core of common culture, whereas the Romance languages have not been unified within one nation since the collapse of the Roman empire.

The test of mutual intelligibility is often used to define the status of a language: where speakers

WORD ORDER AND NAMES

The basic word order of a language is often reflected in the ordering of names:

In SOV languages, like Korean and Japanese, the surname comes first:

| KIM Il-Sung | (Korean) |
| MATSUMOTO Tada | (Japanese) |

This also applies to titles, as in Japanese:

| Yamata sensei | "Professor Yamata" |
| Watanabe ishi | "Doctor Watanabe" |

Similarly, patronymics (surnames denoting "son/daughter of") reflect the current or earlier word order of the language. In VSO languages such as Scots, Irish, and (Biblical) Hebrew, patronymics take the form "child (or grandchild) of X":

Mac- as in MacAllister	"child of Alistair" (Scots)
O- as in O'Hara	"grandchild of Hara" (Irish)
Ben- as in Ben-Gurion	"child of Gurion" (Hebrew)

In SOV languages such as those of the Caucasus region, such surnames take the form "X's child":

| -ian as in Khachaturian | (Armenian) |
| -shvili as in Basilashvili | (Georgian) |

Many Indo-European languages show a similar order, which may be a relic of earlier SOV word order:

-ová as in Gruberová	"Gruber's daughter" (Czech)
-dóttir as in Sigurðsdóttir	"Sigurd's daughter" (Icelandic)
-son as in Andersson	"Anders' son" (Swedish)

(English names such as Johnson are of Norse origin)

of two related languages can understand each other, the two languages are said to be dialects of the same language. But intelligibility is a matter of degree: typically, a speaker of one language will recognize at least a few words of a related language (as an English speaker will recognize the German words *Finger* and *Haus*). In practice, the distinction between language and dialect is made on socio-political grounds: it has been said that a language is "a dialect with an army and a navy behind it." Recognition as a national language is crucial here: Romansch, for example, is regarded as a language because it is one of the four recognized languages of Switzerland, together with French, German, and Italian. Ladin, another Rhaeto-Romance language spoken in four valleys in the Dolomites of northern Italy, has no such recognition and is regarded as a local dialect.

LANGUAGE NAMES

Many speakers do without names for their own language: many Cantonese speakers, for example, simply call their language *bundei-wa* ("local speech"). The established names of languages are often those given by outsiders, which may be foreign or even offensive to native speakers. The name *German* is the Roman geographers' term, while German-speakers use the word *Deutsch* which, like many

Above: *Language and ethnicity or religion do not necessarily correspond. Jews in different parts of the world, for example, speak Hebrew (Semitic), Russian (Slavic), Yiddish or English (Germanic), and Ladino (Romance).*

THE DUTCH-GERMAN DIALECT CONTINUUM

The most striking difference between Dutch and standard German lies in the so-called "High German Sound Shift" which affects consonants systematically. Whereas the Dutch and Low (north) German forms resemble English (*maken* "make," *pund* "pound"), the High (south) German dialects use -ch for -k, and pf- for p-, as in standard German. In the Central German area the individual isoglosses do not always match, and various combinations of "high" and "low" forms are found. Some Central German speakers claim to enjoy a corresponding advantage in understanding both north and south German dialects.

English	Low German	High German
I	*ik*	*ich*
make	*maken*	*machen*
that	*dat*	*das*
apple	*appel*	*Apfel*
pound	*pund*	*Pfund*

Swiss German is distinguished by a further shift from k- to kch-/ch-, as in *Kchind* or *Chind* for standard German *Kind* "child."

KEY
- LOW GERMAN
- CENTRAL GERMAN
- HIGH GERMAN
- SWISS GERMAN
- DUTCH

language names, means "people." The Russian word for the German language and people is *nemetsky*, derived from an adjective meaning "dumb." Linguists now prefer to use the names given by the speakers to their own languages. The Miao-Yao languages of China and Southeast Asia are now called Hmong-Mien. The Algonquian language named Montagnais by French Canadians is known by the name its speakers use, *Innu-Aimun* (literally translated as "person-word").

LANGUAGE AND GEOGRAPHY

Dialectology is the study of geographical variation within a language. The painstaking examination of local dialects, where the local pronunciations of a single word and the distribution of vocabulary items are carefully investigated, has led to the creation of dialect studies such as the *Linguistic Atlas of New England*. More recently, attention has turned to dialects associated with social groups and the urban dialects of cities such as New York and Belfast. Such dialects are much less amenable to mapping, since they reflect social variables such as socio-economic status, gender, and religion rather than geographical variation.

Dialect divisions are established by isoglosses— lines on a map which represent the divide between the domain of one word, form, or pronunciation from that of another. Differences can be very gradual: for example, the dialects of southeastern France and the Italian dialects just across the border are similar enough to be assigned to the same language. Such dialects form a dialect continuum and the line between them is typically drawn on the basis of political, rather than linguistic factors.

Mutual intelligibility is another important factor. Speakers of Dutch, for example, understand Low German, while speakers of Low German understand the dialects of central Germany, and so on. But the varieties spoken at the two extremes of the continuum, such as Dutch and Bavarian, are mutually unintelligible. This situation can make the linguistic distinction between language and dialect somewhat arbitrary. For example, Swiss German, which speakers of standard German find notoriously incomprehensible, is regarded as a dialect or a set of dialects. One reason is that Swiss German coexists within Switzerland with standard German, used in writing, and a continuum of varieties from local dialect to standard obscures the distinction between them.

LANGUAGE FAMILIES

Since the eighteenth century, when the relationship between the Indo-European languages was discovered, languages have been classified by the family-tree model, in which the descent of languages is traced like that of families. A partial family tree of the Indo-European

languages, for example, can be used to show the relationship of English to the neighboring European languages (*see page 39*).

It can be seen that English and German are "sister" languages, with a common parent, while English and French are "cousins," sharing a common ancestor (Indo-European) but with distinct parent languages. Such a classification is made by identifying related words such as English *mother* and German *Mutter*, French *mère* and Italian *madre*.

Items of basic vocabulary, such as pronouns, numerals, body parts, and kinship terms, are especially important in classifying language families, as these items are the least susceptible to change and borrowing. A striking example of the longevity of kinship terms is the Romanian word

Above: *Sanskrit, an ancient language of India, is today only used for religious purposes. It is the oldest recorded language of the Indic branch of the Indo-European languages. It is the language of the Hindu religion, and a rich array of scientific and philosophical texts are also written in Sanskrit.*

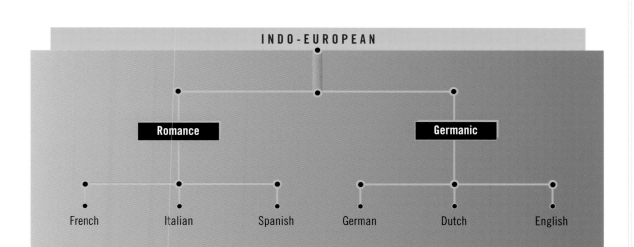

Left: *This partial family tree of the Indo-European languages demonstrates the relationships between neighboring European languages.*

*Above: German is
represented in texts from
the eighth century
onward. Early texts such
as this sixteenth century
legal leaflet are written
in Gothic script.*

nepot ("nephew"), which has the same form as the reconstructed Indo-European root **nepōt-* (as in nepotism): the root has hardly changed in form in the 5–6,000 years since the Indo-European languages split up.

For still more accurate comparison between different language groups, it is customary to take the oldest available text which is representative of each language family: fourth-century Gothic for Germanic; Latin for Romance; Old Church Slavonic for the Slavic family, and so on. Such languages are often preserved for liturgical use, like Latin which was used throughout the churches of Medieval Europe, and like Sanskrit in India.

The family tree model developed for classifying the Indo-European languages has generally worked well for other families. However, languages do not develop in a vacuum, but typically remain in contact with related languages after they have branched off. There is no way to represent this contact in a family tree: the Celtic and Italic families, for example, are more similar than the conventional family tree would suggest. As an extreme case, the language families of Southeast Asia have been described as more like a thicket than a tree. It has also become clear that certain languages do not belong to any one family because they have not been transmitted from generation to generation in the normal way. Creoles, which are born from the sudden juxtaposition of a range of languages, are a clear case: while the vocabulary may derive from a European language, the grammar is created afresh with some input from the other languages involved (*see chapter 8*). "Mixed languages" certainly exist; Michif, a language of Quebec, combines elements of French and the Algonquian language Cree, while in Copper Island Aleut,

Eskimo-Aleut verbs took on Russian inflections. Even Japanese may have arisen as a mixed language of this kind, combining Altaic and Austronesian elements.

RECONSTRUCTION OF PROTO-LANGUAGES

The classification and comparison of a family of languages can help to reconstruct the parts of the ancestral language from which they are descended. The process of reconstruction begins with the assembly of corresponding words from related languages, such as the words for "five" in various Germanic languages:

English	Gothic	Dutch	German	Norwegian
five	fimf	vijf	fünf	fem

ENGLISH AND INDO-EUROPEAN

A set of numbers and kinship terms in four European languages shows the relationship between the Indo-European languages.

English	Italian	Russian	Hungarian
one	uno	odin	egy
two	due	dva	két
three	tre	tri	három
mother	madre	mat'	anya
brother	fratello	brat	testvér
sister	sorella	sestrá	nővér

Notice that certain sounds are similar in pronunciation, such as the English *t* which corresponds to the Italian and Russian *d* in the words for "two": (both are ALVEOLAR STOPS). These correspondences are regular: *t* in Italian corresponds to *th* in English "three," and "brother."

The Hungarian words show no such resemblance. Hungarian, although it is surrounded by Indo-European languages, belongs to the Uralic family, together with languages such as Finnish and Estonian.

THE SHEEP AND THE HORSES: A PROTO-INDO-EUROPEAN FABLE

In perhaps the most ambitious of reconstructions, the nineteenth-century German linguist Schleicher composed a fable in reconstructed Proto-Indo-European. A more recent version, by the historical linguists Lehmann and Zgusta, runs as follows:

Gʷerēi owis, kʷesyo wlhnā ne ēst, ekwōns espeket, oinom ghe gʷrum woghom
Hill-on sheep, whose wool not exist, horses saw, one heavy load
"On the hill a sheep which had no wool saw some horses, one pulling a heavy load,

weghontm, oinom-kwe megam bhorom, oinom-kwe ghmenm ōku bherontm.
pulling, one-also great burden, one-also man fast bearing.
one bearing a great burden, and another carrying a man at speed.

Owis nu ekwomos ewewkʷet: "Kēr aghnutoi moi ekwōns agontm nerm widentei."
Sheep now horses-to said: "heart pains me horses driving man seeing."
The sheep said to the horses: "My heart pains me seeing man driving horses".

Ek'wōs tu ewewkʷont: "Kludhi, owei, kēr ghe aghnutoi nsmei widntmos: nēr, potis,
horses then said: "Listen, sheep, heart pain us seeing man master,
The horses said: "Listen, sheep, our hearts pain us when we see how man, the master,

owiōm r wlhnām sebhi gwermom westrom kʷrneuti. Neghi owiōm wlhnā esti."
sheep's wool himself warm clothing makes. And-not of-the-sheep wool is."
makes the sheep's wool into a warm garment for himself. And the sheep has no wool."

Tod kekluwōs owis agrom ebhuget.
This hearing sheep field fled.
On hearing this, the sheep ran off into the plain."

By separating the roots from inflections, we recognize such words as *owis* "sheep," (compare "ewe"), *wlh-nā* "wool," *e-speket* "see" (compare "inspect"), *oin-om* "one," *moi* "me" and *bher-ontm* "bearing."

Many of the reconstructed forms resemble Latin (*ovis* "sheep," *equus* "horse") or Greek (*mega* "very big," *aner* "man"). These languages are closer to the Proto-Indo-European of around 2500BC represented by the fable.

The syntax reconstructs Proto-Indo-European as an SOV language, also resembling Classical Latin. While it is now thought that the linguistic reconstruction relies too heavily on Sanskrit, and it is not certain that the Indo-Europeans had domesticated horses at this time, the fable helps to bring the science of reconstruction to life.

The endings suggest both a nasal consonant ([n] in German, [m] in Gothic and Norwegian), and a labiovelar one ([v] in English, [f] in German and Dutch). This evidence allows us to reconstruct a Proto-Germanic root *finv- or *fenv- (the asterisk marks it as a reconstruction). This can be compared with other Indo-European words:

Greek	Sanskrit	Latin	Breton	Polish
pente	páñca	quinque	pempe	pieć

With knowledge of sound correspondences (f in Germanic corresponds to p elsewhere as a result of the set of sound changes known as Grimm's Law) a Proto-Indo-European form *penkwe ("five") has been reconstructed. Using this method, it is possible to reconstruct aspects of Proto-Indo-European inflections and even aspects of its syntax. The elaborate case systems of the early Classical languages (and of conservative Indo-European languages such as Lithuanian) suggest that Indo-European had around eight cases for nouns: nominative, vocative, accusative, dative, genitive, instrumental, ablative, and locative. In the case of Indo-European, Classical texts from Sanskrit, Greek, and Latin provide intermediate forms between the proto-language and the modern forms, whereas for most other language families, such evidence is lacking and reconstruction calls for correspondingly more detective work.

LONG-RANGE COMPARISONS

In recent years there has been renewed debate about the classification of the world's languages and the extent to which it can be pursued. For many years it was accepted that the existence of certain families, such as Indo-European and Uralic, had been established beyond reasonable doubt, while that of other families, such as Ural-Altaic and Austric, was questionable. It was widely believed that the evidence was insufficient to allow their classification beyond the time depth of Indo-European history.

Recently, however, interest in distant relationships has revived. Joseph Greenberg, whose earlier work proposed the four African language families, has attempted controversially to group the indigenous languages of America into three great families, corresponding to three successive waves of migration: Amerind, Na-Dené, and Eskimo-Aleut. The Na-Dené language family of America may be related to Sino-Tibetan, and even to Caucasian languages. Greenberg has also proposed a vast Eurasiatic family, viewing the Indo-European, Uralic, and Altaic families as distantly related. Basic vocabulary such as the pronouns me ("I") and te ("you"), which occur widely in Indo-European, Uralic, and beyond, may provide evidence according to some linguists. Such similarities which stretch beyond established groupings may point to long-range relationships.

As an extreme case, "global etymologies," which reach back to a "proto-world language" have been proposed for some items such as body parts and kinship terms. The words for "one" and "finger," for example, are said to go back to a common proto-root tik (reflected in the word "digital"). Some grammatical items such as the

	HUNGARIAN	CHAOZHOU	RYUKYUAN	HAUSA	AKKADIAN	DYIRBAL
	(Uralic)	(Chinese)	(Japanese)	(Chadic)	(Semitic)	(Australian)
*min "what?"	mi	miʔ	mi	mè/mì	mīn	minya

Above: *Resemblances between the same word in different languages are said to indicate a common "proto-world" language. However, this theory is controversial.*

question words *kin* ("who?") and *min* ("what?") are also proposed (*see example on page 28*).

Skeptics suggest other possible explanations for these resemblances. Some sounds are symbolic: the widespread use of nasal sounds in words expressing negation, for example, might be due to an intrinsic or natural association, and the *mi(n)* pattern might have arisen independently for

analyses of human populations with linguistic classifications. Naturally, genetic and linguistic boundaries do not necessarily match. However, the long-range linguistic classifications seem broadly consistent both with population genetics and with archeological evidence of the spread of human populations. Archeological findings suggest that America, for example, may have been

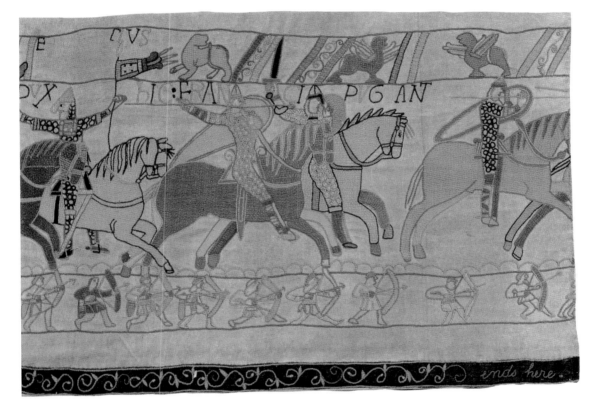

Left: *The Norman Conquest of England in 1066, depicted here in the Bayeux tapestry, was the start of nearly a millennium of close contact between the English and French, which has had a profound influence on the vocabulary of both languages. The commentary in medieval Latin states:* hic Franci pugnant—*"here the French are fighting."*

similar reasons, perhaps involving a reflex opening of the mouth. Another difficulty is distinguishing whether a shared word is the result of common inheritance or more recent borrowing. Finally, it needs to be demonstrated that the similarities are more pronounced than would be expected simply by chance. Given these difficulties, it seems unlikely that such proposed long-range groupings as Amerind or Eurasiatic will be established or refuted by linguistic criteria alone.

Language classification is becoming an interdisciplinary field, with attempts to match archeological evidence and genetic and anatomical

populated as recently as 12,000 years ago by peoples from Eurasia, making hypotheses about American language families and their connections to Eurasian language families at least plausible.

LANGUAGE CONTACT

A recurrent theme in this book is contact between adjacent languages and its effects. No language exists in a vacuum: even geographically isolated languages such as Basque in the Pyrenees and Burushaski in the Himalayas have been influenced by the surrounding languages. Although English and French are related only distantly through the Indo-European family tree, the contact between

CODE-MIXING

Code-mixing/switching is a colorful feature of bilingual societies and individuals. Mixing of Spanish and English is common in North American Hispanic communities: the following examples are typical.

"...*those friends are friends from Mexico que tienen chamaquitos.*" [who have little children]

"*All of a sudden I started acting real curiosa [strange], you know.*"

Such mixing occurs out of linguistic necessity, when the speaker cannot think of the words in the original language, but also for reasons of identity.

In Hong Kong, where most of the population speaks some English, those who are fluent in both Cantonese and English mix the two in a characteristic way which marks them as more or less bilingual.

This mixing is also found in Cantonese texts, as in the popular novel *Diary of a Yuppie*. The text uses English names (*Angie*), adjectives (*happy*), and half-digested idioms (*in another word* for "in other words"). The letter D is used to represent the Cantonese word *dī* meaning "a bit" and the colloquial verb *mit* "tear," for which no standard Chinese character exists, is written phonetically.

我忍無可忍，終於爆發，我同 Angie 講：「你咁問我當然係咩呀？我係你老公喎！我講ロ的 happy 嘢俾你聽係想你同我 share D 開心，唔係俾你搵盆冷水照頭淋嘅！」

Angie 一邊 mit 面膜，一邊就住唔發脾氣，佢怕有皺紋，佢話：「超，我想客觀ロ的同你分析啫！」

「客觀？你係我老婆，你唔係要嚟客觀，係要嚟主觀嘅！你要識得欣賞你老公！」

Angie 答案係「我欣賞你咁單純！」

又過份咗叻！即係話我幼稚！我用個指甲鉗指住 Angie 話：「你一直睇小我！」

Angie 好「叻」，即刻調轉嚟講：「In another word，我係鼓勵緊你！」

呵呵呵呵！我好似做大戲咁笑！我唔再睬 Angie，翹埋雙脚ロ係床上面睇電視！我唔

them in the centuries since the Norman Conquest of England has led to much shared vocabulary. Similarly, Chinese and Japanese are related not through a common origin but by cultural contacts, leading to the borrowing of much Chinese vocabulary together with the Chinese writing system. Language contact takes a number of forms which have come to be more fully understood in recent research. In particular, borrowing occurs when languages come into contact for trading purposes and through bilingualism. Language shift occurs when speakers of one language come to speak another over the course of several generations. Borrowing affects primarily vocabulary, while language shift can have deeper effects on the structure of the language and often leaves clear marks in the grammar.

BILINGUALISM AND MULTILINGUALISM

It has been estimated that around half the world's population is bilingual or multilingual. While relatively unusual in countries such as France, Britain, and the U.S.A., bilingualism is the norm in many parts of the world—Thailand, for example, is home to some 80 languages. In areas such as India, West Africa, and Papua New Guinea, it is common for individuals to speak a local language, a regional language, and a colonial language: in the Cameroon, for example, most people speak two or more African languages, and the educated also speak French. This does not necessarily lead to discord, as harmoniously multilingual countries such as Switzerland and Thailand demonstrate.

While bilingualism has sometimes been seen as a handicap, linguists have accumulated evidence that, in addition to the obvious practical advantage of enabling communication with a wider range of cultures, bilingualism also offers cognitive advantages. It certainly raises awareness

Above: *Contact between speakers of different languages, for example in a multi-ethnic society such as the U.S.A., can lead to the introduction of foreign loan words into the dominant language. For example the words "renegade" and "mosquito" originate from the Spanish language.*

of language: bilingual children, for example, are aware that the names we give to things are largely arbitrary, so that a horse could equally have been called a dog. Bilingual education is seen as an important means of promoting cultural integration, at the same time preserving the use of minority languages and their associated cultural traditions. For these and other reasons, linguists are almost unanimous in their support for bilingual education and oppose legislation attempting to enforce monolingualism, such as laws making the use of English in the workplace compulsory.

LOAN WORDS AND BORROWING

All kinds of language contact give rise to "loan words," foreign words adapted and added to the vocabulary of the "borrowing" language (the terms are misleading in that the words are rarely returned to the "lending" language). English is full of loan words reflecting spheres of cultural influence, as in the case of French cuisine (*see map, pages 32–33*), or the word zero, from Arabic mathematics. Expressions such as "lose face" and "long time no see!" are loan translations from Chinese, derived by translating separately each part of the corresponding Chinese expressions.

While English has long welcomed loans and continues to do so, some languages have resisted them as a threat to linguistic purity. French is protected by the Académie Française and the French government has introduced legislation to outlaw the use of English words (franglais) in official media. Computer terminology, for example, is created in French to avoid borrowing English words (*l'ordinateur* "computer," *le logiciel* "software", *le courriel* "e-mail").

More extensive contact, especially when bilingualism is widespread, gives rise to structural borrowing in which not only vocabulary but

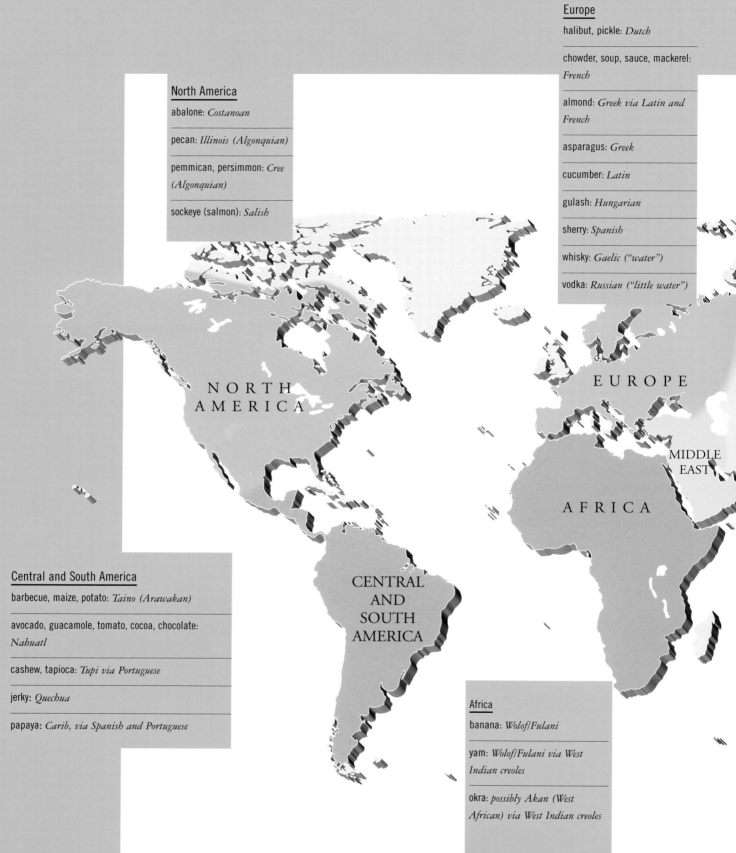

Europe

halibut, pickle: *Dutch*

chowder, soup, sauce, mackerel: *French*

almond: *Greek via Latin and French*

asparagus: *Greek*

cucumber: *Latin*

gulash: *Hungarian*

sherry: *Spanish*

whisky: *Gaelic ("water")*

vodka: *Russian ("little water")*

North America

abalone: *Costanoan*

pecan: *Illinois (Algonquian)*

pemmican, persimmon: *Cree (Algonquian)*

sockeye (salmon): *Salish*

Central and South America

barbecue, maize, potato: *Taino (Arawakan)*

avocado, guacamole, tomato, cocoa, chocolate: *Nahuatl*

cashew, tapioca: *Tupi via Portuguese*

jerky: *Quechua*

papaya: *Carib, via Spanish and Portuguese*

Africa

banana: *Wolof/Fulani*

yam: *Wolof/Fulani via West Indian creoles*

okra: *possibly Akan (West African) via West Indian creoles*

NORTH AMERICA

EUROPE

MIDDLE EAST

AFRICA

CENTRAL AND SOUTH AMERICA

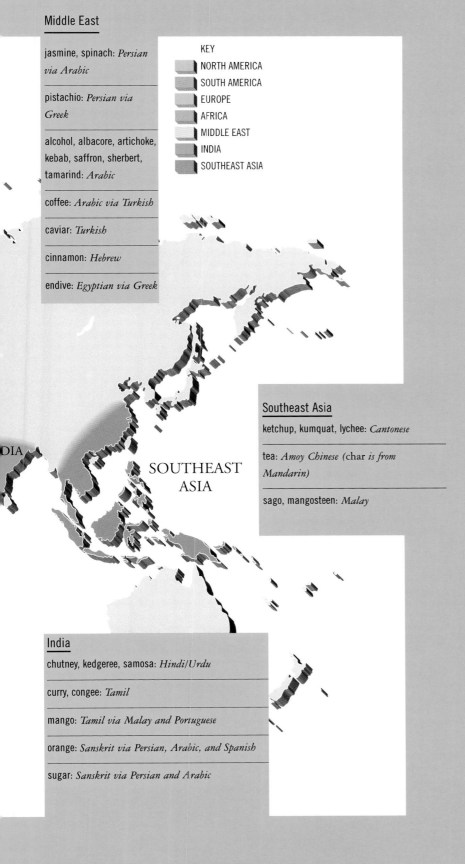

Middle East

jasmine, spinach: *Persian via Arabic*

pistachio: *Persian via Greek*

alcohol, albacore, artichoke, kebab, saffron, sherbert, tamarind: *Arabic*

coffee: *Arabic via Turkish*

caviar: *Turkish*

cinnamon: *Hebrew*

endive: *Egyptian via Greek*

KEY
NORTH AMERICA
SOUTH AMERICA
EUROPE
AFRICA
MIDDLE EAST
INDIA
SOUTHEAST ASIA

SOUTHEAST
ASIA

Southeast Asia

ketchup, kumquat, lychee: *Cantonese*

tea: *Amoy Chinese* (char *is from* *Mandarin*)

sago, mangosteen: *Malay*

India

chutney, kedgeree, samosa: *Hindi/Urdu*

curry, congee: *Tamil*

mango: *Tamil via Malay and Portuguese*

orange: *Sanskrit via Persian, Arabic, and Spanish*

sugar: *Sanskrit via Persian and Arabic*

GASTRONOMIC LOAN WORDS

Food names are among the most easily borrowed items, partly for reasons of fashion and prestige. The Norman Conquest of England introduced the French terms "pork" and "beef," which replaced the Germanic words. Many loan words have been assimilated so that their foreign origins are not obvious. The word "hamburger" (German: "[sausage] from Hamburg") has been mis-analyzed as being a combination of "ham" and "burger," giving rise to words such as "cheeseburger." In addition to the hundreds of French loans, some everyday food names come from exotic sources:

chocolate (Nahuatl, via Spanish and French)
tea (Amoy Chinese)
tomato (Nahuatl, via Spanish)
chutney, kedgeree (Hindi)
ketchup (Cantonese: "tomato-juice")
kebab (Arabic)
mango (Tamil, via Portuguese)

One of the words given as evidence for a long-distance relationship between Indo-European, Uralic, and other language families is the root *madw-* "honey" (as in English mead, a drink made from honey):

Sanskrit	(Indo-European)	**mádhu**
Russian	(Indo-European)	**med**
Hungarian	(Uralic)	**méz**
Tamil	(Dravidian)	**mattu**
Etruscan	(unclassified)	**maθ**

Although these resemblances are striking, this is the kind of word which could easily be borrowed, in which case the forms would not be evidence of a genetic relationship. The word *maθ* "mead," for example, is not sufficient to show that Etruscan is related to the Indo-European languages.

aspects of grammar are adopted. After Danish immigrants settled in Britain in the eighth and ninth centuries, for example, the influence of their Norse on Old English led to the borrowing of the pronouns "they," "them," "their," the form "are" of the verb "be," and the spread of phrasal verb constructions such as "pick up."

LANGUAGE SHIFT AND SUBSTRATES

The substrate phenomenon occurs as a result of language shift, when speakers of language A adopt language B, whether for cultural, political, or other reasons. Naturally, the first generation to adopt language B will be bilingual and will mix the two languages, as in the case of Cantonese and English in Hong Kong. Their use of B will show some features of A. The children of this generation will become native speakers of B, but retain some of the A-like features—a substrate derived from language A. An example of language shift occurred when the Franks, a Germanic tribe, colonized northern France and shifted to speaking French. They brought to their French the verb-second rule, familiar to learners of German, resulting in the inversion of subject and verb in questions such as *Que voulez-vous?* ("what do you want?"). The result is a Germanic substrate which distinguishes French from the other Romance languages.

Language shift is happening in many parts of the world today. In Scotland and Ireland, the shift from Gaelic to English continues, leaving some marks such as the construction "he's after drinking" meaning "he's been drinking" in Irish English. In California, many Hispanic families and communities are shifting from Spanish to English, and in Central America, from native American languages to Spanish. Successive generations of immigrants to North America—Norwegian, Polish, Hungarian—have discarded their languages for English, often with only surnames betraying their ancestry. In fact, language shift is now the principal way in which languages become extinct.

LINGUISTIC AREAS

As an extreme case of language contact, the languages of an area may come to share similar characteristics regardless of their genetic affiliation. A well-known example is the Balkan *Sprachbund*, the German term meaning a "bundle of languages" sharing common features. Unlike most of the surrounding languages, Greek, Romanian, Bulgarian, and Albanian lack an infinitive form of the verb. Most have a suffixed definite article (Romanian *om-ul* "the man"), and an unusual case system in which one form serves as both subject and object and another as either dative ("to") or genitive ("of"). Such similarities result from a combination of contact influences, bilingualism, and language shift, which have taken place over a long period of coexistence. In the case of the Balkans, successive migrations following the conquests and colonization of the Ottoman Empire led to widespread bilingualism. Similar situations are found in South and Southeast Asia: the use of tone, for example, is an areal feature of Southeast Asia which is not associated with any one language family.

OVERVIEW

Chapters 2 to 8 examine the language families of the regions of the world. Since it is not feasible to give the locations and affiliations of all 6,000 or so languages, the family trees and maps show

Above: *Lothair I (795–855), emperor of the Franks, a Germanic tribe who colonized northern France and who brought to the French language Germanic features such as the verb-second rule.*

only major languages or those specifically mentioned in the text. The book is organized primarily by geographical area, and secondarily by language families. Since they rarely coincide completely, the two kinds of classification, geographical and linguistic, need to be carefully distinguished: the terms European languages and Indo-European languages, for example, refer to two distinct sets of languages. European languages are merely those which happen to be spoken in

Europe, and include Uralic languages such as Hungarian, Finnish, and Estonian as well as the isolated Basque; the Indo-European languages are a family of related languages, and not merely those of India and Europe as the name might suggest.

Chapter 9 traces the origins and development of writing systems. The Epilogue considers the prospects for the survival of languages and linguistic diversity.

THE BALKAN LINGUISTIC AREA

The Balkan languages belong to four different families of Indo-European: Slavic, Romance, Greek, and Albanian. Nevertheless, they have come to share several features which are otherwise unusual, including a suffixed definite article and a case form which functions as both dative (to) and genitive (of).

ROMANIAN

lup-ul *"the wolf"*
lup-ul-ui *"to/of the wolf"*

BULGARIAN

žena-ta *"the woman"*
na bâlgarija *"to/of Bulgaria"*

ALBANIAN

mik-u *"the friend"*

GREEK

tu anthrópu *"to/of the man"*

KEY
- CROATIAN & SERBIAN
- ROMANIAN
- MOLDAVIAN
- ALBANIAN
- MACEDONIAN
- BULGARIAN
- GREEK
- TURKISH

Europe
and Eurasia

The Eurasian land mass is home to the Indo-European, Uralic, and Altaic families, together with several obscure and isolated languages of uncertain origin. The Indo-European languages form the world's most widely distributed language family; it is also the best understood thanks to a long history of recorded texts. On the other hand, the Caucasus' "mountain of tongues" has the region's greatest linguistic diversity, while the Altaic family has a remarkable uniformity of structure. In the Far East, Japanese poses its own unique puzzle.

A man in Hungarian costume asserts his national identity. Hungarian does not belong, like most European languages, to the Indo-European family but to the Finno-Ugric group.

The Eurasian linguistic area, consisting of Europe and northern and central Asia, is home to the Indo-European, Uralic, and Altaic language families.

It has long been suspected that distant relationships exist between these families. The Nostratic and Eurasiatic hypotheses, for example, both seek to establish such genetic linkages, the former suggesting that Eurasiatic is itself a branch of a greater Nostratic family (*see box below*). This hypothesis dates the spread of these languages across Eurasia to the end of the last Ice Age, some 15,000 years ago.

While the three main Eurasian families share some similarities, exceptions are presented by the highly diverse Caucasian languages and by isolated languages without known living relatives: examples include Basque, which is spoken in the French and Spanish Pyrenees, and Nivkh, which is spoken in eastern Siberia.

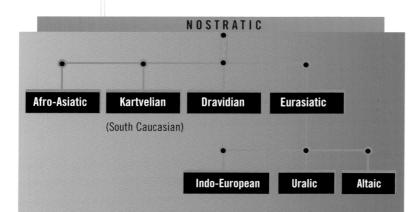

NOSTRATIC

Afro-Asiatic	Kartvelian	Dravidian	Eurasiatic

(South Caucasian)

Indo-European	Uralic	Altaic

The evidence for a relationship between Eurasian language families begins with similarities in the pronouns (first person *me/mi*, second person *te/ti*), and extends to a wide range of vocabulary items, such as the verb root *man-* "live" (as in the Latin-based word *mansion*):

Indo-European	Dravidian	Afro-Asiatic	Altaic
(Latin)	(Telugu)	(Hebrew)	(Mongolian)
manēre "live"	*manu* "live"	*ʔāmen* "remain"	*mana* "keep watch"

In some cases the meanings must be presumed to have changed substantially, making the relationship much more speculative:

Indo-European	Uralic	Dravidian
English *milk*	Hungarian *mell* "breast"	Tamil *melku* "chew"

The Indo-European Language Family

The Indo-European family was recognized when a British colonial judge, Sir William Jones, came across the Sanskrit language in eighteenth-century India. Sanskrit was extinct as a spoken language but still used for religious purposes. It clearly resembled Latin and Greek, not only in its vocabulary but also in its grammatical system and inflections. Jones concluded that all three ancient languages had "sprung from some common source," which had also given rise to Germanic and Celtic.

Following this discovery, the Baltic and Slavic families were added, together with Armenian and Albanian, single languages which represent distinct branches. More recently, the long-extinct Tocharian and Hittite languages have also been shown to have sprung from the same single source. Tocharian appears in Buddhist writings from China's Xinjiang province, showing Indo-European's early eastward expansion, while Hittite, known from inscriptions in modern Turkey (ancient Anatolia), has been identified as Indo-European's tenth branch.

THE CELTIC LANGUAGES

Although spoken widely in western Europe in the first millennium BC, the Celtic languages have been in gradual decline since Roman times, when Latin replaced Gaulish in France. They survive as minority languages in the northwestern extremities of Europe, the most vigorous being Welsh, with half a million speakers, and Breton, with almost a million.

Left: *Over half a million Welsh speakers are served by bilingual Welsh-English signs, such as this signpost at Devil's Bridge Station on the Rheidol Railway in Dyfed.*

THE INDO-EUROPEAN LANGUAGES

The Indo-European is the most widely spoken established language family in the world. The tree shows only major languages, others being listed in the sections devoted to each sub-family. Extinct languages are shown with the symbol +.

Within the Indo-European family, some groups are more closely related than the conventional family tree model implies: the Italic branch, to which Latin belongs, is particularly close to Celtic, presumably due to their close proximity in pre-Roman times.

INDO-EUROPEAN

Celtic	Italic	Greek	Germanic	Balto-Slavic		Armenian	Albanian	Indo-Iranian		+Tocharian	Anatolian
				Baltic	Slavic			Indic	Iranian		
Scots	+Latin		English								+Hittite
Irish			German								
Welsh			Dutch	Baltic	Slavic			Indic	Iranian		+Luwian
Breton	Italian		Danish								
	Spanish		Norwegian	Lithuanian	Russian			+Sanskrit	+Avestan		
	Portuguese		Swedish	Latvian	Polish						
	French		Icelandic		Czech			Hindi/Urdu	Persian		
	Provençal				Bulgarian			Bengali	Pashto		
	Romanian				Serbian/Croatian			Punjabi	Kurdish		
	Rhaeto-Romance										

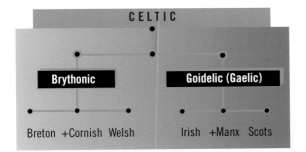

CELTIC

Brythonic			Goidelic (Gaelic)		
Breton	+Cornish	Welsh	Irish	+Manx	Scots

Breton spread to Brittany from southwest England in the seventh century AD. Cornish, a close relative, became extinct in the eighteenth century, and Manx, formerly spoken on the Isle of Man, died out in 1974, although both have since been revived from written records. Scots and Irish Gaelic survive on the Hebridean Islands of Scotland and along the west coast of Ireland.

The Celtic languages are characteristically of the VSO (verb-subject-object) type. In Welsh, for example, the verb normally comes first in the sentence: *Collodd Siôn ddwy bunt* (literally, "lost Siôn two pounds," translated as "Siôn lost two pounds"). Similarly, the noun comes before adjectives which modify it: *Bws coch mawr* (literally, "bus red big," translated as "a big red bus").

THE ROMANCE LANGUAGES

The Romance languages are derived from the "Vulgar," or vernacular, Latin of the Roman empire, which would have differed from the literary Latin of Classical texts just as the English spoken around the British Empire differed from standard British English. Italian remains closest to Latin, while many of the other Romance languages have been subject to external influences: French by Celtic and German; Romanian by surrounding Slavic languages; and Spanish by Arabic. Among the minority languages, the Rhaeto-Romance tongues of the Swiss and Italian Alps are so distinctive that they cannot be accommodated as dialects of major languages. Occitan (Provençal)

Above: *Sir William Jones, who first recognized the Indo-European language family.*

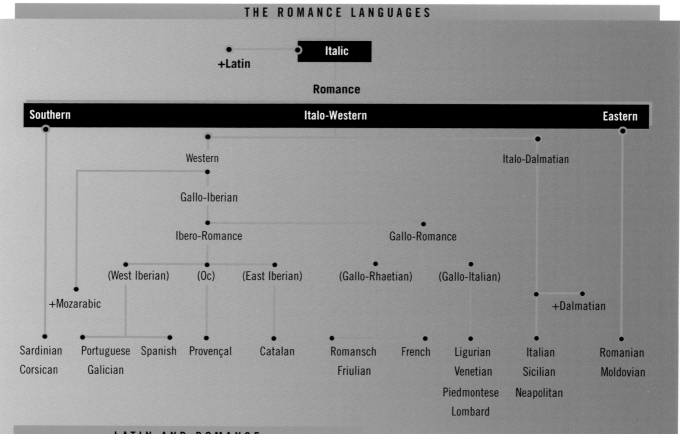

THE ROMANCE LANGUAGES

Italic

+Latin

Romance

Southern	Italo-Western	Eastern

Western

Italo-Dalmatian

Gallo-Iberian

Ibero-Romance

Gallo-Romance

(West Iberian)   (Oc)   (East Iberian)

(Gallo-Rhaetian)   (Gallo-Italian)

+Mozarabic

+Dalmatian

Sardinian	Portuguese	Spanish	Provençal	Catalan	Romansch	French	Ligurian	Italian	Romanian
Corsican	Galician				Friulian		Venetian	Sicilian	Moldovian
							Piedmontese	Neapolitan	
							Lombard		

LATIN AND ROMANCE

The Romance languages clearly show their Latin ancestry, with Italian especially close to Latin in its sounds and vocabulary; typologically, however, they are very different. They have lost the case inflections of Latin and have SVO rather than SOV word order. In many instances where Latin used inflected forms of the verb, the Romance languages use separate AUXILIARIES:

	Latin	Italian	
Perfect	*canta-vi*	*ho cantato*	"I have sung"
Passive	*canta-tur*	*è cantato*	"it is sung"

While Latin had three genders, the modern languages have two. Nouns denoting neither males nor females are assigned more or less arbitrarily to either masculine or feminine gender:

	Latin	Italian	
Masculine	*homo* "man"	*uomo* "man"";	*vino* "wine"
Feminine	*domina* "mistress"	*donna* "woman";	*guerra* "war"
Neuter	*vinum* "wine",		
	bellum "war"		

was spoken thoughout southern France, but is now restricted to remoter parts of Provence and the Massif Central. In Spain, Catalan and Galician, which have much in common with Occitan and Portuguese respectively, are increasingly recognized as separate languages. Moldavian is a dialect of Romanian which was written in Cyrillic script in the times of the Moldavian Soviet Socialist Republic. Dalmatian, a Romance language spoken on the Adriatic coast of Croatia until the nineteenth century, is now extinct.

Right: *St. Jerome (AD 320–420), born in Dalmatia, was a scholar of Chaldee, Hebrew, and Greek. His great work was the Vulgate, the first complete translation of the Bible into Latin (from Hebrew).*

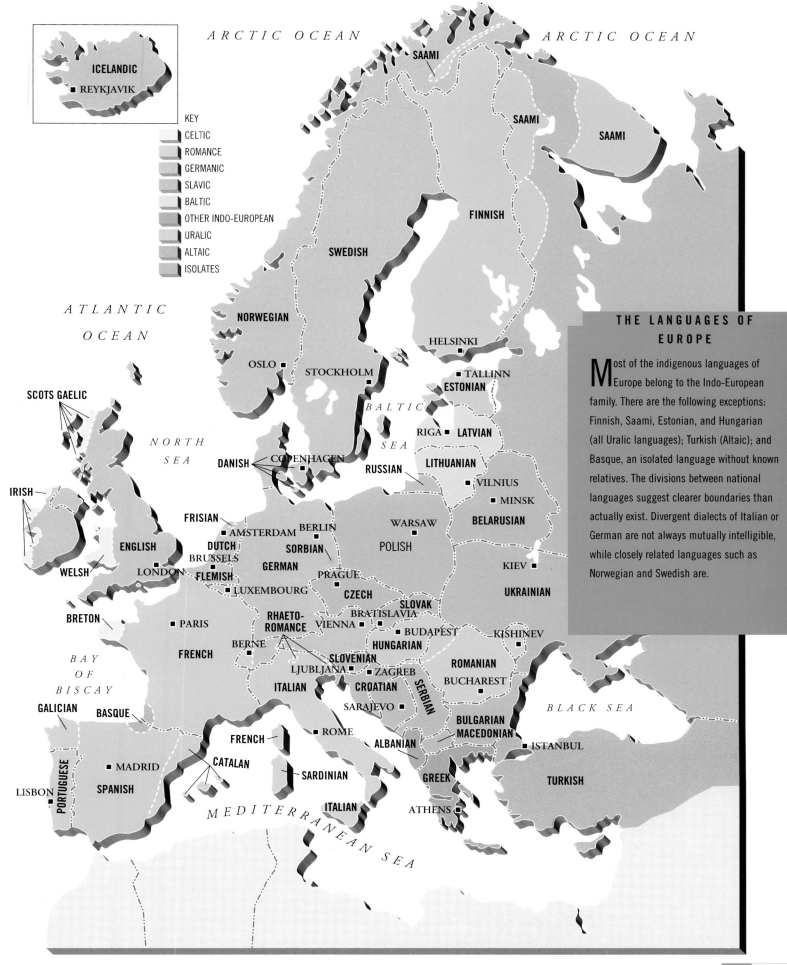

ARCTIC OCEAN

ARCTIC OCEAN

ICELANDIC
REYKJAVIK

SAAMI

SAAMI

SAAMI

KEY
CELTIC
ROMANCE
GERMANIC
SLAVIC
BALTIC
OTHER INDO-EUROPEAN
URALIC
ALTAIC
ISOLATES

ATLANTIC
OCEAN

FINNISH

SWEDISH

NORWEGIAN

HELSINKI

OSLO
STOCKHOLM
TALLINN
ESTONIAN

BALTIC
SEA

SCOTS GAELIC

NORTH
SEA

RIGA   LATVIAN

DANISH   COPENHAGEN

RUSSIAN

LITHUANIAN

VILNIUS

IRISH

MINSK

FRISIAN

AMSTERDAM   BERLIN

WARSAW

BELARUSIAN

ENGLISH
DUTCH
BRUSSELS
WELSH   LONDON   FLEMISH
LUXEMBOURG

SORBIAN

GERMAN

POLISH

PRAGUE

CZECH

KIEV

BRETON

RHAETO-
ROMANCE

SLOVAK
BRATISLAVIA

UKRAINIAN

PARIS

VIENNA

KISHINEV

FRENCH

BERNE

BUDAPEST

HUNGARIAN

BAY
OF
BISCAY

SLOVENIAN
LJUBLJANA   ZAGREB

ROMANIAN
BUCHAREST

ITALIAN   CROATIAN

SERBIAN

GALICIAN   BASQUE

SARAJEVO

BLACK SEA

FRENCH

ROME

BULGARIAN
MACEDONIAN

ALBANIAN

ISTANBUL

CATALAN

SARDINIAN

PORTUGUESE   MADRID

GREEK

TURKISH

LISBON   SPAIN

ITALIAN

ATHENS

MEDITERRANEAN SEA

THE LANGUAGES OF EUROPE

Most of the indigenous languages of Europe belong to the Indo-European family. There are the following exceptions: Finnish, Saami, Estonian, and Hungarian (all Uralic languages); Turkish (Altaic); and Basque, an isolated language without known relatives. The divisions between national languages suggest clearer boundaries than actually exist. Divergent dialects of Italian or German are not always mutually intelligible, while closely related languages such as Norwegian and Swedish are.

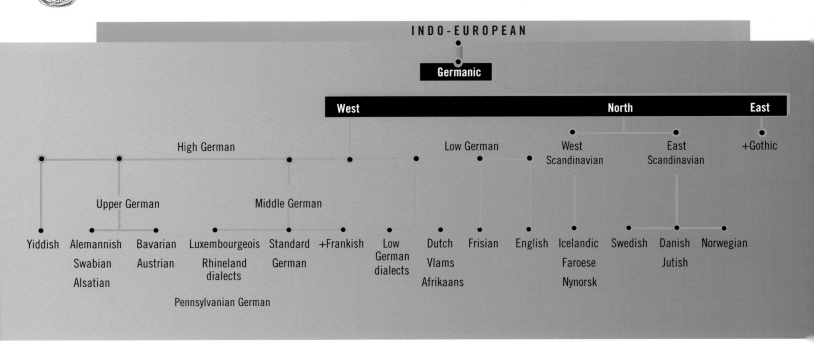

INDO-EUROPEAN

Germanic

West | North | East

High German | Low German | West Scandinavian | East Scandinavian | +Gothic

Upper German | Middle German

Yiddish | Alemannish Swabian Alsatian | Bavarian Austrian | Luxembourgeois Rhineland dialects | Standard German | +Frankish | Low German dialects | Dutch Vlams Afrikaans | Frisian | English | Icelandic Faroese Nynorsk | Swedish | Danish Jutish | Norwegian

Pennsylvanian German

THE GERMANIC LANGUAGES

The oldest records of Germanic, apart from the few Runic inscriptions, come from Gothic. Known largely from parts of a fourth-century translation of the New Testament, Gothic was still spoken around the Black Sea in the sixteenth century, but became extinct soon afterward. English, German, and Dutch are the main representatives of the western branch of Germanic. Frisian, which is spoken on the North Sea coast of Holland and Germany and on the neighboring offshore islands, is akin to the Anglo-Saxon brought to Britain after the departure of the Romans, and is thus the closest continental relative of English.

Afrikaans developed from the Dutch of seventeenth-century settlers in South Africa, where it is spoken by over half the white population and by many of mixed European and African descent. It has undergone some simplification but remains partially intelligible to Dutch-speakers. Yiddish, spoken by Jews of Central and East European extraction, is also considered a Germanic language; although it has adopted much vocabulary from Slavic and other sources, its grammar displays characteristically Germanic features.

The mainland Scandinavian languages, Swedish, Norwegian, and Danish, are mutually intelligible to some extent. Swedish is also spoken in Finland, and much of the population is bilingual in Swedish and Finnish (a Uralic language). Together with some varieties of Norwegian, and Serbo-Croatian, Latvian, and Lithuanian, Swedish is one of the few European languages with tone: different "tonal accents" distinguish pairs such as *bur-en* "the cage" and *buren* "carried."

WORD ORDER IN GERMANIC LANGUAGES

Most Germanic languages are not easily classified as SVO or SOV. Instead, they have a general rule that the verb comes second in a main clause:

German
Gestern war ich zu Hause
Yesterday was I at home
"I was at home yesterday"

Swedish
I dag kommer jag inte
today come I not
"I'm not coming today"

While Old English was a typical Germanic language in this and other respects, Modern English preserves only relics of this rule:

"Along came a procession of cows."

"Never have I seen such a range of talent in one place."

Below: *Afrikaans, seen here on a bilingual sign, is based on seventeenth-century Dutch, and is spoken by half the white population of South Africa.*

PASOP VIR SEEKOEIE
BEWARE OF HIPPOPOTAMUS

The most conservative Germanic languages are Icelandic and Faroese, preserved by remoteness and a proud tradition of resisting international influences. While other European languages all use versions of "telephone" and "radio," Icelandic uses *sími* (from the word "thread") and *útvarp* (literally "throw-out") for these devices. The system of four cases is also more fully preserved than in other Germanic languages. Thanks to this conservatism, the medieval sagas and epic poems in Old Norse are still comprehensible to Icelandic speakers.

THE BALTO-SLAVIC LANGUAGES

The Baltic and Slavic families are closely related branches of Indo-European. The two Baltic languages, Lithuanian and Latvian, compete with Russian in the former Soviet republics (Estonia, the third Baltic state, belongs linguistically to the Uralic group). The Balto-Slavic languages are especially interesting for their conservative nature, which makes them useful in the reconstruction of Indo-European. While most Indo-European languages have lost the verb and noun endings characteristic of Latin and Greek, the Baltic languages preserve complex case systems and in addition have developed tonal distinctions.

The Slavic languages, divided into western, southern, and eastern branches, are also conservative, are inflectional, like Latin and Greek, and their nouns have around six cases. A characteristic and complex feature of Slavic grammar is the division of verbs according to aspect: the "perfective" form indicates a complete

action, usually expressed by a prefix as in *ja pro-chital knigu* "I've read the book (and finished it)."

The recent political changes in eastern Europe have enhanced the status of several Slavic languages. Following the break-up of Czechoslovakia, for example, Czech has become the language of the Czech Republic, and Slovak that of Slovakia. In the former Yugoslavia, the relatively minor differences between Croatian and Serbian are now emphasized by the different writing systems: Serbian, like Russian, Ukrainian, and Bulgarian, is written in Cyrillic script, while Croatian, like Slovenian and the West Slavic languages, is written in a Roman alphabet. This distinction in turn reflects the historic division of Slavic peoples between the Eastern Orthodox and Catholic faiths. Similarly, Ukrainian and Belarusian are now languages of independent states, although they are mutually intelligible with Russian. Upper and Lower Sorbian are minority languages, each with its own written form, spoken in eastern Germany near the Czech border.

The Slavic languages have a reputation for being difficult to pronounce. Asking for an ice cream (*zmrzlina*) in Czech, and even saying "hello" in Russian (*zdrávstvujte*) are not the easiest accomplishments for speakers of other Western European languages. The main sources of this difficulty are the intimidating consonant clusters, together with certain unfamiliar consonants, such as the labiovelar glide *ł* in Polish (for example, *Wałęsa*) and the trilled post-alveolar *ř* in Czech (for example, *Dvořák*). Additional distinctive

Above: *Tablets found at the Cretan palace of Knossos date to the fourteenth century BC. Their inscriptions are written in Linear B, an archaic form of Greek. The tablets were used to record all aspects of the administration of the royal household.*

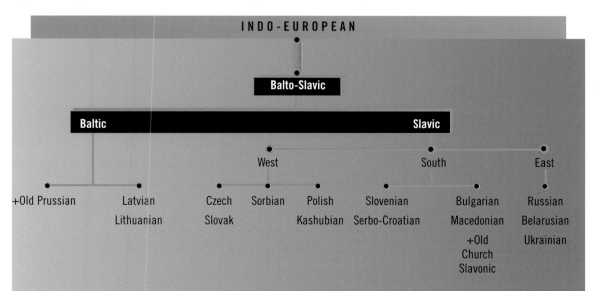

INDO-EUROPEAN

Balto-Slavic

Baltic — Slavic

West | South | East

+Old Prussian | Latvian | Czech | Sorbian | Polish | Slovenian | Bulgarian | Russian
Lithuanian | Slovak | Kashubian | Serbo-Croatian | Macedonian | Belarusian
+Old Church Slavonic | Ukrainian

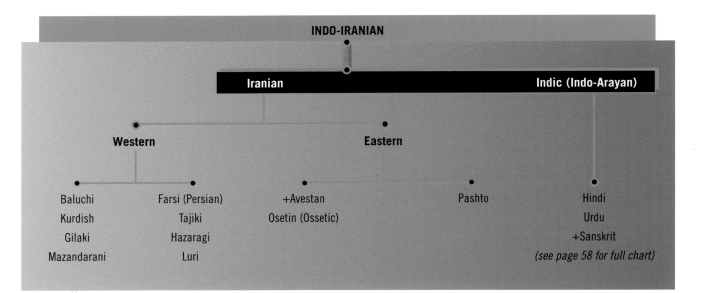

INDO-IRANIAN

Iranian				Indic (Indo-Arayan)
Western		**Eastern**		
Baluchi	Farsi (Persian)	+Avestan	Pashto	Hindi
Kurdish	Tajiki	Osetin (Ossetic)		Urdu
Gilaki	Hazaragi			+Sanskrit
Mazandarani	Luri			*(see page 58 for full chart)*

Slavic features are the palatalized or "soft" consonants, produced by raising the tongue to the roof (palate) of the mouth. In Cyrillic script they are shown by the soft sign ь as in Russian брать (*brat*) "to bring," as opposed to брат (*brat*) "brother."

Greek, Albanian, and Armenian

In the Balkan region are two isolated sub-families of Indo-European: Greek and Albanian. Greek has been spoken in the Mediterranean since at least the fourteenth century BC, indicated by the Linear B inscriptions from the Minoan civilization of Crete (c. sixteenth century BC). Greek, especially the archaic language of the Homeric poems which date back to the seventh or eighth centuries BC, is one of the oldest sources for Indo-European. The differences between modern and ancient Greek are far less drastic than the differences between English and Old English. Modern Greek is also spoken on Crete and Cyprus as well as in immigrant communities in America, Australia, and elsewhere.

There are some 4 million Albanian-speakers in Albania itself, in the Serbian province of Kosovo, and in Albanian settlements in Greece and southern Italy. The Balkan languages share several common features as a result of intense contact and bilingualism (*see page 30–31*).

Armenian is spoken in eastern Turkey and in the southwestern Caucasus. Until the post-Soviet establishment of Armenia, the Armenian people lacked a homeland, and many emigrated to the U.S.A. and elsewhere. Their language, while influenced by neighboring Persian and Turkish, has retained some Indo-European features: it is thought to be the only preserve of the ejective consonants now reconstructed as a hypothetical feature of the Indo-European proto-language.

The Indo-Iranian Languages

Indo-Iranian is a large Indo-European sub-family, with languages spoken in Iran, Afghanistan, India, and Pakistan. The ancient languages of the Indic and Iranian groups,

Left: *Rom, or gypsies, are scattered throughout Europe, having migrated from northwest India from about the ninth century onward. They maintain a nomadic way of life, and speak Romany, a language belonging to the Indic branch of the Indo-European family, usually combined with elements of the language of their adopted country.*

Sanskrit and Avestan, provide valuable clues to the reconstruction of Indo-European.

The Iranian languages are spoken in southwestern Asia and the Middle East. Persian, the national language of Iran, is also spoken in Afghanistan, together with Pashto. Kurdish is spoken in parts of Turkey, Iraq, Iran, and Syria, Ossetic in the northern Caucasus, Tajik in Tajikistan, surrounded by Turkic languages. The Baluchi and Pashto languages extend eastward into Pakistan.

The Indic languages are spoken in South Asia (*see chapter 3*), with the exception of the Gypsy language, Romany, which exists in many forms throughout Europe. Some of these have become mixed, like Anglo-Romani, which combines Romany vocabulary with English grammar.

BASQUE

Basque, spoken in Spanish and French territory at the western end of the Pyrenees, is an isolated language; many inconclusive attempts have been made to link it with other families,

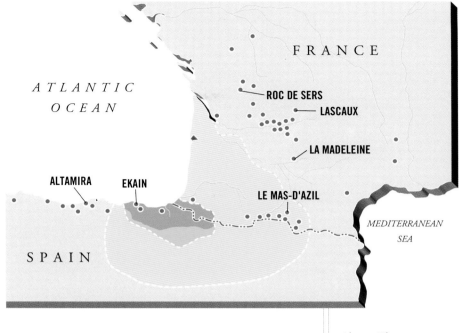

Above: *Place names and historical records indicate that languages related to Basque were once spoken in a wider area of southwest France and northern Spain than today. These areas closely match the distribution of Paleolithic cave art (see illustration on page 12) at sites such as Lascaux and Altamira. Evidence such as this suggests that the Basques were among the first populations of modern humans to settle in Europe.*

BASQUE AS AN ERGATIVE LANGUAGE

Basque is one of the few European languages with an ergative case system, the others being languages of the Caucasus. The "ergative" case is a special form for the subject of a transitive verb:

TRANSITIVE	INTRANSITIVE
Ni-k neska ikusten dut.	Ni etorri naiz.
I-ERG. girl see AUX.	I come AUX.
"I see the girl."	"I have come."

The subject of the first sentence, *ni* ("I"), has the suffix -*k* marking the ergative case, while the object *neska* ("the girl") is not marked for any case, just like the subject of the intransitive sentence, *ni*. This contrasts with the accusative system found in Indo-European languages such as Latin, Russian, and German, where the object of a transitive verb ("girl") is marked with a special case (accusative), leaving the subject of both transitive and intransitive verbs ("I") in the nominative case. While rather less numerous than the accusative type, ergative languages are widespread, especially in the Caucasus, the Far East, South Asia, America, Australia, and the Pacific.

---

especially the Kartvelian group of the Caucasus which it resembles in its grammatical structure. It is likely that other Basque-like languages were spoken more widely in western Europe before the Roman conquest: the French province of Gascony bears a Basque name, and the Gascon dialect shows many clear traces of Basque influence.

The Uralic Language Family

The Uralic family derives its name from Russia's Ural mountains, the presumed homeland of the proto-Uralic language. Uralic languages were formerly widespread in Eurasia, and left their mark on the Baltic and Slavic languages which replaced them in many areas. Most of the languages are now spoken in northern Russia, Siberia, and the Baltic region, while Hungarian was brought to Hungary by the Magyars in about the ninth century.

The Finno-Ugric group includes three national languages of Europe: Hungarian, Finnish, and Estonian. Finnish and Estonian are closely related and Estonian became a national language when

URALIC

| | | | | | | Finno-Ugric | | | | Samoyedic | Yukaghir |

Finno-Ugric **Samoyedic** **Yukaghir**

Finnic	Lappic	Volgaic	Permic	Ugric	Nenets
					Enets
					Nganasan
Finnish	Saami	Mordvin	Votyak	Hungarian	Selkup
Estonian		Mari	Komi	Khanty	Kamas
				Mansi	

Estonia gained its independence from the U.S.S.R. in 1991. Saami is spoken by the nomadic Lapps of northern Scandinavia and the Kola peninsula in Russia. The Ugric branch to which Hungarian belongs has been separated from the Finnic branch for some 3,000 years, and Hungarian shows only distant traces of its relationship to Finnish and Estonian:

Hungarian	Finnish	Estonian	
három	*kolme*	*kolm*	"three"
szem	*silmä*	*silm*	"eye"

Outside Hungary, Hungarian is also spoken by substantial minorities in Transylvania (Romania) and Slovakia, reflecting the borders before World War I. Mansi, Khanty, and Mari are spoken by minorities in northern Russia and northwestern Siberia.

The Samoyedic languages, spoken by around 30,000 inhabitants of Siberia, are more distantly related to the Finnic and Ugric languages.

SOME CASE ENDINGS REPRESENTING SPATIAL RELATIONSHIPS IN HUNGARIAN

	"located at"	"moving toward"	"moving away from"
"in"	*a ház-**ban***	*a ház-**ba***	*a ház-**ból***
	"in the house"	"into the house"	"out of the house"
"on"	*a ház-**on***	*a ház-**ra***	*a ház-**ról***
	"on the house"	"onto the house"	"off the house"
"at"	*a ház-**nál***	*a ház-**hoz***	*a ház-**tól***
	"at the house"	"to the house"	"away from the house"

Yukaghir, spoken much farther east in Siberia, shares certain features with Samoyedic and the Uralic languages (*see box left*), but its genetic relationship to them is uncertain.

The Uralic languages are well known for their complex case systems (15 in Finnish, 17 in Hungarian) which represent spatial meanings like "onto" and "away from" as well as serving grammatical functions, such as indicating the direct and indirect objects of the verb (*see box below left*). While, compared to Latin's six cases, this seems highly complex, the forms taken by case endings are very regular and generally predictable.

Another typical Uralic feature is vowel harmony, a rule according to which a word contains only a certain type of vowel; to meet this requirement, suffixes change their form according to the vowels of the word to which they attach. This is the main respect in which the Hungarian case forms vary: for example the suffix *-on* becomes *-en* in *a hegy-en* ("on the hill") and *-ön* in *a föld-ön* ("on the ground").

The Altaic Language Family

The Altaic languages of Eurasia are spoken by traditionally nomadic peoples over a large area in

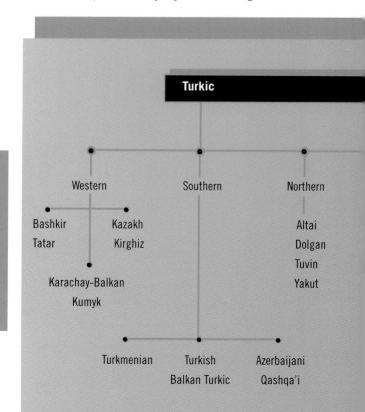

Turkic

Western	Southern	Northern
Bashkir	Kazakh	Altai
Tatar	Kirghiz	Dolgan
		Tuvin
Karachay-Balkan		Yakut
Kumyk		
Turkmenian	Turkish	Azerbaijani
	Balkan Turkic	Qashqa'i

the dry steppe climate, from Turkey to northeastern Siberia. Like the Uralic languages, they are named after their presumed mountain homeland, the Altai range of central Asia. While there is some doubt as to whether they are genetically related, their common features include SOV order, words which are formed by adding separate constituents ("agglutination"), and vowel harmony. The last two features are also shared with Uralic, suggesting either prolonged contact or a distant genetic relationship between the two families. For similar reasons, some scholars include Korean and even Japanese within Altaic (*see chapter 3*). The three main Altaic families are Turkic, Mongolic, and Tungusic, each of which is relatively homogenous.

TURKIC LANGUAGES

Turkic languages are spoken by numerous nationalities in Russia, in several of the Central Asian republics: Uzbekistan, Kazakhstan, Kirghizstan, Turkmenistan, and Azerbaijan; by parts of the population in Iran, Afganistan, and Mongolia; as well as in Turkey itself. Uighur is spoken largely in Xinjiang province of China, while Yakut is found in northeastern Siberia.

Chuvash, a distinctive Turkic language spoken by about 2 million inhabitants of the upper Volga region, is the sole survivor of the Bolgar group and has retained several archaic features; it may represent the "missing link" between Turkic and Mongolic.

YUKAGHIR "WRITING"

Yukaghir is spoken in one of the world's harshest climates, and much of our knowledge of it comes from intellectuals exiled to Siberia who studied the local language and culture to relieve boredom. Among their discoveries are the pictorial "letters" whose meanings were to be guessed at, as in a game of charades.

The "love letter" represents two households and several characters shown as pine trees. A girl (c) is thinking of her sweetheart (b) who is living with a Russian woman (a). The crossed lines represent discord within the households. There is another man (d) interested in the girl, supposedly a warning to (b). Although the drawings are not regarded as true writing because they do not directly represent any aspect of the Yukaghir language, they are comparable to native American pictographs as symbolic representations in a pre-literate culture.

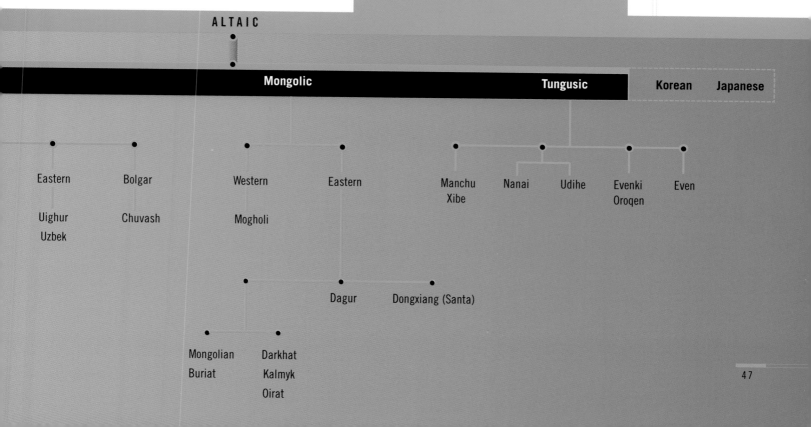

ALTAIC

Mongolic   **Tungusic**   **Korean**   **Japanese**

| Eastern | Bolgar | Western | Eastern | Manchu Xibe | Nanai | Udihe | Evenki Oroqen | Even |

Uighur
Uzbek   Chuvash   Mogholi

Dagur   Dongxiang (Santa)

Mongolian   Darkhat
Buriat   Kalmyk
        Oirat

THE MONGOLIC LANGUAGES

The main Mongolic languages are those of the Mongolian People's Republic and Inner Mongolia, an autonomous region of China. The Mongolian spoken in these two areas differs only about as much as British and American English. The Khalkha variety is the standard form, written today in Cyrillic script. Other Mongolic languages are spoken in China (Oirat and Santa) and Russia (Buriat, in southern Siberia, and Kalmyk, along the Caspian Sea). Together the Mongolic languages have around 3 million speakers and are similar in structure to the better-known Japanese and Korean, with seven or eight cases and SOV word order.

THE TUNGUSIC LANGUAGES

Tungusic languages are spoken by minorities in the north of China (Oroqen and Udyghe), and Siberia and the Far East (Evenki and Even). Until recently they were widely spoken in northern China, where Manchu, the language of the last emperors of China, enjoyed prestige under the Ch'ing Dynasty (1644–1911). During

AGGLUTINATING LANGUAGES

Agglutinating structure, whereby the parts of a word are "glued together," is characteristic of the Altaic languages. In Classical Mongolian, as in Latin, nouns have special forms for different grammatical functions (cases):

	Singular	Plural
Nominative	*bakši* "the teacher"	*bakši-nar* "the teachers"
Accusative	*bakši-yi* "the teacher" (object)	*bakši-nar-i* "the teachers"
Dative	*bakši-dur* "to the teacher"	*bakši-nar-tur* "to the teachers"
Genitive	*bakši-n* "the teacher's"	*bakši-nar-un* "the teachers"
Ablative	*bakši-aca* "from the teacher"	*bakši-nar-aca* "from the teachers"
Instrumental	*bakši-bar* "by the teacher"	*bakši-nar-iyar* "by the teachers"
Comitative	*bakši-luġa* "with the teacher"	*bakši-nar-luġa* "with the teachers"

Each form can readily be separated into component parts, such as the suffix *-nar* denoting plural forms. Apart from some variation in the first vowel or consonant of the suffix, the forms are regular and predictable, quite unlike Latin and Greek where the various forms of the noun declensions have to be learned individually.

KEY
- TURKIC
- TUNGUSIC
- MONGOLIC
- FINNO-UGRIC
- SAMOYEDIC
- CHUKOTKO-KAMCHATKAN
- INDO-EUROPEAN
- OTHER LANGUAGE FAMILIES

BARENTS SEA

SAAMI

NENETS

KHANTY

KARELIAN

KOMI

KOMI

MANSI

VOTYAK

MARI

TATAR

CHUVASH

MORDVIN

UKRAINIAN

KALMYK

KAZAKH

KAZAKHSTAN

UZBEK

TURKEY

TURKMENIAN

TAJIK

TURKISH

SYRIA

AZERI

AFGHANISTAN

IRAQ

IRAN

PAKISTAN

SAUDI ARABIA

this period the classics of Chinese literature were translated into Manchu, which was written in a Uighur syllabic script like that of Mongolian. Manchu is now close to extinction, with Manchu-speakers having shifted to Chinese; northern Chinese dialects often reflect this shift, showing traces of Altaic structure such as SOV word order. Like many Uralic and Altaic languages, Manchu makes much use of vowel harmony, a principle requiring each word to contain the same type of vowel. One of its uses in Manchu is to distinguish male and

EURASIAN LANGUAGE FAMILIES

The Uralic, Altaic, and Indo-European families which extend across the Eurasian continent may ultimately be related to each other as part of a Eurasian phylum. Although spoken over wide areas, many of the Uralic and Tungusic languages are threatened with extinction, as are the language isolates such as Ket, Yukaghir, and Nivkh which may represent relics of earlier families.

KEY
ABKHAZ-ADYGHEAN
NAKH-DAGESTANIAN
KARTVELIAN
ALTAIC
INDO-EUROPEAN

female, or *yin* and *yang* words: *eme* ("mother"), *hehe* ("woman"), and *emhe* ("mother-in-law") are all *yin* words, while *ama* ("father), *haha* ("man"), and *amha* ("father-in-law") are all *yang* words.

The Languages of the Caucasus

The Caucasus, with its vast number of languages located in a small territory, has long attracted the attention of linguists. In the early 1800s, Russian missionaries, ethnographers, and even generals started collecting data on the languages of the area, and their discoveries have become an important foundation on which studies continue to rely. There are over 40 spoken languages belonging to three distinct families, and the phrase "Caucasian languages" denotes a purely geographical grouping. The three main families are Kartvelian, Abkhaz-Adyghean, and Nakh-Dagestanian. In the surrounding lowland areas, Turkic (Azerbaijani and Kumyk) and Indo-European languages (Armenian, Ossetic) are also spoken (*see map above*).

The Kartvelian family includes Georgian, Laz, Svan, and Mingrelian. Georgian has a long and

Left: *A speaker of the Chechen language. With almost a million speakers, Chechen has a rich ergative case system which relates it to other languages of the Nakh-Daghestanian family. It is also one of the written languages that currently use the Cyrillic alphabets.*

well-established literary tradition whose earliest documents date back to the fifth century AD. Kartvelian languages are known for their complex morphology and voice systems.

The Abkhaz-Adyghean family of the northwestern Caucasus includes Abaza, Abkhaz, Adyghe, Kabardian or Circassian, and Ubykh. Ubykh used to be spoken in Turkey but is now considered a dead language; its last known speaker, from whose expertise three generations of linguists were able to benefit, died in 1992. The remaining languages of the family use writing systems based on Cyrillic.

Abkhaz-Adyghean languages are famous among linguists for their inordinately complex system of consonants (some experts distinguish 80 in Ubykh and 69 in the Bzyb dialect of Abkhaz), and for their extremely limited number of vowels (2–3). As vowels undergo reduction in speech (for instance, Kabardian *c'əχ°əf* – "a good person" may be pronounced as *cχ°f*), some linguists have even described these languages as having no vowels at all. Several languages of this family are characterized by ergativity (where the subject of a transitive sentence is marked differently from the subject of an intransitive sentence, which is marked in the same manner as the object in a transitive one).

Most of the languages of the Nakh-Daghestanian family are also ergative. These include Chechen, Ingush, Avar, Chamalal, Dido, Lak, Dargwa, Lezgian, Tabassaran, Archi, Tsakhur, and others. The largest languages are Chechen with close to a million speakers, and Avar and Lezgian with around 400,000 each. For a while, Tabassaran was known to linguists as the language with the world's richest case system. Indeed, all languages of this family have extensive systems of cases, primarily due to the abundance of locatives expressing spatial relations (in Tsez there are around 152 local cases). Cases are formed agglutinatively, and each case form includes a special suffix denoting the position of the reference point ("on," "under," "near," "behind"). This suffix can in turn be followed by another suffix expressing motion ("to," "toward," "from") in relation to the reference point.

Below: *An Armenian villager from Karabagh represents just one of the up to 50 different ethnic groups and nationalities dispersed across the Caucasus region. Language is inseparable from ethnic identity, and is maintained by peoples who may owe more loyalty to clan and family than nation or region.*

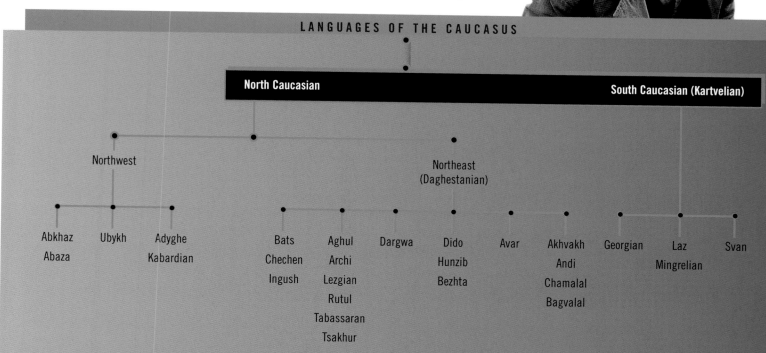

LANGUAGES OF THE CAUCASUS

North Caucasian | **South Caucasian (Kartvelian)**

Northwest

- Abkhaz / Abaza
- Ubykh
- Adyghe / Kabardian

Northeast (Daghestanian)

- Bats / Chechen / Ingush
- Aghul / Archi / Lezgian / Rutul / Tabassaran / Tsakhur
- Dargwa
- Dido / Hunzib / Bezhta
- Avar
- Akhvakh / Andi / Chamalal / Bagvalal

South Caucasian (Kartvelian)

- Georgian
- Laz / Mingrelian
- Svan

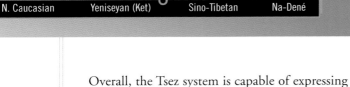

DENE-CAUCASIAN

| N. Caucasian | Yeniseyan (Ket) | Sino-Tibetan | Na-Dené |

Overall, the Tsez system is capable of expressing the following concepts by means of locative case markers: "in a hollow object" (e.g. a room), "in a mass among," "on a horizontal surface," "under," "at, by, near," "to," "from," "toward (a distant point)," "away from (a distant point)," and "through."

In the Nakh-Daghestanian family, Avar, Chechen, Lezgian, Tabassaran, Lak, and Dargwa are written languages which currently use Cyrillic alphabets (some formerly used Arabic script). Another language of the family, Udi, is linked to Old Udi or Caucasian Albanian, a written language that flourished between the sixth and tenth centuries and is found on ceramic fragments and stone tablets; the deciphering of Caucasian Albanian documents is far from complete.

Below: *A view of the Siberian Yenisey River, where the isolated language Ket is spoken by a dwindling number of people.*

The origins of the Caucasian languages remain mysterious. The two northern families, Abkhaz-Adyghean and Nakh-Dagestanian, may be distantly related. The Dené-Caucasian hypothesis links them in turn with the Na-Dené languages of North America and with Sino-Tibetan. At least one part of the Dené-Caucasian hypothesis, linking the Yeniseyan languages of Siberia with the Na-Dené family, is strongly supported by grammatical and lexical evidence.

The Languages of The Far East

The languages of the Far East do not form a single family, but are subdivided into two separate families and several isolated languages including Ket (*see above left*), Yukaghir (possibly Uralic), and Nivkh. The number of people speaking these languages is dwindling, and the study of them undertaken by Russian and Soviet scholars in the nineteenth and twentieth centuries became a salvage operation. Ket, spoken along the Siberian Yenisey River, is partly inflectional,

resembling the languages of the Caucasus more than those of Siberia. Nivkh is spoken by some 2,000 people living along the river Amur and on Sakhalin Island.

The Eskimo-Aleut language family includes Asiatic Eskimo and Aleutian and extends over two continents, Asia and America. Varieties of Eskimo (also known as Inuit, Yupik, or Inuktittut) are spoken as far away as Greenland. In the Far East, due to intense contact, a mixed language known as Copper Island Aleut developed with Aleutian vocabulary and Russian

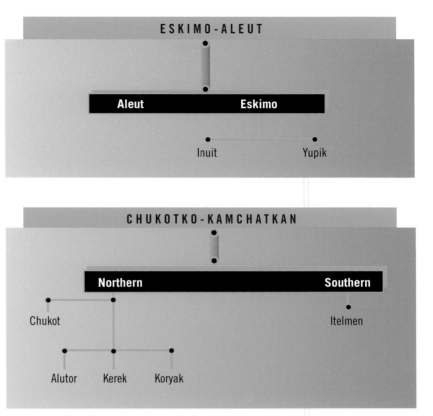

TYPOLOGY OF LANGUAGES

According to their morphology (word structure), languages can be classified into four basic types: isolating, agglutinative, fusional (inflectional), and polysynthetic. The classification is based on three essential criteria:

(1) Does a word divide into smaller meaningful parts (morphemes)?

(2) Are the boundaries between these component parts clear?

(3) Does each component express a single meaning?

● If the answer to the first question is negative, we are dealing with an isolating language, where even grammatical concepts are expressed by separate words which do not divide into smaller units. Chinese and Vietnamese are both examples of this type; in Mandarin *ta bu hui yong dao chi fan* translates literally as "he no can use knife eat rice," ("He doesn't know how to eat rice with a knife.")

● In an agglutinating language, words divide into smaller units (morphemes) with clear boundaries between them, and each grammatical meaning is expressed by a separate morpheme; for example, in Japanese *tabe-sase-rare-ru* translates as "can cause someone to eat"; *tabe* means "eat", *sase* "cause", *rare* "can" and *ru* marks the present tense.

● In an inflectional language, the boundaries between morphemes are fuzzy, and morphemes can express more than one grammatical meaning, as in Latin *pluribus* where the ending *-ibus* indicates both plurality and either dative or ablative case.

● In a polysynthetic language, several morphemes are put together to form complex words which can function as a whole sentence, as in Chukchi *tə-meyŋə-levtə-pəɣt-ərkən*, literally "1st person-big-head-ache-ing" ("I have a fierce headache").

grammar, but this is now practically extinct.

The Chukotko-Kamchatkan family includes Alutor, Itelmen, Kerek, Koryak, and Chukchi. All these languages have undergone significant influence from Russian and the numbers of their speakers have decreased. Chukchi is the most robust, with about 12,000 remaining speakers.

Languages of both the Eskimo-Aleut and Chukotko-Kamchatkan families are characterized by ergativity (*see page 45*), as well as by agglutination and complex verbal categories. An unusual feature found in some languages of both families is incorporation, a process whereby a word (usually a verb) forms a compound with its object and modifiers but retains its original function in the sentence. Incorporation results in the creation of long, internally complex words. For example, the English sentence "Let's play ball all through the night," consisting of seven words, is rendered as a single, long compound word in

Above: *Akankohan village on the Japanese island of Hokkaido is home to the Ainu people. The Ainu language is now virtually extinct—the last known native speaker, Asai Take, died in 1994.*

can express what is normally a sentence by a single compound word (as in the Chukchi example above), they have been characterized as "polysynthetic" (*see page 53*).

JAPANESE AND KOREAN

Japanese is one of the world's major languages, ranking ninth in numbers of mother-tongue speakers at around 120 million. In terms of both its language and its culture Japan is one of the world's more homogenous countries, dominated by a single national language, although regional dialects differ considerably in pronunciation and may even be mutually unintelligible. Ryukyuan, with some 900,000 speakers on Okinawa and the surrounding islands, is considered a separate group of languages, mutually unintelligible with Japanese.

The origin of Japanese is among the most disputed questions of language history. On the one hand, much of Japanese grammar resembles that of Altaic languages such as Mongolian and Manchu. On the other hand, in its use of prefixes and its sound system with a limited set of consonants and a preference for open syllables, Japanese resembles Austronesian languages, which are thought to have originated in the area of Taiwan (*see chapter 5*); certain words also support the Austronesian connection. These two hypotheses can best be reconciled in terms of a mixture of Altaic and Austronesian elements.

Korean is spoken on the Korean peninsula, in the neighboring Chinese province of Heilongjiang, and on the island of Cheju, which possesses a distinctive dialect. The post-war political division of North and South Korea, like the separation of East and West Germany, has led to differences in language policy: the North Korean government has conducted purification campaigns to eliminate Chinese words and the use of Chinese characters.

Japanese and Korean are remarkably similar in structure: they are both agglutinating languages with SOV word order, the verb being placed

Chukchi: *mən-nəke-ure-qepl-uwičwen-mək* (literally, "let-us-night-long-ball-play-we").

Ainu is a virtually extinct language formerly spoken on the northernmost Japanese island of Hokkaido and Russia's Sakhalin Island, where the last known speaker died in 1994. Although some Ainu culture persists on Hokkaido, its people now speak only Japanese. Ainu is more distinct from Japanese and from Korean than the latter two languages are from one another. Its origins pose a problem; it may be an outlying Altaic language, separated from Japanese and from Korean by as many as 10,000 years. The Ainu had a rich oral literature which allows us a glimpse into their past. The archaic language of Ainu epic poems shows that, like Chukchi, it allowed a noun to be incorporated into a verb, as in *ney ta cise-kar-as* (literally, "There we house-made," or "We made a house there.")

Incorporation is not exclusive to languages of the Far East; it is also common in languages of the Americas and of Australia. Since some of these

HONORIFICS

One of the most striking, and for foreigners most difficult, features of Japanese and Korean is their honorific system. All languages have ways of showing politeness, such as the *tu/vous* contrast in French and similar distinctions in most European languages. Japanese and Korean are unusual in the extent to which politeness is encoded in the grammar by the various forms of the verb. Politeness to the person to whom one is speaking is shown in Japanese by the suffix ***masu***:

Taroo-ga	*sono*	*tegami-o*	*yomu*	"Taroo reads that letter"
Taroo-SUBJ	that	letter-OBJ	reads	(neutral)
Taroo-ga	*sono*	*tegami-o*	*yomi-**masu***	"Taroo reads that letter"
Taroo-SUBJ	that	letter-OBJ	reads-	POLITE (polite to addressee)

The Japanese honorific system also allows the speaker to show respect for a person referred to in a sentence. Respect for the subject of the sentence is expressed by a more complex form of the verb with the prefix *o-*:

Sensei-ga	*sono*	*tegami-o*	***o-yom-i ni nat-ta***
teacher-SUBJ	that	letter-OBJ	HON-read-HON-PAST
"The (honorable) teacher read that letter"			

Similar honorific forms are used in Korean, where the ages of the speaker and addressee are especially important, in accordance with the Confucian principle of respect for one's elders.

strictly at the end of the sentence. There are also complex honorific forms which indicate respect to those spoken or referred to. These and other similarities have led some scholars to postulate a genetic relationship between the two languages, but this theory is far from universally accepted.

Both Japanese and Korean have borrowed extensively from Chinese, and both languages were first written with Chinese characters: Japanese script remains a combination of Chinese characters (Kanji) with syllabic systems, while Korean is now written largely in Han'gul, a unique form of phonetic script devised by King Sejong in the fifteenth century. In recent years Japanese has absorbed some English vocabulary, known as *gairaigo* ("foreign-coming language"): for example, *jīnzu* ("jeans"), *fitto suru* ("fit"), *furesshu na* ("fresh"), *repooto suru* ("to report"). Since corresponding Japanese words exist in most cases, these loan words reflect fashion as much as need. They are distinguished by being written in the angular *kata-kana* script, rather than in the cursive *hira-gana* syllabary used for native Japanese forms.

Below: *The traditional greeting of bowing in Japan shows respect. In speech, Japanese, like Korean, includes complex honorific forms which indicate respect to those being spoken to or about.*

South and Southeast Asia

In South and Southeast Asia multilingualism is a way of life, and as a result there has occurred much remarkable linguistic convergence. The Indo-European family extends into South Asia where it meets the Dravidian and Austro-Asiatic languages. In Southeast Asia several language families have mingled in the shadow of China. The various forms of Chinese, one of the region's many tone languages, have more native speakers than any other language in the world; it is perhaps also the language most widely misunderstood.

Tibetans from China's least populated region. The Tibetan language, with about 4 million speakers, has a literary tradition dating back to AD 600.

The languages of South and Southeast Asia reflect the region's cultural antiquity and heavy population density. Although there are numerous language families, they are less diverse than might be expected, often sharing features resulting from contact between speakers over the course of several generations.

The South Asian languages have SOV word order, with retroflex consonants, sounds which are produced by turning up or curling back the tip of the tongue under the hard palate. The Southeast Asian languages belong to the isolating type, where grammatical concepts are expressed by separate words which do not divide into smaller units. These languages have few inflections, many noun classifiers, and use tone to distinguish words. Regional features tend to obscure the genetic relationships between the languages, which sometimes remain unclear.

Right and Below: These family trees show the two main language families of South Asia. Refer to the tree on page 39 to see how Indo-Iranian is related with other Indo-European families.

THE INDIC AND DRAVIDIAN LANGUAGES

South Asia is dominated by two language families, Indo-Iranian and Dravidian, with much smaller groups speaking Munda and Tibeto-Burman. The Indo-Iranian branch of the Indo-European family extends through much of India, Pakistan, and Bangladesh as well as most of Sri Lanka and the Himalayan kingdom of Nepal.

In India and Pakistan, the Indic languages have come into contact with the Dravidian languages, from which they have acquired features such as retroflex consonants and strict verb-final word order. The Dravidian languages in turn have borrowed Indic vocabulary. Tamil has many loan

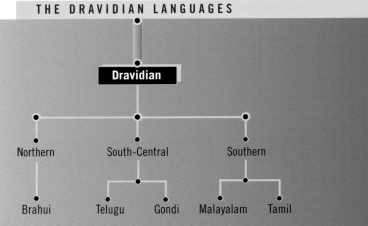

Above: The Tamil Tigers of Sri Lanka have waged a guerrilla war against the majority Sinhalese, seeking an independent Tamil state.

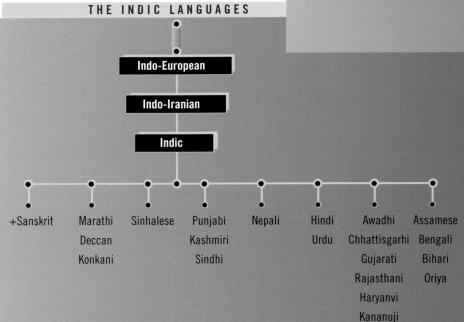

The Indo-Iranian branch of Indo-European is the dominant language family of South Asia. In the south, the languages of the Dravidian family are spoken, while in the northeast there are pockets of Austro-Asiatic and Sino-Tibetan. Most Indians speak two or three languages, with Hindi and English taught in schools. The map shows the major languages in each group.

Burushaski is a unique language with no known relatives, spoken by some 50,000 people in the Karakoram mountains of northern Pakistan. It is an ergative language with a complex system of prefixes and suffixes and some use of tone.

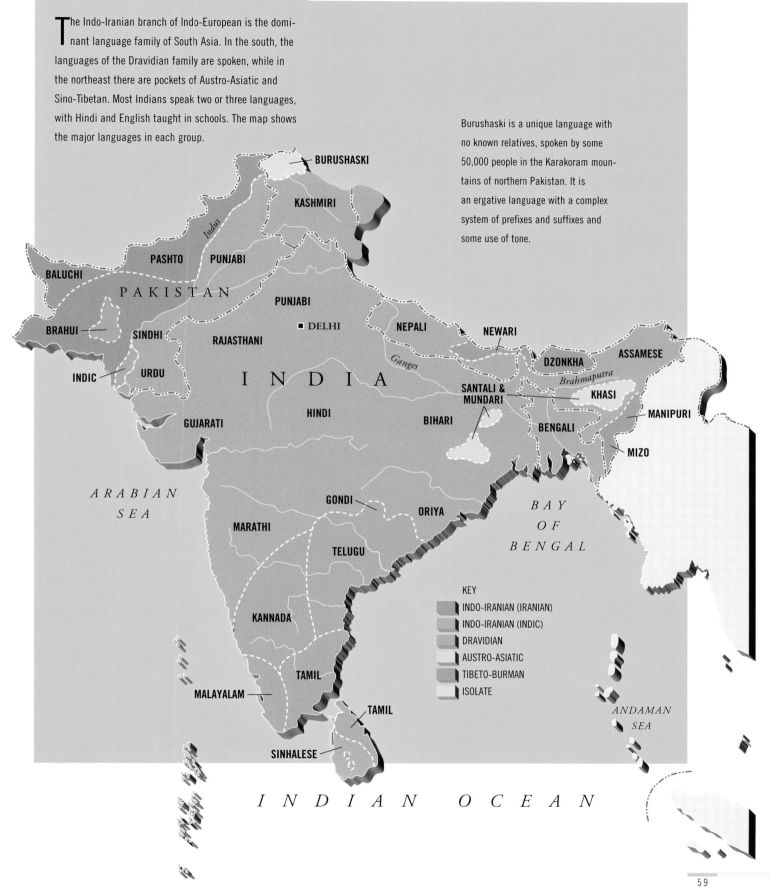

BURUSHASKI

KASHMIRI

PASHTO   PUNJABI

BALUCHI

PAKISTAN

PUNJABI

BRAHUI

SINDHI   ■ DELHI   NEPALI   NEWARI

RAJASTHANI

Indus

Ganges

INDIC

URDU

I N D I A

DZONKHA   ASSAMESE

Brahmaputra

SANTALI &
MUNDARI   KHASI

HINDI

BIHARI   MANIPURI

GUJARATI   BENGALI

MIZO

ARABIAN
SEA

GONDI

ORIYA

BAY
OF
BENGAL

MARATHI

TELUGU

KEY

	INDO-IRANIAN (IRANIAN)
	INDO-IRANIAN (INDIC)
	DRAVIDIAN
	AUSTRO-ASIATIC
	TIBETO-BURMAN
	ISOLATE

KANNADA

TAMIL

ANDAMAN
SEA

MALAYALAM

TAMIL

SINHALESE

I N D I A N   O C E A N

SANSKRIT

Sanskrit underlies the languages of South Asia as Latin does those of western Europe. It represents, albeit in a somewhat artificial literary form, the ancestor of the Indic languages, and its vocabulary has spread widely throughout languages as far east as Thailand and Laos, just as Latin vocabulary has infiltrated English and other European languages. Its cultural significance, again like that of Latin, derives from religious use: the name Sanskrit means "purified." Sir William "Oriental" Jones, who identified the Indo-European language family, described it memorably: "a wonderful structure; more perfect than the Greek, more copious than the Latin, and more exquisitely refined than either." For example, where Latin had six cases, Sanskrit had eight:

Nominative	*devas*	"God"	Dative	*devaya*	"to God"
Vocative	*deva*	"O God"	Ablative	*devat*	"from God"
Accusative	*devam*	"God"	Genitive	*devasya*	"of God"
Instrumental	*devena*	"by God"	Locative	*deve*	"with God"

Sanskrit is typically written in the Devanagari script ("script of the city of the gods") containing the root *deva-* (as in "divine"). Dating from as early as 1500BC, the Sanskrit texts represent crucial evidence in the reconstruction of Indo-European. Among the famous works of Sanskrit literature are the Vedas, the epic Ramayana, and Panini's writings on grammar, in which many concepts of modern linguistics are prefigured.

Above: An extract taken from a Sanskrit manual for high schools, showing conjugations of various verbs. Although only now used for religious purposes, Sanskrit is one of the official languages of India.

words from Sanskrit, such as *pādam* "foot" (related to *pedal* from Latin). Some Tamils have tried to purge their language of these "foreign" words.

The main Indic languages spoken in India are Hindi, Urdu, Punjabi, Sindhi, Bengali, Gujarati, Marathi, Bihari, and Assamese. Hindi and Urdu, the official languages of India and Pakistan, are essentially dialects of a single language and share a common form, Hindustani, promoted by Gandhi as a unifying force. Some Indians resisted the imposition of Hindi/Hindustani, however, and English has been retained as a *lingua franca*. Faced with some 200 indigenous languages, India follows a three-language policy, whereby children learn Hindi and English as well as a local language at school.

Although Urdu is the official language of Pakistan, larger numbers of Pakistanis speak other Indic languages such as Punjabi and Sindhi or the Iranian languages Baluchi and Pashto. Burushaski, isolated in the Karakoram mountains of northwest Pakistan, is unrelated to any other known language. In the Himalayan kingdom of Nepal, the main languages are Nepali, of the Indic family, and Newari, of the Tibeto-Burman, while in nearby Bhutan, Dzongkha, a form of Tibetan, is the *lingua franca*. In Bangladesh, Bengali, one of the major Indic languages, predominates.

The Dravidian languages are concentrated in southern and eastern India, though the isolated Dravidian language Brahui, which is found in Pakistan, suggests that they were spoken throughout the region before the Indo-European expansion. They are agglutinating languages with numerous consonants and as many as eight case forms. The major Dravidian languages are Kannada, Malayalam, Tamil, and Telugu; each has its own established literary tradition and each is the official language of an Indian state. In

Sri Lanka, the Indic language Sinhalese coexists uneasily with the Dravidian Tamil.

The Munda languages are found in the highland regions of northeastern India. They are distantly related to Southeast Asian Vietnamese and Khmer, but have been influenced by the surrounding Indic languages. The main examples are Santali and Mundari.

SOUTHEAST ASIA

Mainland Southeast Asia constitutes a distinct linguistic area: most languages have SVO word order and belong to the isolating type, where most words consist of a single syllable. Many of these languages are also known for their use of tone as a distinctive feature, whereby the pitch at which a syllable is pronounced indicates its meaning: in Mandarin *zhū* with a high tone means "pig," *zhŭ* with a fall-rise means "lord." Typical tone patterns are pitch levels (high, low, or mid-) and contours (falling or rising, fall-rise or rise-fall). Tones can also involve voice quality, as in Burmese which has a "creaky sound," and Hmong with its "breathiness."

Chinese and Indian cultures, with their Confucian and Buddhist belief systems, dominate the languages of Southeast Asia. Chinese loan words are found in most languages of the region, and Sanskrit ones in Thai and Khmer. Chinese writing is, or has been, used to write non-Chinese languages such as Vietnamese, Japanese, and Korean, while scripts of Indic origin are used for Thai and Tibetan.

THE MON-KHMER LANGUAGES

Together with the Munda languages of north-eastern India, the Mon-Khmer languages form the Austro-Asiatic family. Their scattered distribution suggests that they were once spoken over a wide area of mainland Southeast Asia, but were split by the movement of Tai speakers southward. (Tai is the name of a language family to which Thai belongs.)

Vietnamese and Khmer, the latter spoken in Cambodia, are the best-known languages in this group. Mon, the language of an ancient civilization of Thailand, is now spoken in

Above right: *The Indian subcontinent is separated from the rest of Asia by the Himalayan mountain range. In the Himalayan region the Indo-Iranian and Tibeto-Burman language families meet, while Burushaski is the sole survivor of an earlier family.*

Right: *The Uighurs of Northwest China are an Islamic people, speaking a Turkic language. Their main city, Kashgar, was an important trading post on the Silk Road.*

southern Myanmar (Burma), northeast Thailand, and along the border between China and Vietnam. The Aslian languages are spoken in inland peninsular Malaysia.

Although similar in type to Chinese and the surrounding Tai-Kadai languages, the use of tone is not typical of Mon-Khmer: the tones of Vietnamese seem to have developed relatively recently, under the influence of Chinese and/or Tai languages. Many Mon-Khmer languages have a distinction of register, some vowels being pronounced with a low "creaky" voice, rather than of tone.

TAI-KADAI

This family includes two standard languages, Thai and Lao, which are spoken in Thailand and Laos respectively. The Tai languages are thought to have originated in southwest China, and are still spoken by many of the minority peoples of this area; Zhuang, with its own romanized script, has the most speakers (around 14 million in 1992: the Zhuang people also have an Autonomous Region in the province of Guangxi). The Kam-Sui languages of China's Hunan and Guizhou provinces differ more radically than Zhuang from

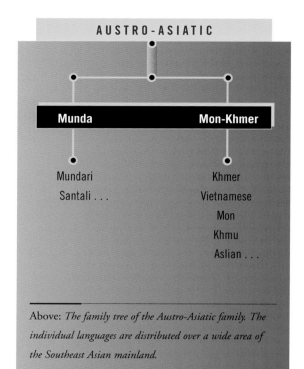

AUSTRO-ASIATIC

| Munda | Mon-Khmer |

Mundari
Santali . . .

Khmer
Vietnamese
Mon
Khmu
Aslian . . .

Above: *The family tree of the Austro-Asiatic family. The individual languages are distributed over a wide area of the Southeast Asian mainland.*

Thai and Lao. The Li and Be languages are indigenous to Hainan island, although Hainan has since been settled by both Yao and Chinese speakers. Shan, a minority language of eastern Myanmar, is also of the Tai family.

The Tai-Kadai languages were once believed to belong to the Sino-Tibetan family because they share some vocabulary and similar sound systems with southern Chinese dialects such as Cantonese. These similarities are now seen as the result of borrowing and language shift, whereby speakers of the Tai-Kadai languages came to adopt Chinese, bringing to it features of their original languages. The Tai-Kadai group are all tone languages:

Left: *Tamil tea-pickers from Sri Lanka. A Dravidian language, Tamil is spoken in both Sri Lanka and the southeast Indian state of Tamil Nadu.*

MAINLAND SOUTHEAST ASIA

The mainland Southeast Asian languages belong to four families: Tibeto-Burman, Tai-Kadai, Mon-Khmer, and Hmong-Mien. Though numerous, the languages are of a similar type due to long proximity and nearly all use tone. In Laos, languages of all four families are spoken, typically at different elevations: the Hmong, for example, live in mountain areas.

KEY
TIBETO-BURMAN
SINITIC
HMONG-MIEN
TAI-KADAI
MON-KHMER

CHINA

MIAO
KAM
SUI
CHINESE (YUE)
DAI
MIAO
YAO
ZHUANG
YAO

LAI
WA
SHAN
Red
Black
HANOI
MIN
MINNAN

MYANMAR
LOLO
KHMU
HMONG
LI
YAO

BURMESE
LAO
SOUTH CHINA SEA

KAREN
Irrawaddy
Ping
Yom
VIENTIANE

RANGOON
THAI
LAOS
Mekong

THAILAND

MON
INDIAN OCEAN
KAREN
BANGKOK
KHMER
Mekong
VIET NAM

CAMBODIA
VIETNAMESE

PHNOM PENH

GULF OF THAILAND

PAK TAY

Thai has five tones, Lao six, while Kam-Sui languages have as many as 15 tones. They are SVO languages but unlike Chinese, modifiers come after the noun, as in *phaasǎa thay* "the Thai language" (the word *phaasǎa* is a loan from Sanskrit). Thai writing, which is based on the Indic script used for Sanskrit, includes special markers for tones.

HMONG-MIEN (MIAO, YAO)

These are languages of minority groups in China and Thailand who have suffered a history of oppression. Their remaining speakers now number about 5 million, mainly dispersed in mountainous areas of southern China. The largest group, the Miao, are found mostly in the provinces Guizhou and Guangxi, and in adjacent areas of Vietnam, Laos, and Thailand. The Yao live in Guangxi and Hunan and in parts of Laos and Thailand, with a small population also on the island of Hainan.

The She people, in small communities near the coast of Fujian and Guangdong, have mostly

Above: *A Zhuang mother and child from the city of Nanning in Zhuang Autonomous Region, southern China. The Zhuang language has its own romanized script; in 1992 there were 14 million Zhuang-speakers.*

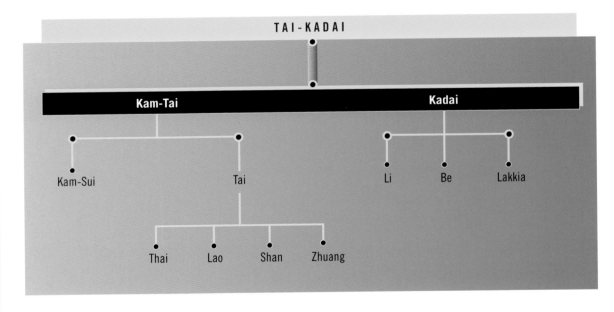

Above: *Tai-Kadai family tree. These languages share some vocabulary and similar sound systems with southern Chinese dialects. However, this is not because they are related, but due to borrowing and language shifts.*

shifted to Chinese: only a few She communities in southeast Guangdong preserve their language, while using the surrounding Hakka dialect of Chinese to communicate with outsiders. This gradual "Sinicization" of the minority groups in southern China has been happening for centuries.

The Hmong-Mien languages are tonal and use SVO order, with Miao being especially close to the Tai-Kadai languages in structure, suggesting either extensive contact or a distant genetic relationship, as assumed in the Austric hypothesis (*see box right*). Hmong is a language of the Miao group spoken in Thailand and Cambodia. It has several writing systems including a unique semi-syllabic script, said to have been revealed to its originator in a divine vision. In recent years Hmong speakers, refugees from the wars in Vietnam and Laos, have settled in the U.S.A, Australia, and France. The two main varieties, "Green" and "White" Hmong, are named after the colors of traditional women's dress.

THE AUSTRIC HYPOTHESIS

This hypothesis links the main language families of Southeast Asia, with the exception of the Sino-Tibetan family.

AUSTRIC
- Austronesian
- Tai-Kadai
- Hmong-Mien (Miao-Yao)
- Austro-Asiatic
  - Mon-Khmer
  - Munda

The inclusion of the Austro-Asiatic family is debated among proponents of the hypothesis; the main difficulty is finding a distinction between the effects of contact and genetic relationships. Some evidence comes from similar infixes and from roots where Austronesian has two syllables, of which Mon-Khmer preserve the first and Tai-Kadai the second:

Proto-Austronesian	Proto-Mon-Khmer	Proto-Kam-Thai
mata "eye"	*mat* "eye"	*taa* "eye"

CLASSIFIERS

In Thai, as in Chinese and most Southeast Asian languages, each noun is assigned a classifier which denotes a class of items or a distinctive feature of the item the noun refers to, for example:

khon	**tua**	**lêm**	**khan**
"person"	"body"	"point"	"objects with handles"
(people, except royal and sacred ones)	(animals, except sacred ones such as elephants)	(sharp and pointed objects, for example needle or sword)	(for example fishing rod or plough)

The classifiers are used, not unlike articles in European languages, when a noun is counted or otherwise modified:

lûuk săam **khon**	*nók* **tua** *yày*
child three "person"	bird "body" big
"three children"	"the big bird"

Above: *Muslims are a minority group in China. Assigned to the Hui ethnicity, most speak local dialects of Chinese.*

THE LANGUAGES OF CHINA

Chinese has spread across China at the expense of the Altaic languages of the remote north and northwest, and the Tai and Miao-Yao languages, which are spoken by ethnic minorities in the mountainous southwest of China. The number of speakers of these minority languages is steadily declining, as the peripheral areas of China become absorbed into mainstream Chinese culture. Nevertheless, the minority languages have left their imprint on local varieties of Chinese, which are as different from each other as individual Romance or Germanic languages in Europe.

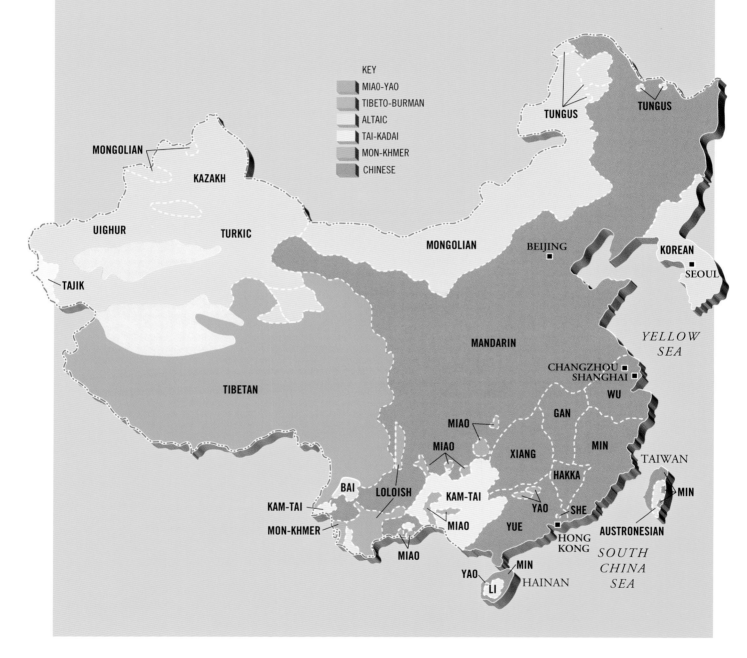

KEY
- MIAO-YAO
- TIBETO-BURMAN
- ALTAIC
- TAI-KADAI
- MON-KHMER
- CHINESE

The Sino-Tibetan Language Family

These languages are spoken across China and in much of Southeast Asia, and have over a billion speakers—more than any family other than Indo-European. In addition to the many varieties of Chinese, Tibetan, and Burmese, the family includes a number of lesser-known minority languages, spoken mostly in southwest China and Tibet. The main branches of Sino-Tibetan are shown below.

The Bai language, with over a million speakers in Yunnan province, is thought to be a distant relative of Chinese; although similar to the neighboring Yi languages in many respects, its word order is SVO, like Chinese, rather than SOV like most of the Tibeto-Burman branch.

Due to the cultural unity of the Chinese people and its standard written form, "Chinese" is often regarded as a single language, both inside and outside China. However, it encompasses an enormous range of dialects, which divide into

SINO-TIBETAN FAMILY

The languages in this family are spoken in China and Southeast Asia. This tree shows the main branches of the family. Chinese divides into eight main dialect groups. Mandarin is the official language of the People's Republic of China, Xiang is spoken in Hunan province, Gan in Jiangxi province, Hakka is spread over the south and southeast, Wu is spoken in Zhejiang province and includes Shanghainese, Northern Min includes Fuzhou, Southern Min includes Xiamen, Taiwanese, and Chiu Chow, Yue (Cantonese) is spoken in Guangdong and Guangxi provinces.

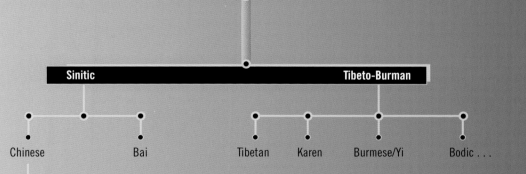

SINO-TIBETAN

Sinitic — Tibeto-Burman

Chinese — Bai — Tibetan — Karen — Burmese/Yi — Bodic . . .

Mandarin
Xiang
Gan
Hakka
Wu
Northern Min
Southern Min
Yue

Right: *A public health announcement is written on a blackboard; of the 50–80,000 characters used at one time or another in Chinese writing, 8,000 are still in use, and a knowledge of 1,000 characters is needed for a basic reading knowledge of the language.*

INDIGENOUS LANGUAGES OF TAIWAN

Successive colonizations of Taiwan have brought various languages to the island including the Min Chinese dialect imported from Fujian in the Ming period, Japanese in the nineteenth century, and Mandarin in the twentieth century. Long before any of these, the indigenous inhabitants spoke Austronesian languages, of which about eight are still spoken in the central mountains, along the east coast, and on outlying islands.

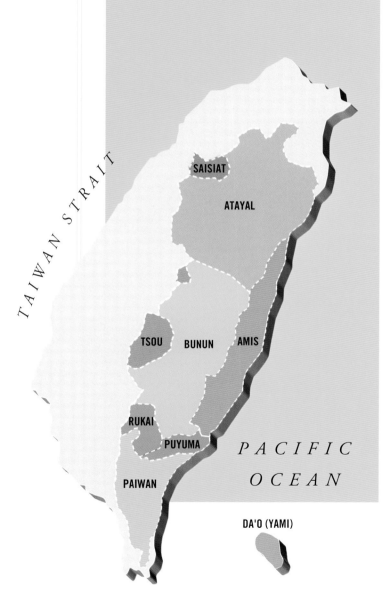

TAIWAN STRAIT

SAISIAT

ATAYAL

TSOU   BUNUN   AMIS

RUKAI

PUYUMA

PAIWAN

PACIFIC
OCEAN

DA'O (YAMI)

eight main groups, each as different from the others as the languages within each branch of Indo-European. Cantonese, for example, differs from Mandarin as much as Italian differs from French or Swedish from German. Dialects from different groups are mutually unintelligible: even within a dialect group, such as Wu or Yue, speakers of one rural dialect may fail to understand speakers of another, though Shanghainese and Cantonese are widely understood within these cities' spheres of influence. The Min dialects of the southeast coast are especially diverse, with some features reflecting the influence of Tai, Miao-Yao, and the Austro-Asiatic languages that were spoken in southern China formerly.

Mandarin Chinese is the official language of the People's Republic of China, where it is termed *Putonghua* meaning "common speech," and of Taiwan, where it is called *Guoyu* ("national language"). Mandarin Chinese has more native speakers than any other language—approaching one billion—and it is widely understood as a second language in most of Chinese territory. Written Chinese, based on Mandarin, is often used by speakers of different dialects and even languages, but while this can overcome some problems—as when Chinese-speakers "draw" characters in the air to confirm their names—Chinese writing is far from universal. The traditional characters, still used in Hong Kong, Macao, and Taiwan, have been simplified in the People's Republic, sometimes beyond recognition. Many dialects use additional characters of their own: writing in Hong Kong, for example, employs hundreds of non-standard characters to represent Cantonese words. As a result of these differences, mainland Mandarin-speakers may have difficulty reading a Hong Kong newspaper and vice versa. Variations in grammar,

Left: *A Taiwanese street scene in Kaohsiung city. A history of invasion has imposed three major languages on the Taiwanese: Japanese, the Min dialect of Chinese, and Mandarin.*

HAINAN

The large tropical island of Hainan, a province of China in the South China Sea, is home to languages from four different families: the indigenous Li and Be languages, belonging to the Tai-Kadai family; Yao, a Hmong-Mien language whose speakers were supposedly brought to Hainan to subdue the Li; Chamic languages belonging to the Austronesian family; and Chinese. The local southern Min and Yue dialects are gradually giving way to Mandarin as the island develops.

vocabulary, and usage between dialects also impede comprehension.

Yue, or Cantonese, the dialect of the southern port city of Canton (Guangzhou), is spoken in most of Guangdong and Guangxi provinces, in Hong Kong, Macao, and in the Chinese communities around the world. The majority of Chinese living in Southeast Asia (Thailand, Vietnam, Malaysia, Singapore, and the Philippines) speak southern dialects such as Hokkien, Hakka, Cantonese, and Chiu Chow.

THE STRUCTURE OF CHINESE

Chinese is one of the clearest examples of an isolating type of language. One feature of this type is that instead of endings indicating grammatical

Above: *A Buddhist monastery in the Tibetan city of Lhasa. There are about 4 million Tibetan speakers; the language is written in a script of Indic origin.*

categories, the grammatical concepts are expressed by independent words, called particles. Thus the possessive relation is expressed by the particle *de* as in *wŏ de fángzi* ("my house"); the pronoun *wŏ* has the same form, whether it means "I," "me," or "my." The verb has no tense forms, but aspect is indicated by particles such as the progressive *zài*, for example *tā zài chī fàn* "She's eating" (literally, "she at eat rice").

Tone, the use of pitch to distinguish words, is a feature of almost all forms of Chinese. The four tones of Mandarin Chinese, for example, give four completely different meanings to the same syllable:

HONG KONG

Cantonese is the dominant language of Hong Kong, with minorities also speaking other Chinese dialects such as Chiu Chow, Hakka, and Shanghainese. Mandarin is increasingly used, symbolizing the reunification with China, while English is the language of education and international trade. Bilinguals mix elements of Chinese and English by, for example, inserting English verbs with the Cantonese suffixes indicating aspect attached to them:

*Léih **present**-gán mātyéh a?*
"What are you presenting?"

*Léih bōng ngóh **keep**-jyuh nī dī lā?*
"Will you keep these for me (for a moment)?"

High level	Rising	Dipping	Falling
fān	*fán*	*fǎn*	*fàn*
"sail"	"trouble"	"turn"	"rice"

This represents a relatively simple system: in some Min dialects of Chinese there are as many as eight tones, which may change according to where the word comes in a sentence. Cantonese has nine tones.

TIBETO-BURMAN

The Tibeto-Burman branch of Sino-Tibetan is separated from the Sinitic (Chinese) branch by around 6,000 years. Comprising eight or nine families and 250–300 languages, it is comparable to Indo-European in size and time depth, but the languages are much less well known. They are spoken primarily in China—where 16 are recognized minority languages—in Myanmar, Nepal, Bhutan, and in northeastern India. Many of them are tone languages, like Chinese, but with SOV (subject-object-verb) word order and sometimes with an ergative case system.

Tibetan and Burmese are the major languages, with around 4 million and 22 million speakers respectively. Both are written in scripts of Indic origin and possess long literary traditions, going back to around AD 600 for Tibetan and AD 1100 for Burmese. Most other Tibeto-Burman languages have far fewer speakers, the most important being Newari in Nepal, Dzhongkha in Bhutan, and Manipuri in India.

Tibeto-Burman minority languages include the Yi (Loloish) group, with some 5 million speakers in the highlands of southwestern China, and across the borders into Myanmar and Thailand; of these, Lisu and Lahu have been extensively studied.

The Karen group, spoken by minority peoples in eastern Myanmar and adjacent areas of Thailand, have SVO word order, unlike most Tibeto-Burman languages, and were probably influenced by neighboring Tai languages.

SINGAPORE

Singapore is a melting pot of cultures, with four official languages: Malay (Austronesian), Tamil (Dravidian), English, and Mandarin. The majority Chinese population speaks a variety of Chinese dialects including Hokkien, Chiu Chow, Hainanese, Cantonese, and Hakka. The government has promoted Mandarin as a means to unify the Chinese population, while English is used between the ethnic groups, in education and business. Singapore English is often mixed with Malay and Chinese elements, such as particles ending the sentence:

A: " One boy, one girl ... going to have some more?"

B: "No! I willing to stop **lah**! Family planning **lah**! No poin[t] more kids **lah**, because we thin[k] of working **ah**, so we have not time with the kids **lah**."

Africa and the Middle East

The origin of language may lie in sub-Saharan Africa with the emergence of modern humans. The present Bantu languages of the region include those of the Zulus and the Shona and *lingua francas* such as Swahili, while the Khoisan languages of the Bushmen, renowned for their "click" sounds, have long been in decline. The Semitic languages of North Africa are of a unique structure, notably reflected in the Arabic writing system.

A Nigerian woman in the largest city, Lagos.
The main ethnic groups in Nigeria are the Hausa,
Fulani, Yoruba, and Igbo, who together make up
65 percent of the population.

Recent research suggests that the people of the world can be divided in terms of their genetic makeup into just two groups: broadly, native peoples of central and southern Africa, and everyone else.

Moreover, linguistic research has shown that the languages spoken by the African peoples belong to three families, none of which has any known relationship to any other language family in the world.

North Africans, however, belong genetically with Europeans and some Asian populations. The languages of these peoples may belong to a single super-family such as Nostratic.

Many scholars also now believe that mankind originated in Africa, and that all living humans must trace their descent from an original African population.

LANGUAGE FAMILIES PAST AND PRESENT

Africa is split by two great physical features, the Sahara desert and the mountains of Ethiopia. Crossing these has always been enormously difficult. North of this divide there are written records going back thousands of years; to the south written records go back only a few hundred years, and few of these are in the native languages of the region, but rather in the languages of foreign traders and invaders. For knowledge of earlier times we must rely on archeology, oral traditions, and the hypothetical reconstructions of linguists based on the living languages of the present.

One study of African history has proposed a grouping of African peoples about 10,000 years ago (*see map page 76*).

Contrast this with the map showing the present day distribution of African language families (*see map page 77*). Each language family can be correlated with one of the population groups: Afro-Asiatic with North Africans, Niger-Congo with West Africans, Khoisan with Bushmen, and Nilo-Saharan with Nilotics.

Undoubtedly the greatest change in the map on page 77 results from the eastward and southward expansion of the West African peoples. The pygmies were surrounded and few now remain as identifiable populations. The Bushmen were pushed to the south and then engulfed by European settlement and by the resulting conflicts between Europeans and the descendants of the original West African migrants.

Though there are still pygmy peoples, there are no known pygmy languages. As for the Bushmen, few remain, and even fewer speak their ancestral languages.

Today the languages of the former European colonial powers are widely used in African countries. Some native languages, such as Swahili in East Africa and Hausa in West Africa, are also used as *lingua francas*.

NILO-SAHARAN

This family still remains close to the position it occupied 10,000 years ago. It comprises 100 or so languages in three branches: Songhai, a single language, and two language groups Saharan and Chari-Nile. As can be seen on the map on page 77, Songhai is isolated from the other branches.

Few languages in this family have even a million speakers; the languages are often very different from one another and many have been little studied.

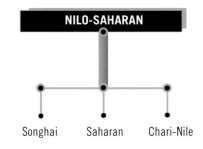

GENETIC GROUPS AND LANGUAGES

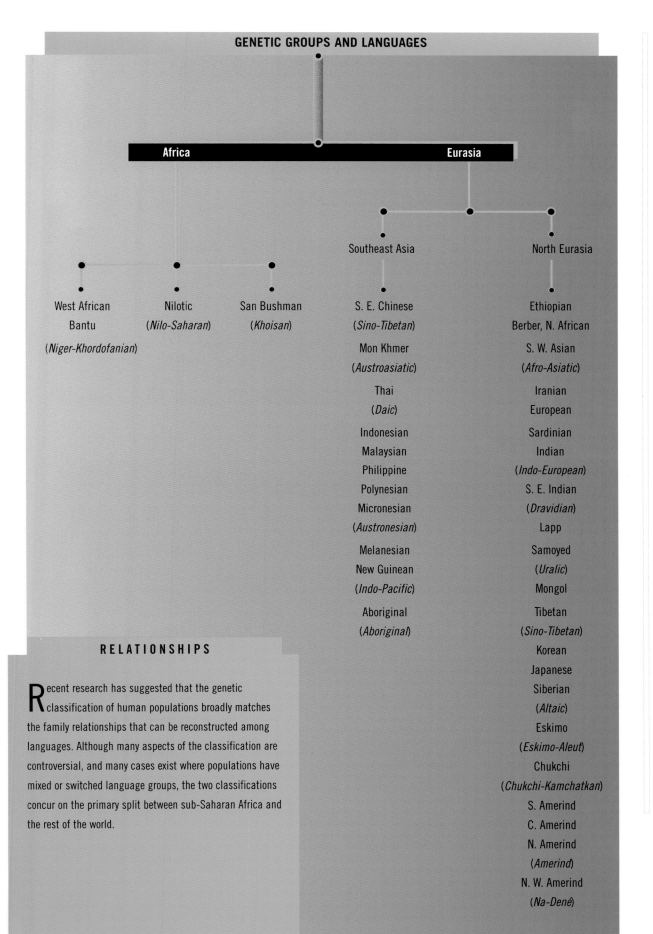

Africa

Eurasia

Southeast Asia

North Eurasia

West African
Bantu

(*Niger-Khordofanian*)

Nilotic

(*Nilo-Saharan*)

San Bushman

(*Khoisan*)

S. E. Chinese
(*Sino-Tibetan*)

Mon Khmer
(*Austroasiatic*)

Thai
(*Daic*)

Indonesian
Malaysian
Philippine
Polynesian
Micronesian
(*Austronesian*)

Melanesian
New Guinean
(*Indo-Pacific*)

Aboriginal
(*Aboriginal*)

Ethiopian
Berber, N. African

S. W. Asian
(*Afro-Asiatic*)

Iranian
European
Sardinian
Indian
(*Indo-European*)

S. E. Indian
(*Dravidian*)

Lapp
Samoyed
(*Uralic*)

Mongol

Tibetan
(*Sino-Tibetan*)

Korean
Japanese
Siberian
(*Altaic*)

Eskimo
(*Eskimo-Aleut*)

Chukchi
(*Chukchi-Kamchatkan*)

S. Amerind
C. Amerind
N. Amerind
(*Amerind*)

N. W. Amerind
(*Na-Dené*)

RELATIONSHIPS

Recent research has suggested that the genetic classification of human populations broadly matches the family relationships that can be reconstructed among languages. Although many aspects of the classification are controversial, and many cases exist where populations have mixed or switched language groups, the two classifications concur on the primary split between sub-Saharan Africa and the rest of the world.

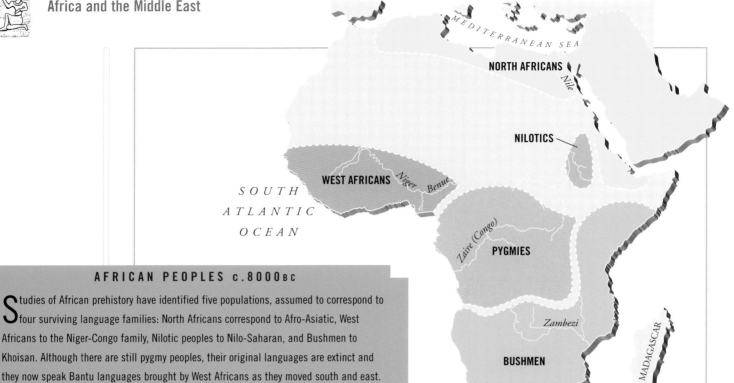

MEDITERRANEAN SEA

NORTH AFRICANS

Nile

NILOTICS

WEST AFRICANS

Niger *Benue*

S O U T H
A T L A N T I C
O C E A N

Zaire (Congo)

PYGMIES

Zambezi

MADAGASCAR

BUSHMEN

Orange

I N D I A N
O C E A N

AFRICAN PEOPLES c.8000 BC

Studies of African prehistory have identified five populations, assumed to correspond to four surviving language families: North Africans correspond to Afro-Asiatic, West Africans to the Niger-Congo family, Nilotic peoples to Nilo-Saharan, and Bushmen to Khoisan. Although there are still pygmy peoples, their original languages are extinct and they now speak Bantu languages brought by West Africans as they moved south and east.

CLICK SOUNDS

Click sounds are a characteristic of the Khoisan languages, some of which have up to 80 different types. Clicks are used in many languages, for example as interjections or indicators of disapproval, but what makes them remarkable in Khoisan is their use as ordinary sounds, equivalent in function to other consonants as constituents of words.

Clicks are best known to the world through the Bantu languages of South Africa, which are thought to have borrowed them from Khoisan-speakers, probably through intermarriage. Some readers may have heard the click song of the South African singer Miriam Makheba, in which the clicks sound like an accompaniment to the words of the song but in fact are intrinsic to the lyrics.

Zulu and Ndebele each have three basic click sounds: the dental (like the English "tsk, tsk"), the lateral (made from one side of the mouth, often used in English to call a large animal like a horse), and the palatal (a cork-popping sound made by placing the tongue against the roof of the mouth and sucking). These are written "c," "x," and "q," respectively. In the following examples the letters standing for clicks are capitalized.

iCala	fault
iXaXa	frog
iQanda	egg

More complicated clicks can be made by combining "c," "x," or "q," with one of two different nasal sounds, or with an almost simultaneous "k" or "g." The result is a total of 15 different click sounds.

In the Khoisan languages themselves there are other basic clicks—such as the bilabial click, which is a kissing sound—and further possibilities for combining with other sounds.

Below: *In 1959 Miriam Makheba's Xhosa click song was a U.S. hit. An exiled figurehead of the anti-apartheid movement, she returned to South Africa in 1991.*

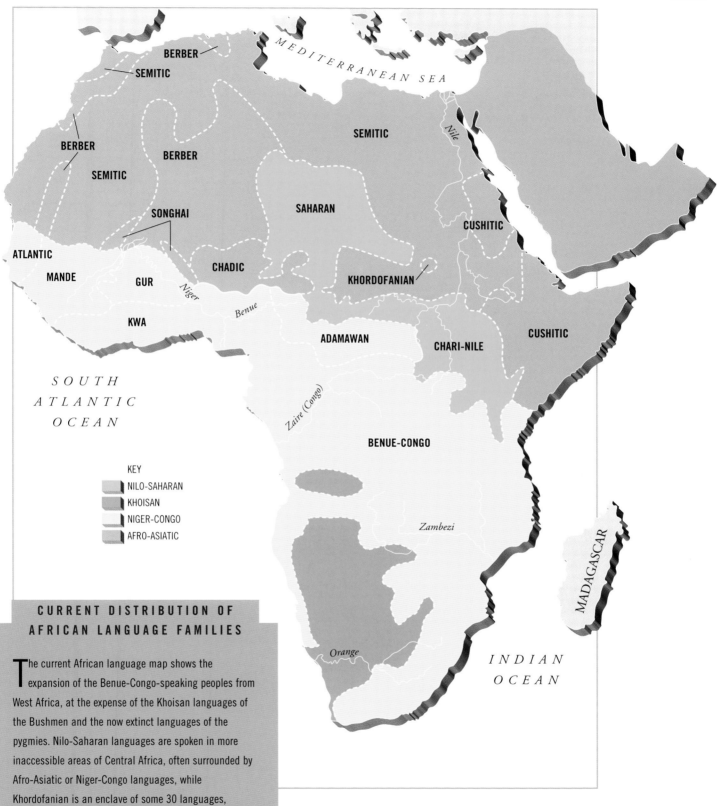

MEDITERRANEAN SEA

BERBER

SEMITIC

SEMITIC

Nile

BERBER

BERBER

SEMITIC

SAHARAN

CUSHITIC

SONGHAI

ATLANTIC

CHADIC

KHORDOFANIAN

MANDE

GUR

Niger

KWA

Benue

CUSHITIC

ADAMAWAN

CHARI-NILE

SOUTH
ATLANTIC
OCEAN

Zaire (Congo)

BENUE-CONGO

KEY

NILO-SAHARAN

KHOISAN

Zambezi

NIGER-CONGO

AFRO-ASIATIC

MADAGASCAR

Orange

INDIAN
OCEAN

CURRENT DISTRIBUTION OF AFRICAN LANGUAGE FAMILIES

The current African language map shows the expansion of the Benue-Congo-speaking peoples from West Africa, at the expense of the Khoisan languages of the Bushmen and the now extinct languages of the pygmies. Nilo-Saharan languages are spoken in more inaccessible areas of Central Africa, often surrounded by Afro-Asiatic or Niger-Congo languages, while Khordofanian is an enclave of some 30 languages, related to the Niger-Congo family, spoken in the Sudan.

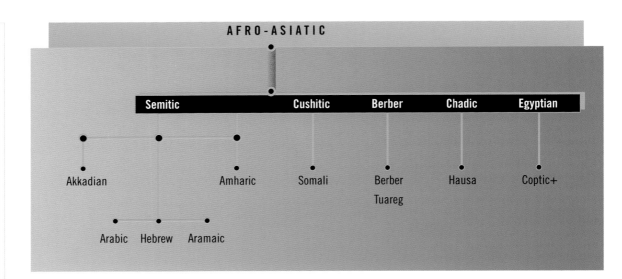

AFRO-ASIATIC				
Semitic	Cushitic	Berber	Chadic	Egyptian
Akkadian	Amharic	Somali	Berber Tuareg	Hausa	Coptic+

Arabic   Hebrew   Aramaic

KHOISAN

Most languages of this family are completely or nearly extinct. Only Damara in Namibia has a significant number of speakers (163,000, about 10 percent of the population). In 1990 it was standardized as a national language and renamed Khoekhoe.

AFRO-ASIATIC

The most important of the Afro-Asiatic languages is Arabic, spoken in one form or another by more than 200 million people. Arabic and Hebrew are great cultural languages, and the languages of two of the great religions of the world. Hebrew, which for many centuries had no home but survived as the religious language of the Jewish diaspora, has found new life in Israel, where it has become the country's national language.

CONSONANTS AND VOWELS IN ARABIC

The distinctive sounds of the Arabic language are the pharyngeals proper, pronounced at the back of the throat, and a whole range of sounds spoken with pharyngealization.

The Afro-Asiatic languages are well known for the extent to which vowel changes are used in the formation of words. Vowel changes are used in

English too, but only to a limited extent: for example the plural of "foot" is not "foots" but "feet."

A verb in Arabic generally has three sets of forms: present, past, and present participle; many verbs also have past participle forms. This is not unlike English where the verb "kick" has the present forms "kick" and "kicks," the past form "kicked," the present participle "kicking," and the past participle "kicked." Here are four examples, one from each set for the Arabic verb meaning "to write:"

1. *ti-ktib*   she writes   present
2. *katab-it*   she wrote   past
3. *kaatib*   writing   present participle
4. *ma-ktuub*   written   past participle

The prefix *ti-* and the suffix *-it* of the first two words mean "she." The prefix *ma-* of the last word is used with past participles.

Grammarians often say that what is common to a set of words when the affixes are removed is the root. So in English if we remove the affixes from "kick," "kicks," "kicked," and "kicking" we are left with the root "kick." But in the case of the four Arabic words it is not as simple. If we remove the affixes we are still left with the four different forms *ktib*, *katab*, *kaatib*, and *ktuub*.

In fact the only thing that is common to all four forms are the consonants "k," "t," and "b:" "kt-b" in (1) and (4), and "k-t-b" in (2) and (3), where the hyphens stand for the missing vowels. Because these consonants are all that the four different forms have in common, they are regarded by grammarians as constituting the root in each of these words. Thus the root is often written simply as *ktb*.

Of course *ktb* is a strange, "discontinuous" root, for its consonants never all occur next to one another, but are separated by one or two vowels. In each word the vowels are also regarded as expressing a meaning of their own. In the second word the vowels are "- a - a -" (now using hyphens to stand for the missing consonants), and this vowel pattern expresses the past tense; similarly the vowel pattern "- - i -" expresses the present tense in the first word, "- aa - i -" the present participle in the third word, and "- - uu -" the past participle in the fourth.

These Arabic verbs thus each contain two meaningful but discontinuous word parts, the consonants expressing the root meaning and the vowels expressing a grammatical meaning:

ktb	"write"
- - i -	the present tense
- a - a -	the past tense
- aa - i -	the present participle
- - uu -	the past participle

Is there anything like this in English? Yes: 200 or so irregular verbs take the past tense or the past participle forms by using a different vowel. For example we have "swim, swims, swimming" but

LANGUAGES OF WEST AFRICA

West Africa is home to several hundred languages, mostly belonging to the Niger-Congo group but not to the Bantu family. An important exception is Hausa, belonging to the Chadic branch of Afro-Asiatic.

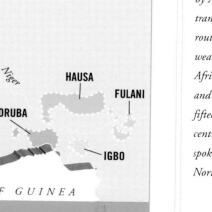

FULANI

HAUSA

FULANI

AKAN   YORUBA

IGBO

Niger

GULF OF GUINEA

Above: *Students at a Koranic school, in Zinder, southern Niger. Over 80 percent of the population of Niger is Muslim, a religion introduced to the region by Arab traders, whose trans-Saharan caravan routes brought great wealth to the West African empires of Mali and Songhay in the fifteenth and sixteenth centuries. Arabic is still spoken widely across North Africa.*

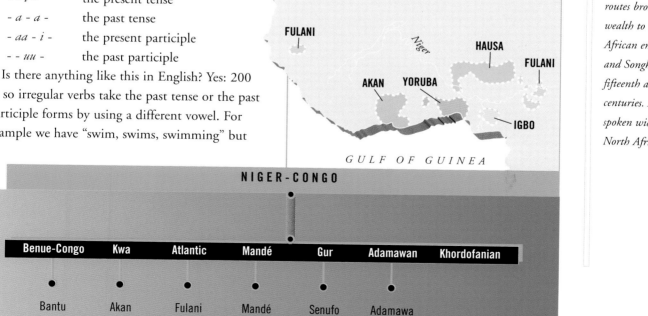

NIGER-CONGO

Benue-Congo	Kwa	Atlantic	Mandé	Gur	Adamawan	Khordofanian
Bantu	Akan	Fulani	Mandé	Senufo	Adamawa	
	Ewe	Wolof	Bambara	Dogon	Gbaya	
	Igbo					
	Yoruba					

"swam" and "swum." However, there is only one vowel in each word which changes; there are only two forms (past tense and past participle) which change; and there is only a small number of such verbs. By contrast, in Arabic more than one vowel in a word may change; each set of forms has its own vowel pattern; and such word formation is normal and widely used.

Not only verbs but also nouns and other word classes show a similar use of roots consisting of consonants which alternate with vowel patterns which express other meanings. In Arabic the plurals of nouns are often formed by alternating the consonants of the root with one vowel pattern in the singular, and another in the plural. For example the noun *xalifa* (the loan word "caliph") has as its plural *xulufu*. Thus the parts of these words are:

xlf "caliph"	the discontinuous root
- a - i - a	the singular part
- u - u - u	the plural part

There are nouns derived from verbs, so that in addition to the patterns of the verb, there are further patterns for the noun. From the verb "write" derives the noun "book" with the same root consonants, giving *kitaab* as the singular, and *kutub* as the plural.

ktb	"book"
- i - aa -	singular
- u - u -	plural

This account of consonant roots may be relevant to an understanding of early Semitic writing systems discussed in chapter 9 of this book. In these writing systems only the consonants were written, and the reader was left to infer the vowels from the context. This, as we have seen, means that the reader is always given the roots, but may be left without any explicit indication of numbers and tenses.

NIGER-CONGO

There are more than 200 million speakers of languages in this family, and more than 900 languages, of which only the most important are shown. The sub-groups stretch from southern and central Africa (Benue-Congo), along the coast of West Africa (Kwa) to the Atlantic coast (Atlantic), then back along the edge of the Sahara (Mandé, Gur, Adamawan). Finally there is an isolated group in the east called Khordofanian.

Half of the Niger-Congo speakers belong to the Bantu sub-group of Benue-Congo which covers much of central and southern Africa. Many of these are important as national languages, but few are spoken by large numbers of people.

The word "Bantu" means "people," and the group was given this name because of the occurrence of this, or some similar word, in most of the languages of the group. We are fortunate to have a major comparative study of the Bantu languages, the result of a lifetime's work by Malcolm Guthrie.

Three languages in particular are referred to more extensively in this chapter: Fulani in the north, Shona in the center, and Zulu in the south of Africa.

Fulani speakers are found all across West Africa from the Atlantic coast to beyond the eastern border of Nigeria. Two of the main groups are found in the east of Nigeria and in Cameroon. As can be seen from the table, Shona has the largest number of native speakers of any Bantu language. It is principally spoken in the central African republic of Zimbabwe, as well as in Mozambique. There are

Right: King Lobengula, pictured here with his favorite wife, broke away from the Zulus in the nineteenth century. These people and their language are now known as Ndebele.

several major dialects; in Harare, the capital of Zimbabwe, the dialect is called Zezuru.

In the south, Zulu is a major language, and is closely related to Xhosa, its even more southerly neighbor. In the nineteenth century a group of Zulus broke away from the main Zulu nation and headed north to what is now Zimbabwe, where they established an independent state. Their king—Lobengula—and his capital Bulawayo (now a great city of southern Zimbabwe) are known to British history under the heading "Matabele wars." These Zulus called themselves "amaNdebele," anglicized as "Matabele." In this chapter both people and language are termed "Ndebele." Ndebele is often referred to as a separate language, but is mutually intelligible with Zulu spoken 700 miles to the south.

TONE FOR LEXIS AND GRAMMAR

Tone is an important mechanism found in hundreds of Niger-Congo languages. Differences of pitch are used to distinguish both word meanings and grammatical patterns. Most African languages south of the Sahara are tonal in this way, with the relative pitch of a word's syllables being fixed, either high or low.

Hausa, from a non-tonal family, uses tone, perhaps acquired through contact with neighbors. Fulani, on the other hand, has lost its tones, as has another important language, Swahili, which is spoken more than 2,000 miles away in Kenya and Tanzania. It is even possible for some dialects of the same language to have tone, and some not. The Ndau dialect of Shona spoken in Mozambique has no tones, but the other Shona dialects do.

To illustrate a typical Niger-Congo tone language, we shall describe some of the characteristic features of one language in which tone is used extensively—the Zezuru dialect of Shona. A dash is written beneath each low-toned

MAJOR LANGUAGES OF SUB-SAHARAN AFRICA

The table below lists national languages with more than 5 million speakers.

LANGUAGE	NUMBER OF SPEAKERS (in millions)	COUNTRY
AFRO-ASIATIC LANGUAGES		
Hausa	25	Nigeria, Niger
NIGER-CONGO NON-BANTU LANGUAGES		
KWA GROUP		
Akan	6.7	Ghana
Yoruba	24.2	Nigeria
Igbo	20.2	Nigeria
ATLANTIC GROUP		
Fulani	10.7	Nigeria (and other countries)
NIGER-CONGO BANTU LANGUAGES		
Gikuyu	5.0	Kenya
Rwanda	7.6	Rwanda
Rundi	5.1	Burundi
Kongo	5.0	Congo, Angola, DR Congo
Luba Lulua	6.5	DR Congo
Swahili	6.0	Tanzania
Makua	6.0	Mozambique
Chewa/Nyanja	8.2	Malawi
Shona	9.2	Zimbabwe
Zulu	7.0	Republic of South Africa
Xhosa	7.0	Republic of South Africa
Ndebele	1.5	Zimbabwe

The major languages of central and southern Africa belong to the Bantu family. Some are used widely as second languages: Swahili is an official language of Tanzania and Kenya and also serves as a *lingua franca* in neighboring countries.

vowel and a slash beneath each high-toned vowel:

havabike   they don't cook

- / - /

Stems and affixes have to be distinguished, because the tones which a word has are determined partly by the stem, and partly by the affixes. The word above is divided into a stem and affixes thus:

prefix	prefix	stem	suffix
ha	*va*	*bik*	*e*
-	/	-	/
not	they	cook	(present tense)

Shona and all the Bantu languages are quite unlike English since they never have a lone verb stem used as a word. In English the stem "cook" is used as a word in all kinds of contexts, but there is no Bantu word which consists of just a stem, such as *bik* in the example above. This means that in the Bantu languages every word with a word stem also has at least one affix.

There are over 600 Shona verb stems with the same phonetic shape as *bik*, that is having a consonant-vowel-consonant structure, and there are many more longer ones. If we keep the affixes the same, we can substitute these stems for *bik* in the structure above. For example:

ha va	*bik*	*e*	they don't cook
	tem		strike
	tor		take

But there are only two different tone patterns:

1. | *ha* | *va* | *bik* | *e* |
   |------|------|-------|-----|
   | - | / | - | / |

2. | *ha* | *va* | *tor* | *e* |
   |------|------|-------|-----|
   | - | / | / | / |

Since the stem itself has a low

tone in (1) but a high tone in (2), all the stems with pattern (1) are called low stems, and all the stems with pattern (2) high stems. There are no exceptions; every verb stem is either low or high. It is the same with longer stems: there are only two patterns, and every verb is used with either the one or the other. If we compare the two words above, it is clear that we could still distinguish their meanings without tonal variations, because their constituent sounds differ.

However, if there were two stems with exactly the same three sounds, then the tone could be a way of marking a difference. In fact in Shona and other Niger-Congo languages, there are a number of stems with the same sounds, but one a low stem and one a high stem. Two such stems are

1.   *par* (low)   to offend
2.   *par* (high)   to scrape

If these stems are used with the above affixes, they form two words with the same consonants and vowels, but with different tone patterns. Here, only the tone gives the meaning; without tone, the two words would be pronounced identically:

1.   *ha va par e*   they don't offend
      - / - /
2.   *ha va par e*   they don't scrape
      - / / /

One count of verb stems having a consonant-vowel-consonant structure in the Karanga dialect of Shona lists 634 different stems. But there are only 31 pairs of stems which differ solely in tone like *par* (low) and *par* (high). Shona verb stems are listed in dictionaries with their tone properties, called "lexical" tone. In Karanga verbs, for example, lexical tone distinguishes meanings for about 10 percent of stems. In other stems the differences are redundant, and meanings can be distinguished without lexical tone. A second important use of tone in

Right: A school in Malawi teaches Chewa, the language of one of the main ethnic groupings. Chewa shares official language status with English, a legacy of the period when Malawi was a British colony, from 1891 to 1964.

Bantu languages, usually called the "grammatical" use, is to distinguish different meanings of two or more words, where all the words have the same stem, and the affixes all have the same consonants and vowels. For example:

va no bik a   they cook
/ -   -   -

va no bik a   the ones who cook
-   /   -   -

In these words *no* and *a* together express a present tense meaning. Pairs or triplets of words like this are very common. In the Niger-Congo languages grammatical tone is more extensive and important than tone used to distinguish the meanings of stems.

Characteristically in Niger-Congo languages, the lexical and grammatical uses may be combined so that three words or more can be distinguished by tone alone. This is illustrated by a final example of four Shona words with just two different stems, and with the same affixes as the previous examples:

1.   *va no par a*   they offend
       / -   -   -

2.   *va no par a*   the ones who offend
       -   /   -   /

3.   *va no par a*   they scrape
       / -   /   /

4.   *va no par a*   the ones who scrape
       -   /   /   /

(1) and (2) have different grammatical tones, (1) and (3) have different lexical tones, (1) and (4) have different lexical and grammatical tones, and similarly for the remaining pairs.

NOUN CLASSES AND AGREEMENT SYSTEMS

The Niger-Congo languages are famous for two related features: a large number of noun classes and an extensive agreement system.

In most Bantu languages a noun typically begins with a prefix which marks its class. When a

SINGULAR AND PLURAL PREFIXES

One important function of the prefixes is to mark singular and plural nouns. The table below shows all the possibilities for prefixes in Ndebele. A singular prefix need not always pair with the same plural prefix. The table below right shows Ndebele noun classes.

PREFIX PAIRS

Nouns with Singular Prefix	Nouns with Plural Prefix	Translation
i - yezi	ama - yezi	cloud(s)
i* - bheka	ama - bheka	baker(s)
in - doda	ama - doda	man, men
in - komo	izin - komo	cow(s)
isi - lwane	zi - lwane	lion(s)
u* - seko	izin - seko	custom(s)
u - khokho	o - khokho	ancestor(s)
um - fazi	aba - fazi	woman, women
um - Ndebele	ama - Ndebele	Ndebele(s)
um - fula	im - fula	river(s)

Just two prefixes, "ubu" and "uku," are never paired.

ubu - khulu	bigness
uku - pheka	cooking

With some stems a singular or plural prefix occurs alone:

Singular Prefixes:	Translation
i - zulu	rain
i* - tiye	tea
isi - Ndebele	the Ndebele language
u* - Nkulunkulu	God
u - chago	milk
um - khathi	sky
i* - tiye	tea

Plural Prefixes:	Translation
ama - zolo	dew
im - thombo	yeast
izi - khihli	sour milk
izin - yembezi	tears

NOUN CLASSES

Noun	Translation
aba - fazi	women
ama - yezi	clouds
i - yezi	cloud
i* - bheka	baker
im - fula	rivers
in - komo	cow
isi - lwane	lion
izi - lwane	lions
izin - komo	cows
o - khokho	ancestors
u - khokho	ancestor
u* - seko	custom
ubu - khulu	bigness
uku - pheka	cooking
um - fazi	woman
um* - fula	river

noun is used in a sentence, the words which agree with the noun also have a prefix similar in form to that of the noun. In any sentence most of the words are either nouns or words that agree with nouns, so that a majority of the words of the sentence will have one of these prefixes.

European languages like French or German do, of course, have noun classes. But French has only two classes (masculine and feminine) and German only three (masculine, feminine, and neuter). Compared to European languages the noun classes of Niger-Congo languages are much more numerous, and the agreement between nouns and other words is not only more extensive but is expressed in a much clearer way.

The noun classes of Ndebele—spoken in Zimbabwe—are given on page 83 as an example of such a system. In all the examples a prefix is separated from the remainder of the word by a hyphen.

There are 16 different prefixes in Ndebele. One noun illustrating each prefix is listed alphabetically in the table on page 83. Three prefixes have the same form but different grammatical properties, so they are distinguished by marking one with an asterisk and one without; thus prefix *i-* is different from prefix *i*-*. In other

Bantu languages the corresponding forms are often different.

NOUN CLASSES AND THEIR MEANINGS

It is natural to wonder if there is any property common to all of the nouns with the same prefix, and some generalizations can be made: nouns with prefixes *aba-* or *um-* refer to people; nouns with prefixes *um*-* or *im-* do not refer to people; and almost all nouns with prefixes *uku-* or *ubu-* are abstract.

Names, nations, and denominations are just three examples of how meaning can determine the prefixes used with a particular stem. If other names need to be created, or other denominations or nationalities need to be named, they take the same prefixes as all other previous words of similar meaning.

NON-BANTU NOUN CLASSES

Not only Bantu, but many other Niger-Congo languages have complicated class and agreement systems. In this chapter Fulani is used to illustrate such a non-Bantu language.

In Ndebele the noun class markers are prefixes, but in Fulani they are found as suffixes. We see a similar difference of position in closely related

---

NDEBELE NAMES

People's names are all found with the prefix *u-* : *u-Mako*, for example, is borrowed as "Mark." Since names usually identify individuals, the plural *o-Mako* may mean "Mark and the people with him." Ndebele given names often derive from nouns, adjectives, or verbs which describe the parents' feelings or circumstances at the child's birth.

For girls

u-Jabulani	Rejoice
u-Linda	Take-care (of the village till father's return)
u-Sakhile	We-have-made-a-good-home
u-Senzeni	What-have-we-done
u-Sithembil	We-are-hopeful
u-Sibahle	We-are-beautiful
u-Thandiwe	She-is-loved (that is by God, because she survived difficult times)
u-Thokozile	We-are-happy (to have a child)

For boys

u-Themba	Hope
u-Zenzo	Things (happened when he was in the womb)

For both

u-Zibusiso	Blessings (are given us by God)

The Ndebele prefixes for neighboring or foreign peoples are *um-* (singular) and *ama-* (plural): *um-Khalanga*, "a Kalanga," *ama-Amelika*, "Americans."

Left: *Makishi dancers entertain tourists at the Victoria Falls in Zimbabwe. The two main ethnic groupings in Zimbabwe are the Ndebele in the north and the Shona, who outnumber the Ndebele by about four to one, in the south.*

languages like English and Norwegian, where the definite article comes before the noun in English but after it in Norwegian. There are 18 noun classes in Fulani and one example of each is given in the table below. They are listed in the alphabetical order of the suffixes, each of which identifies a different noun class, just as each different prefix identified a different noun class in Zulu or Ndebele. The letters B and D stand for implosives, ʔ is a glottal stop, *N* is like the "ng" of "singer" and *ng* like the "ng" of "finger."

Just as in Ndebele there are singular and plural prefixes, in Fulani there are singular and plural

FULANI NOUN CLASSES

Stem	Suffix	Translation
laam	- Be	chiefs
loo	- De	storage-pots
Bow	- Di	mosquitoes
laam	- Do	chief
Biraa	- Dam	milk
nood	- a	crocodile
njar	- am	a drink
les	- di	country
yiit	- e	fire
nyor	- go	cover-mat
taador	- gol	girdle
nyala	- hol	calf
ngas	- ka	hole
daN	- ki	grass shelter
loo	- Nde	storage-pot
ʔen	- ndu	breast
Dem	- ngal	tongue
hottoll	- o	cotton

NDEBELE ANIMAL NAMES

A list of sample Ndebele animal names indicates that it is difficult to discover a property common to all the animals with the same prefixes:

Prefixes	Translation	Stem
i ama	caracal	duha
	cheetah	hlosi
	jackal	khanka
	polecat	qaqa
	rat	gundwane
	roan	thaka
	wild cat	gola
in izin	baboon	dwangu
	buffalo	nyati
	eland	pofu
	elephant	dlovu
	giraffe	tundla
	hippopotamus	vubu
	leopard	gwe
	wildebeest	konkone
isi izi	lion	lwane
	mongoose	tsikibololo
	water buck	dumoka
u o	bat	malulwane
	rhinoceros	bhejane
	shrew	tswebe
	spring hare	mayelani
um im	antelope	ziki
	hare	vundla
	reed buck	tshwayeli

singular suffixes must pair with one of the two remaining plural suffixes *-De* or *-Di*: *loo-Nde*, "storage-pot," *loo-De*, "storage-pots," and *Bow-ngu*, "mosquito," *Bow-Di*, "mosquitoes."

SMALL THINGS AND BIG THINGS

Fulani illustrates another common Niger-Congo feature: there are special "diminutive" and "augmentative" suffixes for indicating smallness and bigness, or importance and unimportance. These "secondary suffixes" replace the nouns' normal "primary" ones (*see box below*).

This is the only important way in which the Fulani noun class system differs from that of Ndebele and Zulu. But many Bantu languages work similarly, with the suffixes of Fulani becoming prefixes. This is the case in Shona, for example. Here, however, there is a further twist: the secondary prefixes not only replace the primary ones, but may also be added to them. Some secondary prefixes from the Karanga dialect of Shona are shown in the table opposite.

Special diminutive forms are found in many languages around the world, but augmentatives are rarer. In English we find diminutives like duckling, gosling, and princeling, but the -ling suffix is used with very few words, and there is no generally-used diminutive. Secondary prefixes make a noun class system more complicated, and some Bantu languages have even more secondary prefixes than those noted above, but they also generate an increase in expressive and creative possibilities by allowing the formation of new words.

suffixes. In both, the number of singular affixes (8 and 16 respectively) is greater than the number of plural ones (6 and 3), with the ratio higher in Fulani. This occurs in many languages: more differences are marked in the singular than in the plural. It is more important, it seems, to distinguish between single entities, than between grouped ones. In Fulani one singular suffix (*-Do*) and one plural suffix (*-Be*) are always paired together, and nouns with these refer only to people: *laam-Do*, "chief," *laam-Be*, "chiefs." All of the other 15

FULANI SECONDARY SUFFIXES

	Singular	**Plural**	
Primary suffixes	*laam - Do*	*laam - Be*	chief(s)
Secondary suffixes:			
Diminutive	*laam - ngel*	*laam - kon*	petty chief(s)
Augmentative	*laam - nga*	*laam - ko*	mighty chief(s)

SHONA SECONDARY PREFIXES

	Singular	Plural	
Primary suffixes	*mu-komana*	*va-komana*	boy(s)
Secondary suffixes:			
Diminutive	*ka-komana*	*tu-komana*	little boy(s)
Double diminutive	*ka-mu-komana*	*tu-va-komana*	tiny little boy(s)

AGREEMENT MARKERS AND PRONOUNS

A group of words which can replace a single noun in a sentence is a noun phrase. In a noun phrase the noun is the most important word, about which the other words, or "modifiers," give further information. English nouns have different forms for the singular and the plural, and there are just two modifiers, "this" and "that," which change respectively to "these" and "those." We say that these modifiers "agree with" the nouns for number. But in English no other modifiers change in this way.

In Bantu languages the situation is quite different. In fact most of the words which modify nouns change when the noun changes. Just as nouns have an affix which shows their class, so the modifiers too have an affix which shows their noun's class, the class affix of the modifier being determined by the class affix of the noun. In the following four noun phrases of Ndebele, the prefix of the adjective is different for each different noun prefix; in Ndebele all the modifiers commonly follow the noun and there are no words for "the" or "a."

um-fazi	*om-khulu*	the big woman
aba-fazi	*aba-khulu*	the big women
i-yezi	*eli-khulu*	the big cloud
isi-lwane	*esi-khulu*	the big lion

The adjective stem is *khulu* which means "big." The class affixes of the modifiers are called "agreement markers."

If instead of an adjective we use the word for "my" then we will see that once again the agreement markers change when the noun changes. The Ndebele words for "my" all begin with an agreement marker.

um-fazi	*w-ami*	my woman
aba-fazi	*b-ami*	my women
i-yezi	*l-ami*	my cloud
isi-lwane	*s-ami*	my lion

Another thing that can be seen from these examples is that the agreement markers are not always exactly the same with different modifiers, although they often are. In these four words for "my," every agreement marker is different from the corresponding agreement marker with the adjective stem *khulu* given earlier, though there is usually some recognizable similarity of form between the agreement markers which occur with the same noun prefix.

When we translate a Bantu noun and its modifiers, the prefix and the agreement markers are not translated; they simply identify the noun's class. Similarly, in a sentence with a subject and a verb, the verb's agreement marker is not translated. For example in the sentence *Um-fazi u-pheka,* "the woman cooks," the agreement marker *u* is not translated. However, if the subject is omitted, the verb functions like a complete sentence in English and the agreement marker is now translated by the English pronoun "she:" *U-pheka,* "She cooks."

In the same way, we may omit the noun from an adjective-plus-noun combination and translate the agreement marker as the English pronoun "one:" *um-fazi om-khulu*, "the big woman," or *om-khulu*, "the big one."

Agreement markers regularly have this double function: when the noun is present they are just agreement markers, but when the noun is absent they take on the role of a pronoun.

Noun class and agreement markers together constitute the famous and distinctive class and agreement system which, in its expressive clarity and its ubiquity, probably makes the Niger-Congo languages unique.

Right: *A young student learns Portuguese, the* lingua franca *in Guinea-Bisseau, where there are some 23 indigenous languages.*

Below: *A village meeting in Niger where the official language is French.*

LANGUAGES CATEGORIZE THE WORLD

It is often said that languages differ in the way they categorize the world. We shall briefly discuss some characteristic properties of African languages in relation to sex, relatives, and the ways people walk.

Most languages of sub-Saharan Africa mark no distinction between males and females in their pronominal (pronoun-like) forms. The Shona sentence *Unobika* means either "He is cooking" or "She is cooking." The pronominal is the first letter *U*, and there are no equivalents to the English pronouns "he" and "she." Of course it is the same with many other language families. In Mandarin, *Ta shi wode pengyou* means "he/she is my friend," with "*Ta*" meaning either "he" or "she."

In Africa the kinship systems are very different from those of Europe, and the differences are seen in the languages. In Ndebele, for example, there are three distinct words each for "mother" and "father:"

u-baba	my father
u-yihlo	your father
u-yise	his father
u-mama	my mother
u-nyoko	your mother
u-nina	his mother

An individual may also have more than one father or mother since your father's brothers are also your "fathers," and your mother's sisters are also your "mothers." These "fathers" and "mothers" can be distinguished from your natural mother and father by using the additional epithets "small" for brothers and sisters younger than your father or mother, and "large" for older ones, giving the terms listed above right.

Our last example illustrates the complexity of African vocabulary. In Shona there are more than 200 different words for walking, just a few of which are listed in the table (*see right*).

NDEBELE KINSHIP TERMS

Ndebele	Literal Translation	English
u-baba	my father	my father
u-baba (omncinayane)	my (little) father	my uncle
u-baba (omkhulu)	my (big) father	my uncle
u-mama	my mother	my mother
u-mama (omncinyane)	my (little) mother	my aunt
u-mama (omkhulu)	my (big) mother	my aunt

SHONA WALKING WORDS

Shona Word	Translation
chakwair	walk with a squelching noise through a muddy place
chwakatik	walk making a noise of breaking sticks
dowor	walk for a long time on bare feet
donzv	walk with a stick
duduk	walk backward
kokonyar	walk bent double with an arched back
kunzvur	walk about restlessly
mbey	walk all around an area
mbwembwer	walk with your body or buttocks shaking about
minair	walk with swinging hips
panh	walk a long way
pfumbur	walk raising dust
pushuk	walk with a very short dress
rauk	walk with long steps
rindimar	walk haughtily
seser	walk along with the flesh rippling
shwitair	walk naked or almost naked
svavair	walk huddled up with cold and wet
tabvuk	walk like a grasshopper with thighs so thin you seem to be jumping
vefuk	walk bent under a heavy load

Pacific

The Indo-Pacific region is home to the greatest diversity of languages on earth. The Philippines have 70 languages, Indonesia 200, and New Guinea and the Melanesian islands over a thousand. Here, the linguistic history is also that of the conquest of the Pacific: the evidence of Austronesian languages has helped researchers trace the prehistoric Polynesian mariners' odyssey to the ocean's remotest islands. The indigenous languages of New Guinea remain the least known in the world, and their history and inter-relationships still pose unsolved puzzles.

A monumental statue
from Easter Island in the
South Pacific. The main
colonization of the Pacific
took place between 4,000
and 1,000 years ago, but
early Polynesian settlers
did not reach remote
Easter Island until
about AD 400.

The number of Austronesian languages still remains a point of contention, primarily because linguists are still uncertain about differentiating separate languages from their dialects. This is in turn due to the lack of actual data on some Austronesian languages, particularly those spoken in New Guinea and certain islands of Indonesia. In other instances, political factors interfere with the identification of dialects or languages; the national languages Bahasa Malaysia (Malay), spoken in Malaysia, and Bahasa Indonesia (Indonesian), spoken in Indonesia, are sufficiently similar to be considered merely dialects of a single language (*see map below*).

Similarities between the languages of Indonesia, Polynesia, and Madagascar were first noticed as early as the eighteenth century, but the first systematic classification of Austronesian languages was produced by the German scholar Otto Dempwolff in 1934–38. This classification underwent a number of changes in the works of Isidore Dyen, Otto Chr. Dahl, Robert Blust, and others. The classification presented here is based on Robert Blust's proposal, according to which the primary division in Austronesian languages is between the languages of Taiwan (the so-called Formosan territorial grouping, which in turn is divided into the Atayalic, Tsouic, and Paiwanic groups) and all the remaining languages.

INDONESIA AND MALAYSIA

The languages shown here all belong to the Austronesian family, with the exception of the Aslian group spoken in the interior of peninsular Malaysia. The national languages Bahasa Indonesia and Bahasa Malaysia (standard Malay) are spreading at the expense of local languages. Also spoken are southern Chinese dialects including Hokkien, Hakka, and Teochew, and Malay-based creoles.

The Southern Philippine languages, Sama, Bonggi, and Bajau, have spread to coastal areas of Borneo and Sulawesi.

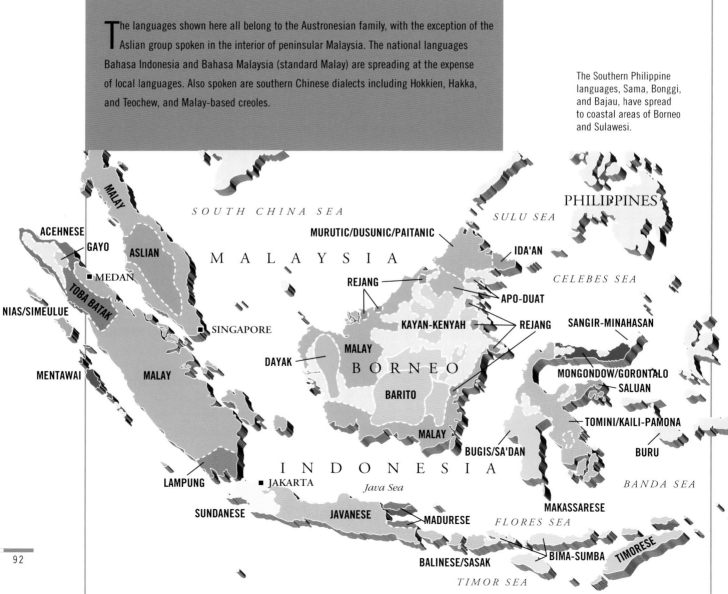

SHARED WORDS IN MODERN AUSTRONESIAN LANGUAGES

This table shows a sample of shared words (also known as cognates), including their hypothetical form in Proto-Austronesian.

Tagalog	Malay	Fijian	Samoan	Proto-Austronesian	English
dalawa	dua	rua	lua	*Duwa	"two"
apat	empat	vaa	faa	*e(m)pat	"four"
lima	lima	lima	lima	*lima	"five; hand"
anim	enam	ono	ono	*enem	"six"
manok	manu	manu-manu	manu	*manuk	"bird"
mata	mata	mata	mata	*mata	"eye"
daan	jalan	sala	'ala	*Zalan	"road"'
pandan	pandan	vadra	fala	*panDan	"pandanus"
niyog	nior	niu	niu	*niuR	"coconut"

THE SETTLEMENT OF POLYNESIA

The acceptance of a primary division between the Formosan languages and the Malayo-Polynesian languages is consistent with archeological evidence indicating that Proto-Austronesian (the language from which modern Austronesian languages descended) was spoken in and around Taiwan about 5–7,000 thousand years ago. A combination of linguistic and archeological findings allows us to reconstruct to a certain extent the way of life led by speakers of Proto-Austronesian. They apparently relied on fishing and agriculture, and cultivated taro, yams, bananas, sugarcane, breadfruit, coconuts, and possibly rice. They kept pigs and probably dogs and chickens, but had no domesticated sheep, goats, or cattle. They made pottery. They were in their element in their maritime environment, developing excellent navigational skills and using outrigger canoes for transportation, which to this day are found throughout the Austronesian-speaking area.

It is these early navigational skills that played a crucial role in the expansion of Austronesian-

Above: *Pandanus is a widespread plant with useful leaves and edible fruits which can be stored after cooking, an important factor for sailors and inhabitants of infertile lands. The name itself is Austronesian, and is shared by languages as far west as Tagalog in the Philippines and as far east as Samoa.*

speakers. The first waves of migration, which probably took place between 3000 and 2000 BC, were from Taiwan to the Philippines and on to the Moluccas. Seaborne migrations then moved southeast, and Oceania was settled during the first millennium BC. Many settlers were either traders or young warriors for whom sailing to remote lands was part of the initiation into adulthood. The expansion of early Austronesian speakers into the islands of the Pacific Ocean is associated with a number of prehistoric cultures; one of the best known is the so-called Lapita. Distinctive Lapita pottery is found on numerous islands from New Guinea all the way east to Samoa.

The last expansion of Austronesian speakers was west to Madagascar, which was settled in the first millennium AD. (The name Madagascar is

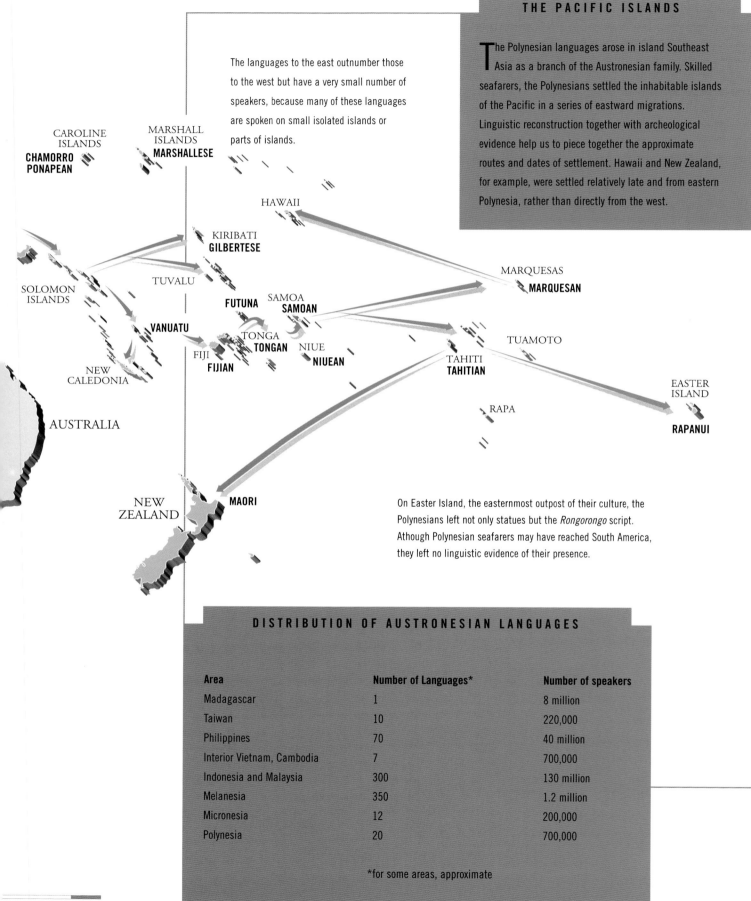

The languages to the east outnumber those to the west but have a very small number of speakers, because many of these languages are spoken on small isolated islands or parts of islands.

THE PACIFIC ISLANDS

The Polynesian languages arose in island Southeast Asia as a branch of the Austronesian family. Skilled seafarers, the Polynesians settled the inhabitable islands of the Pacific in a series of eastward migrations. Linguistic reconstruction together with archeological evidence help us to piece together the approximate routes and dates of settlement. Hawaii and New Zealand, for example, were settled relatively late and from eastern Polynesia, rather than directly from the west.

CAROLINE ISLANDS
CHAMORRO
PONAPEAN

MARSHALL ISLANDS
MARSHALLESE

HAWAII

KIRIBATI
GILBERTESE

MARQUESAS
MARQUESAN

TUVALU

SOLOMON ISLANDS

SAMOA
SAMOAN

FUTUNA

TUAMOTO

VANUATU

TONGA
TONGAN

NIUE
NIUEAN

FIJI
FIJIAN

TAHITI
TAHITIAN

NEW CALEDONIA

AUSTRALIA

RAPA

EASTER ISLAND

RAPANUI

MAORI

NEW ZEALAND

On Easter Island, the easternmost outpost of their culture, the Polynesians left not only statues but the *Rongorongo* script. Although Polynesian seafarers may have reached South America, they left no linguistic evidence of their presence.

DISTRIBUTION OF AUSTRONESIAN LANGUAGES

Area	Number of Languages*	Number of speakers
Madagascar	1	8 million
Taiwan	10	220,000
Philippines	70	40 million
Interior Vietnam, Cambodia	7	700,000
Indonesia and Malaysia	300	130 million
Melanesia	350	1.2 million
Micronesia	12	200,000
Polynesia	20	700,000

*for some areas, approximate

probably a distortion of the African placename Mogadishu, brought to Europe by Marco Polo.) The Austronesian-speakers living on the island call themselves and their language Malagasy. While Malagasy is clearly an Austronesian language, it has borrowed heavily from the Bantu languages of Africa—the Malagasy had intense trade contacts with Bantu-speakers. For example, the name for chicken in Malagasy is *akoko*, a borrowing from the Bantu -*koko*. Like Bantu languages, Malagasy has all open syllables, whereas other Western Austronesian languages tolerate closed syllables.

There are a large number of borrowings from Arabic in the languages of Malaysia and Indonesia, due to the early influence of Islam. There are also borrowings from the Indo-European languages of India, primarily through trade. Despite such borrowings, Austronesian languages remain strikingly similar in their core or basic vocabulary, the very vocabulary that is unlikely to be affected by cultural contacts or migrations.

AUSTRONESIAN LANGUAGE FEATURES

Despite the vast geographical area they span, Austronesian languages continue to have much vocabulary in common and to share many grammatical features. Many languages of the family have rather small inventories of both vowels and consonants, and Polynesian languages are the most economical in that respect. Hawaiian, for example, has only eight consonants (w, m, p, l, n, k, h) and the glottal stop, represented as ', for example, *'ala* in the table on page 93, and five vowels (a, i, u, e, o). Western Austronesian languages have several more consonants but make up for that by a four-vowel system (i, a, u, ə). This final vowel is similar to the sound of the last vowel in the English word "sofa." More complex consonant systems, found in Melanesia for example, are sometimes attributed to the influence of neighboring non-Austronesian languages. Open syllables predominate in Austronesian languages, and this tendency is apparent in well-known Polynesian names such as Ta-hi-ti, Sa-mo-a, Ho-no-lu-lu, u-ku-le-le, and a-lo-ha.

Austronesian languages make heavy use of agglutination. The technique of making new compound words by combining existing words allows Austronesian languages to create their own words for new concepts, rather than borrow such

Above: *Little was known in the West of the peoples or languages of the Far East until Marco Polo, shown here on a Catalan map, traveled overland to China (1271–75).*

ALIENABLE AND INALIENABLE POSSESSION

Alienable possession implies that an object can be transferred to another's ownership. Inalienable possession is viewed as an inseparable, indispensable characteristic of the owner. Inalienable possession includes such concepts as body parts, kinship terms, and some valuable items. In Samoan, for example, "my arm" (an inalienable body part) is expressed differently from "my biscuit," which could readily become someone else's biscuit:

le masi	a	a'u
the biscuit	POSSESSIVE	me
"my biscuit"		

le lima	o	a'u
the arm	POSSESSIVE	me
"my arm"		

words. This tendency is apparent, for instance, in Malagasy, where the creation of native Malagasy words has long been preferred over direct borrowing. Often new words are extremely long, for example: *zava* "to be lit, illuminated," *fahazavana* "illumination, brilliance" (*faha* is a nominal prefix expressing state), *fahazavan-tsaina* "intelligence" (*saina* "mind"). Of course, this example is not intended to show that Malagasy never borrows words; it actually has quite a few borrowings, from Bantu, Arabic, and later from French and English. Some French nouns were borrowed by Malagasy complete with an article, hence *latabatra* "table" (*la table*), or a preposition, hence *dipaina* "European bread" (*du pain*).

Reduplication (a full or partial repetition of a word) is a widespread phenomenon in Austronesian languages. As a result, these languages often have long words; for example, the Samoan word *mata* "unripe," is reduplicated to become *fa'amatamata* "raw." Reduplication is sometimes accompanied by a change in the initial sound of the reduplicated element; in Bolaang Mongondow (Indonesia) *bontat* "hack open, hack through" becomes *mo-montat* "cut open a new path through vegetation"; in Malagasy *hendratra* "startled" becomes *hendra-trendratra* "very scared."

Widespread Austronesian features include the distinction of inclusive first person pronouns (indicating the speaker and the addressee or several addressees) and exclusive first person pronouns (indicating only the speaker(s) and excluding the people who are addressed). Pronominal suffixes mark the possessors of nouns (for example, in the Polynesian language West Futuna, *tupu-u* "your grandparent," *tupu-na* "his/her grandparent"). A distinction is also made between alienable and inalienable possession (possession which can be transferred as opposed to possession which cannot be transferred, *see page 95*).

A number of Austronesian languages rely heavily on passive constructions; in Malagasy and Maori the percentage of passives in a narrative text can reach up to 70 percent (for comparison,

FOCUS CONSTRUCTION IN TAGALOG

Tagalog (also known as Pilipino) is one of the largest languages of the Philippines and its national language. In Tagalog the predicate, which occurs at the beginning of a clause, can be followed by one or more nouns; one of the nouns is preceded by the particle *ang*, and this noun is the topic of the sentence (the information component that the sentence is about). Depending on the noun chosen as topic, the verb also changes its form. There are several possible ways of representing the situation "The woman will give the rice to the child" (the topic of each sentence is in **bold**):

mag-bibigay	**ang**	**babae**	ng	bigas	sa	bata
AGENT TOPIC-will give	TOPIC	woman	ARTICLE	rice	to	child

"The woman will give rice to the child."

i-bibigay	ng	babae	**ang**	**bigas**	sa	bata
OBJECT TOPIC-will give	ARTICLE	woman	TOPIC	rice	to	child

"The rice, the woman will give it to the child."
("The rice will be given to the child by the woman.")

ibigy-an	ng	babae	ng	bigas	**ang**	**bata**
will give-GOAL TOPIC	ARTICLE	woman	ARTICLE	rice	TOPIC	child

"The child, the woman will give him/her the rice."
("The child will be given the rice by the woman.")

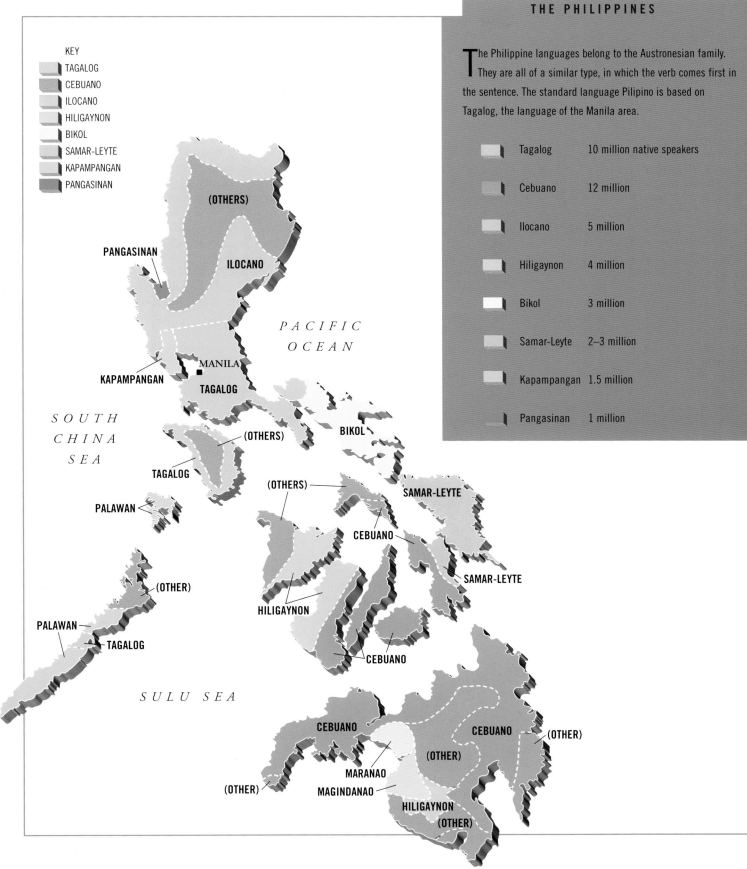

THE PHILIPPINES

The Philippine languages belong to the Austronesian family. They are all of a similar type, in which the verb comes first in the sentence. The standard language Pilipino is based on Tagalog, the language of the Manila area.

	Tagalog	10 million native speakers
	Cebuano	12 million
	Ilocano	5 million
	Hiligaynon	4 million
	Bikol	3 million
	Samar-Leyte	2–3 million
	Kapampangan	1.5 million
	Pangasinan	1 million

KEY
- TAGALOG
- CEBUANO
- ILOCANO
- HILIGAYNON
- BIKOL
- SAMAR-LEYTE
- KAPAMPANGAN
- PANGASINAN

(OTHERS)

PANGASINAN

ILOCANO

PACIFIC OCEAN

KAPAMPANGAN

MANILA

TAGALOG

SOUTH CHINA SEA

(OTHERS)

TAGALOG

BIKOL

PALAWAN

(OTHERS)

SAMAR-LEYTE

CEBUANO

SAMAR-LEYTE

(OTHER)

PALAWAN

TAGALOG

HILIGAYNON

CEBUANO

SULU SEA

CEBUANO

CEBUANO

(OTHER)

(OTHER)

MARANAO

(OTHER)

MAGINDANAO

HILIGAYNON

(OTHER)

the use of passives in scholarly English seldom goes beyond 6–8 percent and is even lower in spoken language). In addition to regular passives such as "The fish was caught" (by the fisherman), Austronesian languages use passive in requests (the so-called "passive imperative"). Compare the following requests in Malagasy:

Manaraha   *ny*   *mpampianatra*
be-followed   the   teacher
"Let the teacher be followed."

Araho   *ny*   *mpampianatra*
follow   the   teacher
"Follow the teacher."

The former request, which uses the passive imperative, is far more polite; the latter sounds

---

Below: *The Philippines encompass over 100 distinct ethnic groups, and over 70 languages are spoken. Chinese make up just 2 percent of the population but over 120 Chinese schools ensure that they retain their cultural and linguistic identity.*

more harsh and uncompromising and has to be used carefully.

Some Austronesian languages (for example, Motu and West Polynesian languages), are ergative, and scholars are still debating whether or not Proto-Austronesian was also ergative. Some languages demonstrate the so-called "split ergativity," where pronouns have accusative marking and common nouns have ergative marking. Research has found that the use of the ergative form varies with social factors such as the relationship between the speaker and hearer: the case marker is used more in formal situations than in the home, and more by men than by women.

West Austronesian languages and Philippine languages in particular are famous for their use of the so-called "focus construction," illustrated on page 93 by Tagalog examples. These examples point to another interesting feature of Austronesian: a number of languages of the family have a verb-initial word order. In Tagalog and Maori, this order is VSO ("Caught the cat the mouse" rather than "The cat caught the mouse"); in Malagasy, it is VOS ("Caught the mouse the cat"); finally, in some languages (certain Fijian dialects and Samoan) it can be both VSO and VOS. As the list of languages exhibiting these orders shows, verb-initial orders in Austronesian languages are not confined to a single geographical location but are found in all parts of the area. These orders alternate with SVO and, more rarely, SOV (the occurrence of SOV in some Melanesian languages is explained by the influence of the neighboring Papuan languages).

Linguists have numerous opportunities to study such grammatical features of Austronesian languages, which are solidly represented in modern languages of the family. Certain features, however, have almost disappeared and must be studied primarily through early grammars compiled by travelers and missionaries, or through comparative analysis of Austronesian languages. One such feature is distinct vocabulary subsystems (and probably some distinct grammatical elements) for different social castes. In Oceania, this is known as "the chiefs' language"; in speaking to or of chiefs, people had to use special words for "eat," "sleep," "walk," "dwelling," and so on. It is also possible that only chiefs were allowed to use some words, which were considered sacred and forbidden for the common man. This special vocabulary is still very much alive in Javanese, a Western Austronesian language.

Austronesian languages still pose a number of other puzzles. One question concerns remote relationships between this family and other languages of the world. There are various theories; a hypothetical link between the Austronesian and Austro-Thai family has been suggested, and a possible link between Austronesian and Japanese is also proposed. Another puzzle is Easter Island, a remote island in the South Pacific, famous for its enigmatic stone monuments and statues, dating to between AD 1000 and 1600. Current theories link the mysterious devastation of this island culture to the exhaustion of its ecology. Wooden boards found there exhibit the script known as *rongorongo*, which probably developed as a formal emulation of European writing (of which the Spanish treaty of annexation of 1770 was the most likely source). It is thought that the script was used for ornamentation or for mnemonic purposes, and was not used for writing down the Rapanui language spoken on the island. The link between the culture of Easter Island and South American cultures, proposed by the Norwegian scholar Thor Heyerdahl, seems implausible in the light of both archeological and linguistic evidence.

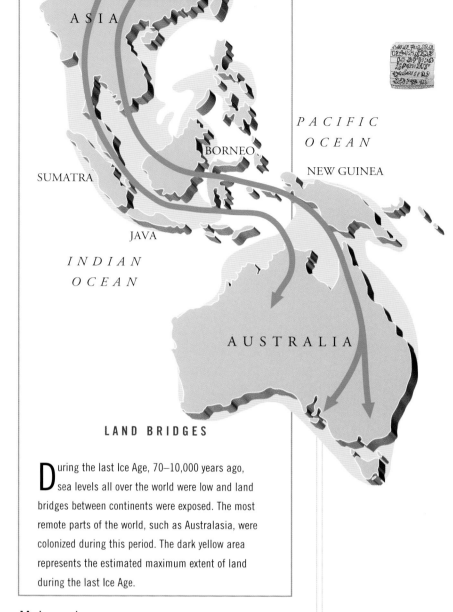

LAND BRIDGES

During the last Ice Age, 70–10,000 years ago, sea levels all over the world were low and land bridges between continents were exposed. The most remote parts of the world, such as Australasia, were colonized during this period. The dark yellow area represents the estimated maximum extent of land during the last Ice Age.

Melanesia

The Melanesian Islands are situated in the southwestern Pacific, and were so named by early explorers because of their inhabitants' dark skin (from the Greek *melas*, "black"). The largest land mass is vast, mountainous New Guinea, to the east of which lie the hundreds of smaller islands of the Bismarck Archipelago, the Solomons, Vanuatu, and New Caledonia. The western limit of the Melanesian population is indeterminate, as there has been much intermixing with other populations, but a Melanesian element can be found throughout eastern Southeast Asia. To the east, the Fijians are apparently Melanesian in physical appearance, but have a culture and language which more closely resemble those of their Polynesian neighbors. At the northern tip of Australia, the Torres Strait Islanders appear to be Melanesian physically, linguistically, and culturally, although as Australians their recent history has been different.

Human society is very ancient in Melanesia. Radiocarbon dating of prehistoric sites such as Kosipe in Papua have indicated 26,000 years of settlement, with some estimates ranging up to 40,000. This timespan corresponds to dates suggested for the peopling of the Australian continent. Indeed, until about 6,000 years ago, a land bridge connected New Guinea and the Australian land mass, whose populations were then continuous, and it is likely that the original migrations to Australia followed this route. Linguistic evidence supports this hypothesis, as links have been found between the languages of the Central Highlands and Proto-Australian (*see chapter six*).

Below: *The* rongorongo *script of Easter Island is thought to be an emulation of European scripts introduced by Spanish colonists. It was probably used as a memory aid or for decorative purposes, not for recording the Rapanui language of the islanders.*

For the linguist, the most remarkable feature of Melanesia is the extreme diversity of its languages. Vanuatu has a population of little over 150,000, but boasts 105 identifiable languages, making it the world's most linguistically diverse country, with an average of one language for every 1,500 speakers. The Solomon Islands have similarly small language groups: nearly 90 languages are spoken by a population of about 300,000. According to the Summer Institute of Linguistics' latest survey, in Papua New Guinea there are over 860 languages in a population of around 4 million. Many of these are still undescribed or incompletely known to outsiders, so for this reason alone care must be taken when making universal generalizations about human language. For example, SOV languages nearly always have case systems, but the Haruai language in Papua New Guinea does not. Phonologically, some Chimbu languages of the New Guinea Highlands have the highly unusual "lateral velar affricate," which can be thought of as a kind of scraped "g" sound made with the side of the tongue, while the Rotokas language of the North Solomons (*see page 106*) appears to lack distinct nasal phonemes, once thought to be universal.

Taking Papua New Guinea as an example, how do we account for this incredible diversity? Why should an area with only one-tenth of one percent of the world's population harbor almost one-sixth of the world's languages? The fragmentation is frequently explained in terms of the tribal groups' isolation by the mountainous, rugged terrain and by constant warfare, but for a number of reasons this cannot be the full story.

To begin with, the largest language group in Papua New Guinea is Enga, with approximately 160,000 speakers. Yet the Engans live in the Central Highlands in some of the most rugged and remote areas in the country, or indeed anywhere on Earth. On the other hand, the region of greatest linguistic diversity is probably Sepik, near the mainland north coast, where it is not unusual for villages to speak very different languages despite close proximity and easy social contact. The idea that before the Europeans' arrival, the tribal groups were unaware of outsiders, has been greatly exaggerated. Anthropologists and archeologists have clearly demonstrated that complex and extensive trading networks had already existed.

In many of these societies, great pride is taken in small cultural differences. It seems there is a tendency to emphasize linguistic peculiarities for the sake of identity, and over the millennia this has doubtless generated difference. The phenomenon of word taboo may also have been a contributing factor: in-laws, for example, are commonly forbidden to utter one another's names; similarly, those of the recently deceased may be taboo. Since personal names can also be ordinary words, alternatives may be substituted, creating an accelerated rate of change.

The late Don Laycock, who made a life-long study of Papua New Guinean languages, suggested that perhaps the problem should be approached from another direction. Instead of wondering why Melanesia has so many languages, maybe we should ask why the rest of the world has so few, or how some languages become established over such wide areas. Most of the conditions required to establish a dominant language—centralized political power, standardization, a writing system, and a literary tradition—were absent in Melanesia, and thus could not allow any one language to become pre-eminent.

Above: *Fijians, though apparently Melanesian in physical appearance, have a language which closely resembles that of their Polynesian neighbors.*

THE LANGUAGES OF MELANESIA

The main division is between the Austronesian and non-Austronesian, or Papuan languages. The Austronesian languages are part of the huge group stretching from Madagascar in the west to Polynesia in the east. It is thought that Austronesian speakers moved through the southwestern Pacific some 3,000 years ago, although the details of these migrations are still being debated by linguists, archeologists, and pre-historians (*see pages 93–5*).

Many of the Austronesian languages of the area have been in close contact over a long period with other non-Austronesian languages, and have been extensively influenced by them, becoming atypical of Austronesian languages as a whole. Indeed, some cases, like Maisin of the northeast Papuan coast, defy classification and are best described as "mixed languages."

The late arrival of the Austronesian languages in Melanesia is reflected in their distribution. Most are spoken by groups living in coastal or island locations, although there has been considerable penetration inland in northeastern New Guinea (*see map opposite*). Further east, as the uninhabited islands were colonized, the whole of Polynesia became an Austronesian-speaking area.

MIXED LANGUAGES: THE CASE OF MAISIN

The Maisin language has caused problems for linguists as it shares features of both Austronesian and Papuan languages. It has alternatively been described as an Austronesian language strongly influenced by Papuan features, or as a Papuan language strongly influenced by Austronesian. Professor A. Capell, a life-long researcher of New Guinea languages, viewed Maisin as a "mixed language." However, this theory has been rejected by many linguists, as it does not fit the "family tree" model. Since little is still known about language mixing, this rejection may be premature, and it may be the model which eventually proves to be inadequate. Other languages have also been described as mixed, such as Magori in southeastern Papua and the Reef-Santa Cruz family in the Solomon Islands. There may be some relationship to the processes of pidginization and creolization as described in chapter 8.

PAPUAN LANGUAGES

Nearly all the languages of the Solomon Islands, Vanuatu, and New Caledonia are Austronesian, but the majority of those of New Guinea are not. The latter used to be classified simply as non-Austronesian languages, but recent research has shown that many are related as families, or more distantly as stocks, or phyla (*see chart opposite*).

CHARACTERISTICS OF PAPUAN LANGUAGES

As can be expected, with such an enormous group of languages there are few universal features. However, some generalizations can be made. Professor W. A. Foley, one of the world's leading authorities on Papuan languages, has described in detail the phonology, morphology, and syntax typically found in the group.

Papuan languages usually have subject-object-verb (SOV) word order, or at least have the verb in final position. This is in contrast to many of the surrounding Austronesian languages, which typically have SVO order. The verb morphology may be complex (*see page 104*), but the morphology of nouns is usually simpler, and restricted to some case marking. Dual pronouns are often distinguished to represent two people, for example "we two" and "you two," as well as the more familiar singular and plural. Within these broad generalizations, there is a multitude of individual grammatical features which makes the study of Papuan languages endlessly fascinating.

MULTILINGUALISM

How have the people of Melanesia adapted to such linguistic diversity? One way of overcoming the problems of communication has been a traditionally high rate of multilingualism. It is still not unusual in Melanesia for people to have a working knowledge of four, five, or even more languages. Since many language groups only have

LANGUAGES OF NEW GUINEA

The map shows the languages mentioned in the text and the main language phyla that have been tentatively identified. Of the 750 or so Papuan languages (shown in green), Enga has the largest number of speakers, some 157,000. The Austronesian languages (shown in pink), scattered around the coast and on surrounding islands, arrived some 3,000 years ago and many have changed radically through contact with Papuan languages.

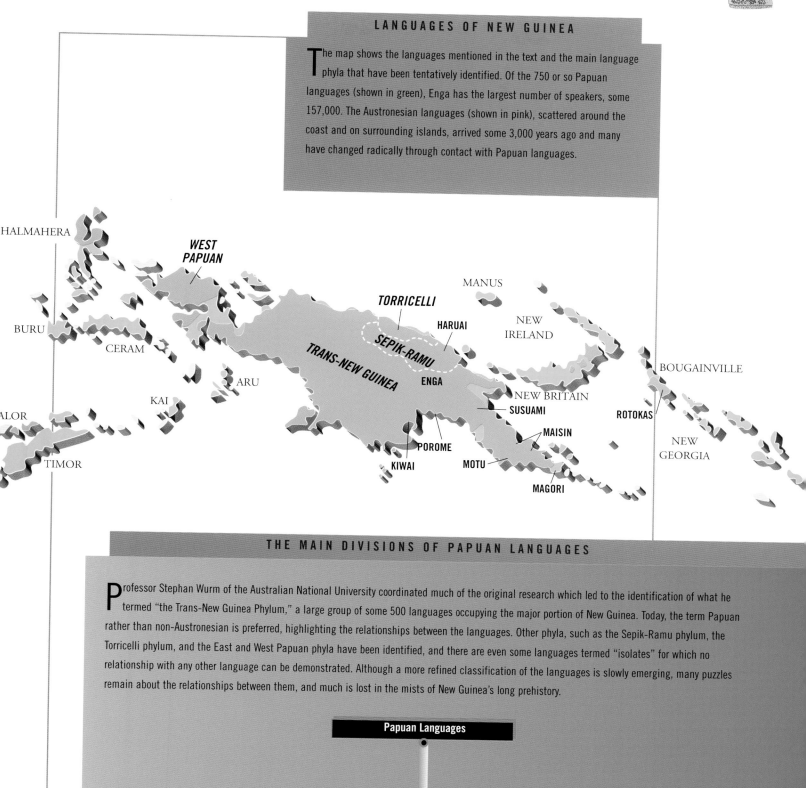

HALMAHERA

WEST PAPUAN

MANUS

TORRICELLI

HARUAI

NEW IRELAND

SEPIK-RAMU

BURU

CERAM

TRANS-NEW GUINEA

ENGA

BOUGAINVILLE

ARU

NEW BRITAIN

KAI

SUSUAMI

ROTOKAS

ALOR

MAISIN

NEW GEORGIA

POROME

TIMOR

KIWAI

MOTU

MAGORI

THE MAIN DIVISIONS OF PAPUAN LANGUAGES

Professor Stephan Wurm of the Australian National University coordinated much of the original research which led to the identification of what he termed "the Trans-New Guinea Phylum," a large group of some 500 languages occupying the major portion of New Guinea. Today, the term Papuan rather than non-Austronesian is preferred, highlighting the relationships between the languages. Other phyla, such as the Sepik-Ramu phylum, the Torricelli phylum, and the East and West Papuan phyla have been identified, and there are even some languages termed "isolates" for which no relationship with any other language can be demonstrated. Although a more refined classification of the languages is slowly emerging, many puzzles remain about the relationships between them, and much is lost in the mists of New Guinea's long prehistory.

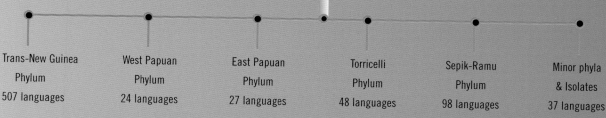

Papuan Languages

| Trans-New Guinea Phylum 507 languages | West Papuan Phylum 24 languages | East Papuan Phylum 27 languages | Torricelli Phylum 48 languages | Sepik-Ramu Phylum 98 languages | Minor phyla & Isolates 37 languages |

a few hundred speakers, it is almost impossible for some individuals to find marriage partners from within their own group. As a result, their children have parents who speak different languages, and as they grow up they may acquire more in communication with relatives from other groups. Adults may have widespread trading networks and acquire at least a working knowledge of their trading partners' languages. In some cases simplified trade languages emerged, such as a simplified Motu in the Gulf of Papua or simplified Yimas or Iatmul in the Sepik. More recently, other languages of wider communication have become established: mission *lingua francas*, Melanesian Pidgin, and the languages of European colonialism.

MISSION LINGUA FRANCAS

Missionaries were some of the earliest European visitors to Melanesia, and by the late nineteenth century, there was already a significant missionary presence in many coastal areas. Often the missionaries would take an interest in the local

languages with the aim of spreading the Christian message more effectively, and some of the earliest linguistic material from the region consists of word lists and sometimes grammar sketches prepared by the missionaries. In Papua New Guinea, a number of local vernaculars were adopted as languages of wider communication for mission-related activities (*see map opposite*). Even today, the Summer Institute of Linguistics, a Christian organization, carries out much of the field investigation of Papua New Guinea languages, as workers describe the grammars of local languages and cooperate with local language-speakers to produce vernacular versions of the gospels.

MELANESIAN PIDGIN

While multilingualism may have been an adequate solution to the problems of Melanesian language diversity when communities were isolated, the twentieth century saw an opening-up of the area, and new opportunities for travel. Laborers from the New Hebrides, the Solomon

Above: *This fisherman from the Fly River delta is one of around 25,000 speakers of the Kiwai language.*

KIWAI VERBS

Languages of the Kiwai family are spoken around the delta of the Fly River in southwestern Papua by about 25,000 people. The verb morphology of Kiwai is one of the most complex in the world. Various prefixes and suffixes indicate subtle differences of tense, mood and aspect, and the number of agents or objects, as these examples from Stephen Wurm's research on Island Kiwai demonstrate:

asidim-ai	"cover one object once"
asidim-o	"keep on covering one object"
i-asidim-ai	"cover more than one object once"
i-asidim-uti	"cover more than one object in separate actions"

Sometimes this process can lead to very long verb forms. The most complex so far encountered are the following:

odi	"string a bow"
ri-mi-bi-du-mo-i-odi-ai-ama-ri-go	"in the remote future, they three will definitely string two bows at a time"
atate	"move, remove"
g-a-bi-duru-mo-iw-ar-atate-ai-ama-go	"in the near past they three had the habit of removing many, one at a time"

Fortunately, other aspects of the language, such as phonology and the structure of the noun phrase are not so complex.

POROME: A LANGUAGE WITH NO KNOWN RELATIVES

The Porome language isolate is spoken by some 1,000 people in a remote corner of the Gulf Province in western Papua. So far, it has not been linked with any of the other languages of the area. Its vocabulary and grammar are quite unlike the surrounding languages from the Kiwaian family. It has a number of unusual features, such as the presence of nasal vowels and absence of subject marking on the verb.

The origin of Porome continues to be one of the fascinating unsolved mysteries facing linguists in this part of the world. However, as more and better data become available, it is possible that relationships will eventually be established.

Islands, and the New Guinea islands were recruited to work on the plantations of Queensland and the Central Pacific, giving rise to the various varieties of Melanesian pidgin (*see chapter 8*). Originally pidgin was a means of surviving in a multilingual plantation environment, but when laborers returned to their home communities it had immediate currency as a language of wider communication in areas where inter-tribal contact was increasing rapidly due to mission and government activity. The descendants of this early pidgin, Tok Pisin in Papua New Guinea, Pijin in the Solomon Islands, and Bislama in Vanuatu, are now firmly established as languages of national unity in the emerging democracies of the southwestern Pacific. A variety known as "Broken" is widely spoken in the Torres Strait in northern Australia, but has no official status.

HIRI MOTU

Another interesting development of a pidgin language is the case of Hiri Motu. Motu is a native Austronesian language spoken by people in 12 coastal villages near the Papua New Guinea capital, Port Moresby. Early missionaries attempted to learn Motu, but it was later apparent that what the locals taught them was just a simplified version. This supports the suggestion made by some theorists that "foreigner talk" is important in the formation of pidgins. Later, a pidginized form of the language was used by the administration, especially the police, on patrols to other parts of Papua, giving rise to its alternative name, Police Motu. The somewhat romanticized

Below: *Mission* lingua francas *developed in the nineteenth century as a means of communication between European missionaries and the local peoples. Most of the early study and recording of Papuan languages was undertaken by missionaries.*

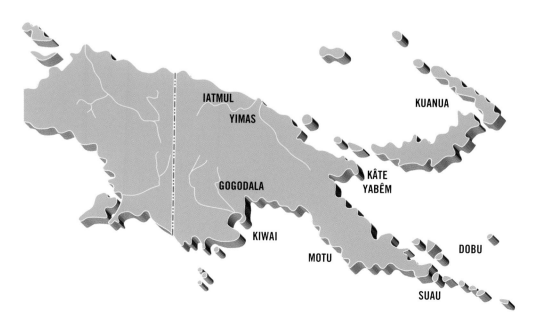

name Hiri Motu is a reflection of the past trading activity of the Motuan people, who used a simplified form of their language on expeditions known as *hiri*, sailing large canoes westward to the Gulf of Papua, where they traded pots for sago. However, it is doubtful if the language used on such expeditions was in fact a direct ancestor of today's Hiri Motu, which is formally recognized as one of the country's official languages alongside Tok Pisin and English.

HIRI MOTU: A PIDGIN LANGUAGE FROM PAPUA

A simplified form of some local languages was used on trading expeditions (*hiri*) to the Gulf of Papua. Later, the name Hiri Motu was applied to the language based on Motu used by the colonial administration in other areas of Papua. It was also sometimes known as "Police Motu." The following examples show how Hiri Motu is simplified as morphological features of Motu are omitted.

Motu	Hiri Motu
umui iboumuiai	*umui ibounai*
"you [plural] all"	"you [plural] all"
idia iboudiai	*idia ibounai*
"they all"	"they all"

In Hiri Motu, number and person inflections are lost and the general adverb *ibounai* is used with all pronouns.

Similarly, in "pure" Motu, a distinction is made between *ruma ibounai* meaning "the whole house" and *ruma iboudiai* meaning "all the houses," while in Hiri Motu, *ruma ibounai* is used for both. A further example:

Motu	Motu Hiri
lau ese baina abia	*dohori lau abia*
"I [subject] I [future] get it"	"[future] I get"
ia ese baine abia	*dohori ia abia*
"he [subject] he future get it"	"future he get"

EUROPEAN COLONIAL LANGUAGES.

Like many other parts of the world, Melanesia has a complex history of colonization by outside powers, especially the nineteenth-century Europeans. The western half of the island of New Guinea was colonized by the Dutch in 1828. In the late nineteenth century, Britain occupied the south-eastern quarter of the mainland, first known as British New Guinea and later Papua. Germany took control of the north-eastern quarter of the mainland and the islands of New Britain, New Ireland, and Bougainville. Following World War I, the whole of the eastern part of New Guinea and the adjacent islands came under Australian administration. In 1963 Dutch New Guinea became the Indonesian province of Irian Jaya. The Solomon Islands eventually became a protectorate of Britain long after the Spanish, who originally claimed the discovery of the fabulous "Isles of Solomon," failed to rediscover the location of their prize. The New Hebrides became

THE SOUNDS OF ROTOKAS

Generally the phonology of Papuan languages is relatively simple compared with other language groups. It is quite common, for example, for there to be only five vowels. One of the Papuan languages of Bougainville in the North Solomons, Rotokas, has achieved fame in *The Guinness Book of Records* as the language with the world's smallest number of phonemes. It has 11, compared, for example, with the 44 in English. These 11 distinct sounds consist of 5 vowels and 6 consonants.

Vowels

a	e	i	o	u

Consonants

b	g	k	p	r	t

All Rotokas words are constructed from the above basic sound distinctions. This leads to a certain amount of repetition of the basic elements.

a unique Anglo-French condominium under joint administration, while the French took New Caledonia, which remains a colony today. Thus English, French, German, Dutch, and more recently Bahasa Indonesia, came to be spoken in the region. The Solomon Islands gained independence in 1978, Vanuatu in 1980, and Papua New Guinea in 1975.

SURVIVAL OF MELANESIAN LANGUAGES

As communication, education, and modernization proceed, there is considerable pressure on many of the smaller languages of Melanesia. The use of English in education and of varieties of Melanesian Pidgin as national languages means that many children are failing to acquire their parents' traditional tongues, and since many have fewer than 500 speakers, their future is uncertain. The plight of the Susuami language is typical.

Some steps are being taken to promote language maintenance. The Summer Institute of Linguistics is doing much work on the grammars of local languages, other non-government organizations are involved in the promotion of vernacular literacy, and recent government policy in Papua New Guinea has increased emphasis on preservation of traditional cultural values,

including languages. In several provinces vernacular pre-schools now teach initial literacy in the mother tongue before formal schooling begins. In spite of these encouraging moves, a number of small languages have disappeared in recent years, and many others must be considered to be under acute threat.

SUSUAMI: A MORIBUND LANGUAGE

Susuami is a language spoken in the resettlement village of Manki in the Upper Watut Valley in northeast New Guinea. In 1980 there were approximately 50 speakers, but already the language was threatened by a number of other languages spoken in the same village. Most of the other inhabitants of the village spoke the distantly related languages Hamtai or Angaataha, while many spoke Tok Pisin to communicate with outsiders. Marriage partners speaking half a dozen other languages were also living there.

By 1990, the number of Susuami speakers had shrunk to about a dozen. Children were failing to acquire the language, even the children of the only married couple who were both native speakers of Susuami. The prognosis for this language, like many other Melanesian languages with fewer than 50 speakers, is gloomy indeed.

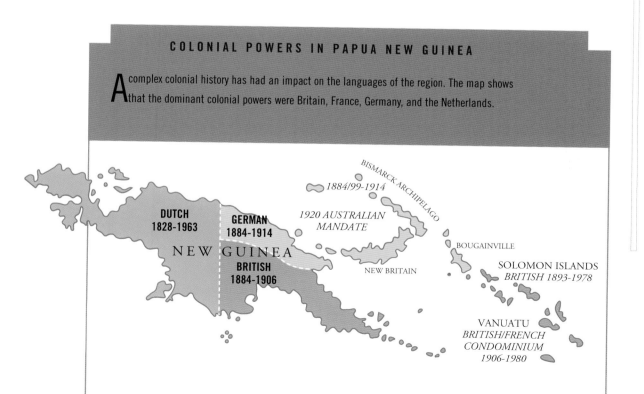

COLONIAL POWERS IN PAPUA NEW GUINEA

A complex colonial history has had an impact on the languages of the region. The map shows that the dominant colonial powers were Britain, France, Germany, and the Netherlands.

Australia

The Aboriginal languages are a repository of ancient knowledge, myths, and traditions, many of which were lost with the colonial breakdown of Aboriginal society. These languages are now known to be highly complex both grammatically and socially, with nuances and taboos reflecting the elaborate kinship systems of Aboriginal communities. Today, their richness is belatedly being recognized, and attempts to halt their decline are under way. Bilingual education may offer a future for the Aboriginal languages and culture which remain.

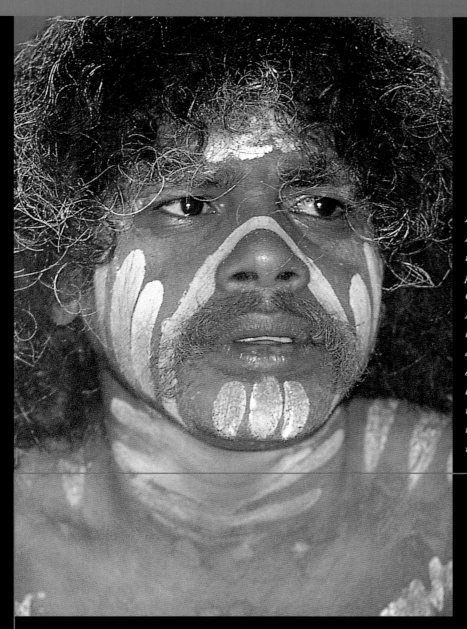

An Australian
Aborigine in
traditional body
paint. Today,
66 percent of
Aboriginal peoples
live in towns,
and there is a
danger that their
long-established
ways of life and
unique languages
will be lost.

Aboriginal people have continuously occupied the continent of Australia for at least 50,000 years. At the time of first contact with European settlers in 1788 there were approximately 700 different tribes living throughout the continent, each speaking their own local dialect. These can be grouped into about 250 different languages which are not mutually intelligible.

Traditionally, Aboriginal people were highly multilingual, with most adults speaking three or more languages. Marriage patterns, where men married women from outside their own tribal group, meant that a child's mother and father would usually speak different languages (but understand each other's), while grandparents, aunts, and uncles would typically speak a number of other languages. Exposure to this rich variety of languages resulted in widespread multilingualism. In addition, each language had a number of styles of speaking, special words or expressions appropriate for different occasions and for use with different people.

The population of Aboriginal Australia is estimated to have been between 500,000 and 1 million in 1788. The people were hunter-gatherers, moving seasonally to exploit fully the unique environments in which they lived. As a result of contact with Europeans, the population declined very rapidly. The original inhabitants were dispossessed of their land, and a large proportion of the population was destroyed by murder, by exposure to European diseases such as influenza and smallpox to which they had no

It has been suggested that the non-Pama-Nyungan language group of northwestern Australia comprises 22 different language families (as different as English from Chinese, or Swahili). The exact nature of the relationships and why such diversity is found is not yet clear.

KEY
PAMA-NYUNGAN
NON PAMA-NYUNGAN

resistance, and by the destruction of both the environment and their means of making a living. People were also placed on missions and government settlements, and their traditional culture and languages were prohibited. In many areas of Australia, especially the southeast and southwest which were settled early, the transmission of culture, including language, from one generation to the next was broken and a great deal of knowledge was lost. Aboriginal languages in some areas are now extinct, or almost so, though in other areas (mainly the center and north) the languages continue to be spoken as the main means of communication and bilingual

THE ABORIGINAL LANGUAGES OF AUSTRALIA

The Aboriginal languages of mainland Australia are not clearly related to any languages outside the continent. They can be classified into two major groups: Pama-Nyungan and non-Pama-Nyungan. The Pama-Nyungan languages are spoken throughout the southern nine-tenths of the continent. The name is derived from two different words for "person:" *pama* in Cape York Peninsula, and *nyungar* in the Nyungar languages of the southwest of Western Australia. The diverse group of non-Pama-Nyungan languages are located in the north and northwest of the mainland, apart from eastern Arnhemland.

Melville Island

Wessel Islands

TIWI

NGARDUKAN

YIWAIDJAN

LIMILNGAN

thurst Island

LARRAKIYAN

GAGADJUAN

Nhulunbuy

DARWIN

BURARRAN

MANGERIAN

UMBUGARLAN

Daly River

NUNGGUBUYU

Groote Eylandt

DALY

GUNWINYGUAN

Numbulwar

MANGARRAYI

ANINDHILYAGUA

WEST MINDI

Roper River

GULF OF CARPENTARIA

MARRAN

Victoria River

River

Vanderlin Island

Daly Waters

Mornington Island

Bentinck Island

EAST MINDI

TANGKIC-MINKINAN

GARRAWAN

NORTHERN   TERRITORY

QUEENSLAND

education programs have been introduced. It is now possible in some regions to hear Aboriginal languages spoken on television and radio, and to read publications in the different languages.

The original inhabitants of the island of Tasmania were subjected to genocidal policies by the British government and driven almost to extinction. Information about the various Tasmanian languages is only fragmentary; however, it appears that they were not connected to those of the mainland. In the Torres Strait region between Australia and Papua New Guinea two different, unrelated traditional languages are spoken.

Since the beginning of the colonial period new languages, called pidgins and creoles, have developed as a means of communication between groups which were brought into contact. These new languages have developed in the northern part of Australia, and for some children have become their first language.

The traditional languages of Australia have rich grammatical systems that seem enormously complex to English speakers. Words show a great deal of variation according to their function in sentences, with elaborate systems of adding suffixes and prefixes to stems to modify meaning. This can sometimes result in long and intricate formations, such as the word in Diyari (South Australia) *wakarripipalumayi* "you two break it for me" (*wakarri* is "broken," *pi* is "cause," *pa* is "for my benefit," *lu* is "you two," and *mayi* is "order"). The order of words in sentences is extraordinarily free, expressing many subtle shades of emphasis.

Traditionally, Aborigines had an extensive oral culture with rich and complex myths, stories, and songs that were passed down by word of mouth for generations. Before European settlement, there

Above: *Nineteenth-century English colonialists brought their language to the Australian continent. They also borrowed words from Aboriginal languages to describe the new flora and fauna they encountered there.*

was no means of writing the languages; writing systems using the Roman alphabet have since been developed for many Aboriginal languages and books have been published. Some of the earliest books were produced by missionaries and include Bible translations dating from the last century; more recently there have been grammatical studies, dictionaries, and collections of stories produced by both Europeans and Aboriginal people themselves.

Aboriginal languages have left their mark on the English spoken in Australia (and, in some cases, throughout the world), both through the large number of placenames that have their origins in the languages of the original inhabitants, and in the many words borrowed from Aboriginal languages to describe the new flora, fauna, and landscapes that the settlers encountered.

LANGUAGE CLASSIFICATION

The Pama-Nyungan languages spoken in most of Australia show a high degree of similarity in their grammatical structures; they all have suffixes and no prefixes. Some similar elements of vocabulary are found across this vast region, for example *mara* or *mala* for "hand" and *pina* for "ear." But other words show a wide variation, even between neighboring groups, or between dialects of a single language. Linguists have suggested that these tongues all descend from an original ancestor language, and have spread throughout the southern part of the continent relatively recently.

The non-Pama-Nyungan languages of northwestern Australia, on the other hand, show great diversity. Some scholars have suggested that all the languages, Pama-Nyungan and non-Pama-Nyungan, are ultimately related and come from an ancestor called Proto-Australian, probably spoken many thousands of years ago. This hypothesis is generally accepted, but has not been proven in detail (unlike, say,

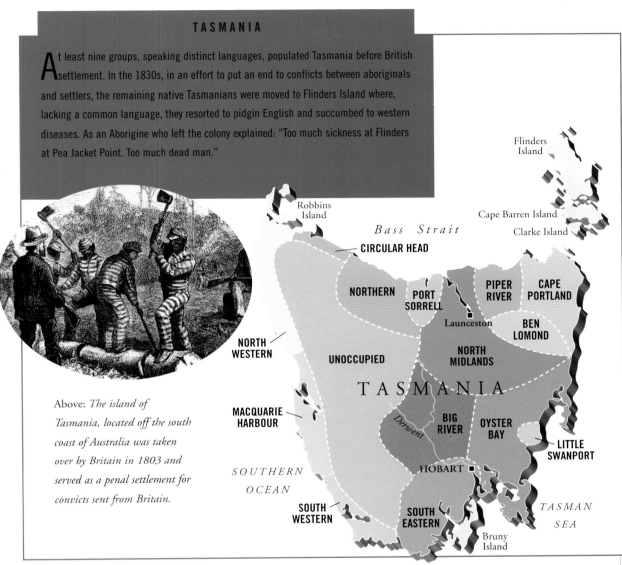

TASMANIA

At least nine groups, speaking distinct languages, populated Tasmania before British settlement. In the 1830s, in an effort to put an end to conflicts between aboriginals and settlers, the remaining native Tasmanians were moved to Flinders Island where, lacking a common language, they resorted to pidgin English and succumbed to western diseases. As an Aborigine who left the colony explained: "Too much sickness at Flinders at Pea Jacket Point. Too much dead man."

Above: *The island of Tasmania, located off the south coast of Australia was taken over by Britain in 1803 and served as a penal settlement for convicts sent from Britain.*

that for Proto-Indo-European, the ancestor of most of the modern languages of Europe).

TASMANIAN LANGUAGES

The Tasmanian Aborigines suffered a terrible fate at the hands of the European settlers and were almost exterminated. They were different in appearance from the mainland Aborigines, and their lifestyle was relatively simpler and adapted to the special requirements of their southerly environment. Archeological records indicate that Tasmania was separated from mainland Australia by rising seas some 10,000 years ago, at the end of the last Ice Age, and remained socially and culturally isolated from the rest of the world until the Europeans arrived in 1804. The Tasmanians, for example, did not have domestic dogs, which were introduced to the mainland some 4,000 years ago.

The materials we have on the languages of Tasmania are fragmentary; they date from the last century and almost all were collected by amateurs who did a very poor job of recording in writing what they heard. However, the records indicate that there were at least nine separate communities living on the island when Europeans arrived, each speaking their own language (*see map above*). The nature of the languages and their grammatical

Above: *Students at the Yirana Aboriginal College, Alice Springs. In 1972 the Australian government established bilingual education in the Northern Territory, and there are now about 30 bilingual programs.*

structure remains unknown, and we are also unable to tell if the Tasmanian languages were related to those spoken on the mainland.

Despite the appalling history of the European colonization of Tasmania, Aboriginal people continued to care for their traditions and preserve what knowledge remained. In 1972, for example, a linguistic researcher, Terry Crowley, recorded a woman in Hobart who taught him some words and one sentence that had been handed down for several generations, even though the language had not been used for daily communication since the 1830s. As in many areas of Australia, the Tasmanian people are working on recovering their lost languages and traditions.

TORRES STRAIT ISLAND LANGUAGES

The people living on the islands in the Torres Strait (between Australia and Papua New Guinea) are primarily Melanesian in origin. Two indigenous languages are spoken there: Kala Lagaw Ya is spoken by people in the western and central islands (including Saibai, Mabuiag, Masig, and Yam), while Meriam Mer is spoken on the eastern islands of Mer, Erub, and Ugar. Kala

Lagaw Ya is related to the Aboriginal languages of the Pama-Nyungan group, while Meriam Mer is completely different and related to languages spoken on the coast of Papua New Guinea. Today, there are about 5,000 speakers of these languages. The Torres Strait island people, including sizeable communities who have migrated to mainland Queensland, strongly maintain their distinctive culture, especially its music, dance, and songs.

A third language, Broken or Blaikman Tok, is spoken in the Torres Strait islands and other neighboring areas. This creole has become the first language of most people under 50 years of age.

NEW LANGUAGES: PIDGINS AND CREOLES

When communities come into contact and they do not share a common language, the need to communicate can sometimes give rise to new languages. This has been the case in Australia, and pidgins and creoles have consequently developed. From the earliest days of settlement, Aboriginal people developed pidgin varieties of English to communicate with the settlers, who showed little interest in learning their speech. These basic languages use words, primarily from English, mixed with words from other languages in rudimentary sentence structures. An example is the following quotation from a Tasmanian Aborigine in an official government report: "Blackfellow no come back. Too much sickness at Flinders at Pea Jacket Point. Too much dead man. Blackman frightened like to crackenny [die] bust."

When a pidgin becomes widely used in a community and children begin to learn it as their first language it can develop into a creole, which is a full language with a developed grammatical system. This has happened in the northern part of Australia, where two creoles are now spoken by many thousands of Aboriginal people. Cape York Creole is spoken in the northern Cape York peninsula and the islands in the Torres Strait, where it is also called "Broken" or "Blaikman Tok." Kriol is spoken from the Kimberley region of Western Australia through into western Arnhemland in the Northern Territory. These two languages have a full grammatical structure that differs in significant ways from English and pidgin. In Kriol, for example, there are several ways to express "we" (as in Aboriginal languages): *yunmi* "we two, you and I," *mintupala* "we two, he and I," *mipala* "we all, including you," and *melabat* "we all, excluding you." The following comment

from a Kriol-speaker, Ralph Dingul, who comes from Ngukurr on the Roper River in northeastern Australia, demonstrates the differences between Kriol and English:

La Ngukurr melabat garrim eitbala langgus. Wen naja traib wandim tok la dis traib, dei tok mijalb garrim Kriol. Jad impotan langgus im Kriol. Olabat gan sabi bla wanim olabat toktok. ("At Ngukurr, we have eight languages. When another tribe wants to talk to this tribe they talk to each other in Kriol. The important language is Kriol. They all can understand whatever they want to discuss.")

WORD ENDINGS IN ABORIGINAL LANGUAGES

Word endings in the Jiwarli language of Western Australia are used to express fine shades of meaning:

ngatha parlirrinyja	"I returned"
ngatha jurla nhanyanyja	"I saw a tree"

ngatha ("I") is used for the subject of a sentence.

thuthungku ngathanha nhanyanja	"The dog saw me"

ngathanha (formed by adding the ending *nha* to *ngatha*) indicates "me" and is used for the object of a sentence.

All pronoun objects take this *nha* ending, as do words referring to human beings and animals (but not other things, which is why *jurla* "tree" has no ending in the example above).

For words other than "I," however, there is a difference in the form of intransitive subjects and transitive subjects (transitive subjects are the subjects of verbs like "hit" or "see" that require an object, intransitive subjects are the subjects of verbs like "go" or "fall" that do not take an object):

thuthu parlirrinyja	"The dog returned"

thuthu "dog" has no ending, but:

thuthungku ngathanha nhanyanyja	"The dog saw me"

The ending *ngku* indicates a transitive subject.

jumangku thuthunha nhanyanja	"The child saw the dog"

thuthu takes the ending *nha*, to indicate a transitive object.

Typically, the ending selected varies according to the shape (pronunciation) of a word: in Jiwarli, words of two syllables take *ngku* for transitive subject, but words of three or more syllables take *lu*.

The subject and object of the sentence can always be identified by the form of the word, so word order is free:

thuthunha jumangku nhanyanyja	"The child saw the dog"
nhanyanyja thuthunha jumangku	"The child saw the dog"

Compare English "The child saw the dog" with "The dog saw the child."

In addition to these endings, nouns and pronouns also take case endings to indicate location, direction, and possession, as in Jiwarli:

thuthungka	"with the dog"
thuthurla	"to the dog"
thuthuparnti	"from the dog"
thuthuwu	"belonging to the dog"

It is possible to attach an ending before the case marker which expresses concepts like the number of items, as in *kutharra* ("two"), *martu* ("small group"), and *nyjarri* ("many"):

*thuthu**kutharra**rla*	"to the two dogs"
*thuthu**martur**la*	"to the group of dogs"

Further subtle expressions of meaning are possible through the use of other suffixes, for example *jaka* "having," or *yirra* "'lacking."

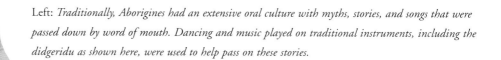

Left: *Traditionally, Aborigines had an extensive oral culture with myths, stories, and songs that were passed down by word of mouth. Dancing and music played on traditional instruments, including the didgeridu as shown here, were used to help pass on these stories.*

Left: *Central Australia is a vast area of arid semi-desert. It was occupied by European settlers on the basis that the land was* terra nullius *(belonging to no-one). As a result of Aboriginal campaigns, the concept of* terra nullius *was rescinded in 1992.*

Bilingual education is now undertaken in Kriol at several centers in northern Australia and publication in the language has been established, including Bible translations, dictionaries, and school books.

STRUCTURE OF THE LANGUAGES

The pronunciation of Aboriginal languages shows a remarkable degree of similarity across the continent. Usually, just three to five vowels are distinguished, and a larger number of consonants. Most languages do not distinguish between *p* and *b, t* and *d, k* and *g,* and *ch* and *j.* Although these sound different to European ears, Aboriginal languages have sounds that are partway between each of these pairs; the result is that often there are two or more spellings in English for a single term because different people wrote down the word. (Thus the Arrernte people of central Australia were formerly called both "Arunta" and "Aranda.") On the other hand, the languages often distinguish sounds which are not found in English, or use familiar sounds in unfamiliar ways. For example, all Aboriginal languages have a sound *ng* (as at the end of English "sing"); frequently words begin with this sound (such as *ngaya* "I" in many languages), creating a problem for English-speakers to copy. Most languages have two *r* sounds: a trilled *r,* as in Scottish English (written "rr" in modern spellings) and a glide *r,* as in American English (written "r" in modern orthographies). In languages of central, western, and northern Australia there are retroflex

r-colored sounds reminiscent of those found in the languages of India; these are written as "rn" and "rt." Aboriginal languages do not normally have sounds such as *s, z, sh, h, th, f,* and *v.* Word forms are relatively straightforward and pronunciation and stress are quite rhythmical.

In their grammars Aboriginal languages show great use of word endings to express fine shades of meaning. Nouns and pronouns characteristically change their endings according to function (*see page 115*). Because of the existence of these endings, the order of words in a sentence is completely free. Word order in these languages is used for stylistic reasons to express emphasis or contrast, not to indicate who does the action and who suffers it.

In northern Australian (non-Pama-Nyungan) languages, nouns and adjectives can take prefixes (elements attached before the word) and these indicate the class or gender of the noun. For example, in Kunwinyku (Northern Territory) *na-* is masculine, *ki-* is feminine, *ma-* is plant, and *ku-* is neuter. In languages of the Kimberley region even more classes are distinguished.

Pronouns in Aboriginal languages also express contrasts not found in English. Typically, three numbers are distinguished: singular (one); dual (two); plural (three or more). To express "we" in the dual and plural forms, the languages make a contrast between including the person spoken to ("inclusive") and excluding that person ("exclusive"). Jiwarli has four forms for "we": *ngali* "we two including you," *ngaliju* "we two excluding you," *nganthurru* "we all including you," and *nganthurraju* "we all excluding you." In some languages the kinship status of the persons speaking can also be reflected in the choice of pronoun used.

Verbs also change their endings to express meaning differences, such as tense. In Jiwarli, for

MAYALI VERB FORMS

A Mayali word can correspond to an English sentence:

abanyawoihwarrgahmarneganjginjeng

aban	*yawoih*	*warrgah*	*marne*	*ganj*	*ginje*	*ng*
"I-them"	"again"	"wrong"	"for"	"meat"	"cook"	"past"

"I cooked the wrong meat for them again."

---

example, tense is expressed as follows: distant past *nhanyaartu* "used to see," recent past *nhanyanja* "saw," present *nhanyinha* "sees," and future *nhanyara* "will see." There is also an ending to express an order, as in *nhanyama* "see! look!" In addition, many Aboriginal languages have endings which express concepts that have no equivalent in European languages. For example, to express the purpose of an action ("in order to ...") the ending *ngku* is added if the same person does both actions, and *puka* if not: *ngatha mirlimirli mananyja nhanyangku* "I brought the book to look at," but *ngatha mirlimirli mananyja nhurralu nhanyapuka* "I brought the book for you to look at."

Among northern (non-Pama-Nyungan) languages verbs typically take prefixes that indicate the subject and object involved in the action, and often take other prefixes or suffixes that express ancillary information. Complex verb forms in these languages correspond to a whole sentence in a language such as English (*see box above*).

These subtle grammatical distinctions give the languages great expressive power that is difficult to convey in translation, especially in the poetic language of mythology and songs.

Many people in Australia believe that Aboriginal languages are simple and have few words, but their vocabularies are in fact large and well developed. A recently published dictionary of Arrernte, for example, is over 750 pages long. The languages are able to express fine shades of meaning and have many words for describing the physical and social world in which the people live. Many specific terms are used for different species of flora and fauna, aspects of the landscape, parts of the body, kinship, and for those items used in people's daily lives. Terms for feelings and emotions are particularly well developed, as are words for different types of actions (the Jiwarli, for example, have three different words for "carry," depending on whether something is carried on the head, in the hand, or on the back). The languages have also developed ways of talking about the modern world, either by borrowing from English or by coining new combinations from old words (the Jiwarli call a dentist *yirrawu wiingkalji*, literally "tooth puller").

KINSHIP AND LANGUAGE

The core of Aboriginal traditional society centers on kinship relations; everyone in the community is classified as a relative through blood or marriage, and there are complex systems of referring to and addressing kin. In addition, rules of appropriate behavior are governed by the kinship system; in all communities, for example, a man must act in a restrained and respectful way toward his wife's mother. In some communities they must completely avoid one another and cannot speak. Contact with other relatives, such as between a man and his sisters, is also restricted and is typically registered by the use of a style of speech which indicates respect. These respect styles have the same grammatical structure as ordinary speech, but they use completely different words, often with more general and polite meanings. In some areas pronouns (words for "I" and "you," and so on) vary according to the nature of the relationship between the people speaking (much as French uses *tu* "you" for intimate friends and family, and *vous* for strangers). Among the Adnyamathanha (South Australia) there are ten sets of pronouns distinguishing such kinship relations.

In some communities there are also respect styles connected with the rituals of male initiation; among the Panyjima of Western Australia, for example, men must use the *paathupathu* respect style in the presence of the man who initiated them.

In addition to kinship relations, Australian Aboriginal communities are also divided into social groups according to the marriage system. Among the Jiwarli of Western Australia there are four groups (called "sections" by anthropologists and "skins" by Aboriginal people): *panaka*,

---

Right: *European settlers borrowed Aboriginal words for the new plants, animals, and landscapes they encountered in Australia. The word "kangaroo" comes from Guugu Yimidhirr, spoken in the Cooktown region, and was recorded in the journals of Captain James Cook.*

PLAINS KANGAROO AND HILL KANGAROO

Here is a traditional story from the Jiwarli people of Western Australia told by the late Jack Butler. It deals with the time of the Ancestral Beings (called in Jiwarli *ngurra pulharalapurra* "when the earth was soft") and explains why the hill kangaroo and the plains kangaroo now live in different places:

Kurrpirli mathanma kumpaja wangkaarni ngana kumpayi parlungka ngana kumpayi parlkarrala. Mathanma wangkaja. Nhurra tharrpama nyirnta walhungka. Ngurntama nhurra nyirnta jumangka walhungka. Kurrpirli ngunha tharrpanyja ngurntayi walhungka ngunhi jumangka parlungka. Kurrpirli wangkaja. Nhaarrinyjarru. Nhurra ngarta ngurntinha jurungka. Kurrpirli wangkaja. Nhurra tharrpama ngurntayi. Pikurta tharrpanyja ngunhipa walhungka ngurntayi. Nhurra ngurntinha pirturarru warrirru mulku nhanyapuka manthartalu kurningurru nhurrampa. Nhurra kumpama parlunyungu. Ngunha wangkaja. Ngaa. Nhurra yanama kumpayi. Kurrpirli wangkaja. Nhurra yanama pukartirarrila kumpayi parlkarrala malungka ngurntayi pukartila kujilarapirrila.

"Plains kangaroo and hill kangaroo were talking to one another about who would live in the hills and who would live on the plain. Hill kangaroo said: 'You go into the cave here. You lie down here in the small cave.' Plains kangaroo went in to lie there in the small cave. Plains kangaroo asked: 'What happened?' 'Your legs are lying in the sun' (replied the hill kangaroo). Plains kangaroo said: 'You go in to lie down.' Hill kangaroo went in there to lie in the cave. 'You are lying hidden so you won't be seen by men looking for you. You should live among the hills.' Hill kangaroo said: 'Yes. You go and live there. You go to live amongst the snakewood on the plain to lie in the snakewood and amongst the mulga trees.'"

karimarra, *palyarri*, and *purungu*. A *panaka* man must marry a *karimarra* woman and their children will be *purungu*; a *karimarra* man marries a *panaka* woman and their children will be *palyarri*. These groupings are reflected in language; a *karimarra* man speaking to two other *karimarra* men will call them *kurtarra*, but if he is speaking to a *karimarra* and a *panaka* man he will say *ngathalkarra*. There are terms for all the other possible combinations of sections.

ORAL CULTURE

Each Aboriginal group has a store of myths, stories, and songs handed down by word of mouth from generation to generation. Much of the traditional mythology deals with the travels and actions of the Ancestral Beings, the ancestors of modern humans, animals, and plants. The Ancestral Beings lived long ago when the Earth was being formed (called "The Dreamtime" in Australian English), and through their actions they created the features of the landscape and established the customs and traditions that Aboriginal people follow today. Throughout Australia the land is covered with sacred sites, placenames, and names for geographical features that reflect these Ancestral actions; the mythology celebrates and retells the past and carries it through to the present. Some of this knowledge is sacred and restricted to people who have been through ceremonies of initiation, while other stories and songs are known to all.

Complex song cycles, often many hundreds of lines long, also have their origins in the Ancestral Beings. In some areas song cycles and myths are shared by neighboring groups with each group owning its own particular section of the song or myth. Traditions can then stretch for many hundreds of miles as the Ancestral Beings traveled from place to place, changing language and style as appropriate for the people whose country they traveled through. Individual Aboriginal people can know dozens of these myths and songs.

VISUAL STORY TELLING

In the language of the Arrernte people of central Australia, *aarwe-iltyinke* ("rock wallabies with their tails tied together") is a game resembling cat's cradle. The designs represent parts of stories chanted by children (*see below*).

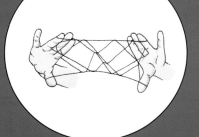

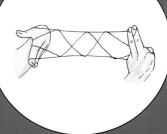

Three eagles: mother, father, and baby in the middle

A well

Curlews wrestling at night

Running water

SIGN LANGUAGE

In many communities sign languages are used alongside the normal oral means of communication in two special circumstances: by hunters to signal messages silently so as not to disturb game, and much more widely, by women who are in mourning. A woman must spend a period of time in mourning after the death of her husband. During this period, she cannot travel about and is not allowed to feed herself or communicate in spoken language, so sign language is used by the women to communicate with one another. It consists of many hundreds of hand shapes and movements to signal words and meanings.

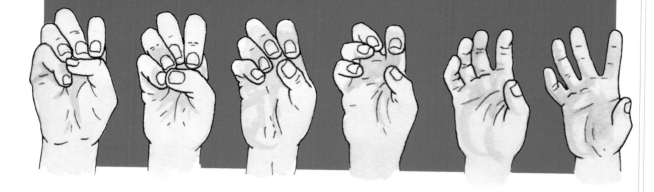

Left: An example of sign language from the Arrernte people of central Australia is the sign for aherre *"kangaroo" which begins as a closed hand and moves to an open shape.*

In some cases there is clear evidence that Aboriginal people handed down their stories and songs for many hundreds of generations. There are stories from Queensland of Ancestral Beings walking across dry land to what are now islands off the coast. It was in fact possible to walk to these places during the last Ice Age, some 10,000 years ago, when the sea level was lower than now, though it has not been possible since the sea levels rose. Similarly, in the Pilbara region of Western Australia people have a word for a dog-like animal whose description matches that of the *thylacine*, or Tasmanian tiger (rock engravings in this region also depict *thylacines*). This animal has been extinct on the mainland for many thousands of years, and survived until the early twentieth century only on the island of Tasmania.

As well as this type of oral literature there are also songs and stories of a more ordinary nature

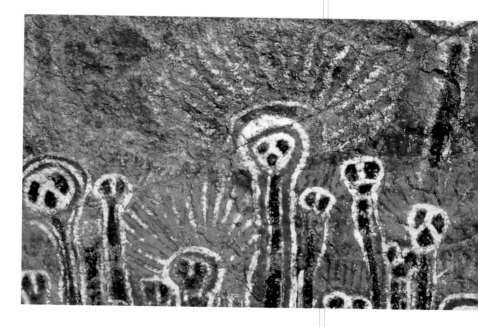

Above: *Cave painting of the Wardaman people of northern Australia. About 50 of these people remain, now speaking mostly Kriol.*

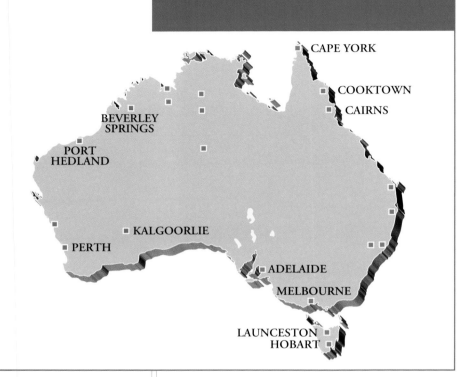

A number of Aboriginal language centers, set up to record and develop disappearing languages, are to be found throughout Australia.

CAPE YORK

COOKTOWN
CAIRNS

BEVERLEY
SPRINGS

PORT
HEDLAND

KALGOORLIE

PERTH

ADELAIDE

MELBOURNE

LAUNCESTON
HOBART

functions, and books, primers, and dictionaries were published in them. Many books were published in the language of the Diyari from Lake Eyre between 1870 and 1910, for example, but from around the turn of the century until 1972 Aboriginal languages in general were given a very minor role in community life. In 1972 the Australian government established bilingual education in the Northern Territory, and there are now around 30 bilingual programs operating in central and northern Australia, with children beginning school in their own languages and gradually being introduced to English (*see map left*). The academic and social success of these programs has been widely demonstrated, as has their role in helping to stem the decline in the number of speakers of traditional languages. Aboriginal groups have also set up language centers throughout Australia to assist with the documentation and development of the languages, and to produce literacy materials. In areas where languages are under threat the centers assist in the preservation and revival of languages.

Today, Aboriginal languages are used in education, publications, films, video, and in the media; the Central Australia Aboriginal Media Association, for example, broadcasts in four languages in Alice Springs, while Imparja television carries Aboriginal language material throughout central Australia. Aboriginal bands have also become popular among young people of all races, with some performers using traditional languages in their songs; the internationally-known band Yothu Yindi, for example, sings popular songs in Gumatj from eastern

that deal with day-to-day matters—stories of love and hate, and rivalries between people and groups, love songs, songs to make rain or increase animal and plant species, and curses to inflict pain and suffering on others. In many areas there are also stories and songs that report on the first contact with European settlers, from amusing anecdotes about the strange actions of the new arrivals to chilling details of massacres and murders carried out by the Europeans as they took away the land and livelihood of the original inhabitants.

LANGUAGE AND EDUCATION

In the early period of contact between Aborigines and Europeans, Aboriginal languages were used in some mission communities for church and school

Right: *Aboriginal bands, such as Yothu Yindi, use traditional languages in their songs and have acquired a worldwide following.*

Arnhemland (see www.yothuyindi.com). In this way Aboriginal languages are facing the challenges of use in the modern Australian community.

ABORIGINAL WORDS IN ENGLISH

A striking feature of the English spoken in Australia is that it contains many words that originate in the Aboriginal languages. As the settlers established themselves they came across many new plants, animals, and features of the landscape that were unknown in Europe, and often borrowed a term from one of the local languages and adapted it into English. Often the pronunciation of the Aboriginal word has been altered somewhat in the process of borrowing (and sometimes the meaning also), but in many cases it is possible to discover which language the word has been taken from. Perhaps the most famous example is "kangaroo" which comes from Guugu Yimidhirr of the Cooktown region through the journal of Captain James Cook, who first saw these unique marsupials when he and his crew put in to the Endeavour River for repairs to their ship.

BORROWINGS FROM ABORIGINAL LANGUAGES IN ENGLISH

The main areas where English has borrowed from Aboriginal languages are the following:

- names for animals, such as: barramundi, dingo, koala, wallaby, wallaroo, and wombat;
- names for birds, such as: brolga, budgerigar, currawong, galah, and kookaburra;
- names for plants, such as: bindi-eye, coolabah, gidgee, karri, and mulga;
- features of the landscape and Aboriginal artefacts, such as: billabong (river pool), gibber (stone), coolamon (bark dish), woomera (spear thrower), and wurley (shelter).

In addition, many hundreds of names of places in Australia come from Aboriginal languages. Some of these have descriptive meanings, while others have origins in the mythology and actions of the Ancestral Beings, and do not have direct translations (despite the often fanciful etymologies given in placename books in Australia). Some examples of descriptive names are:

Boggabri "having creeks" from *bagaaybaraay* (New South Wales)
Coonamble "full of feces" from *gunambil* (New South Wales)
Wonthaggi "fetch!" (Victoria)
Ali Curung "two dogs" from *alikerrenge* (Northern Territory)
Kata Tjuta "many heads" (also called The Olgas, Northern Territory)

The Americas

The languages of the Sioux, Mayans, Incas, and Inuit are just a few of the several hundred native tongues spoken before the Europeans' colonization of the Americas. They are complex and highly diverse with histories that are still being disentangled. Today, although some indigenous languages still thrive in South and Central America, many others are on their way to extinction, and in the North most are already lost.

The U.S.A. welcomed immigrants from all parts of the world and, as a result, the country became a mixture of many different cultures and religions.

The native languages of the Americas, before the arrival of Columbus, were widespread and numerous. Over this vast territory there were, by any reckoning, dozens of language families, more varied than the Indo-European or the African Bantu, and hundreds, maybe thousands, of individual languages. Since the advent of the Europeans, the numbers of speakers of many of these have severely dwindled, with many formerly spoken over large areas now represented only by small isolated elderly groups. Some are no longer spoken at all.

Nevertheless, some languages have survived and retain an old and valuable literary tradition. The importance of these languages and cultures is now being acknowledged, and programs are currently being developed to support the use of native American languages in various settings, including movies such as *Dances with Wolves,* in which actual Lakhota Sioux is heard.

Above: The 1990 movie Dances with Wolves *broke new ground by using the Lakhota language of the Sioux for at least a third of the dialog. Filmed on location in South Dakota, its positive portrayal of Sioux culture was a marked departure from traditional Westerns.*

LANGUAGE GROUPS IN THE AMERICAS

A study of the original distribution and family relationships of these languages can help to establish whether similarities are due to chance, to prolonged contact, or to family relationships. The languages of the Americas will be divided into three separate groups: those of North America, of Mexico and Central America, and of South America. This grouping is arbitrary, for the native peoples themselves did not make the sort of political divisions that the European colonists subsequently imposed, but it does proceed from the languages with which linguists are most familiar (that is, the North American ones) and, perhaps not coincidentally, reflects the increasing vitality of the languages themselves as one goes from best to least known.

LANGUAGES OF NORTH AND CENTRAL AMERICA

The languages of the Americas form a continuous chain from the Arctic Ocean in the North to Tierra del Fuego in the South, and from the Atlantic Ocean to the Pacific, with adjacent languages often, though not always, closely related. Several of the groups of North America also appear in Central America; in Mexico, for example, there are a number of Aztec-Tanoan languages, including Yaqui, and perhaps the best recorded earlier representative, Nahuatl, the language of Montezuma and the Aztec Empire. Hokan-Siouan languages, Penutian languages, and even a member of the Algonquian branch of Algic, a language called Kickapoo (made famous by Al Capp in the comic strip "L'il Abner") are also found in Mexico.

The large Mayan family is spread throughout Central America with numerous branches and many languages within each branch.

Oto-Manguean is found principally in Mexico, where it is represented by seven sub-families comprising around 150 different languages. The Totonac family is small, with only two branches,

Tepehua and Totonac, and fewer than a dozen different languages, yet their number of speakers is estimated at about 300,000, probably more than all the speakers of Native languages in North America. The Totonac languages tend to be spoken by people of all ages, who also speak Spanish, the national language of most of the countries of the region. On average there are several thousand speakers of each language and tens of thousands in each language family. In Mexico alone there are some 240 languages belonging to all of the six major families listed in the table on page 130, as well as the Algic Kickapoo found on the northeastern border.

LANGUAGES OF NORTH AMERICA

The languages of North America, and of the Americas in general, can be subdivided in a few different ways: by geographical region, political affiliation, or familial relationship. The latter method will be employed here, as it gives the best sense of the vast areas over which some languages or language families once ranged. As elsewhere in the world, political boundaries are rarely equated with linguistic ones.

So subdivided, native North American languages form six or seven super-families (*see charts pages 128–129*), leaving only a few isolated languages still defying classification. This scheme is based on the pioneering work of the American linguist Edward Sapir, some of which is still hotly debated by specialists.

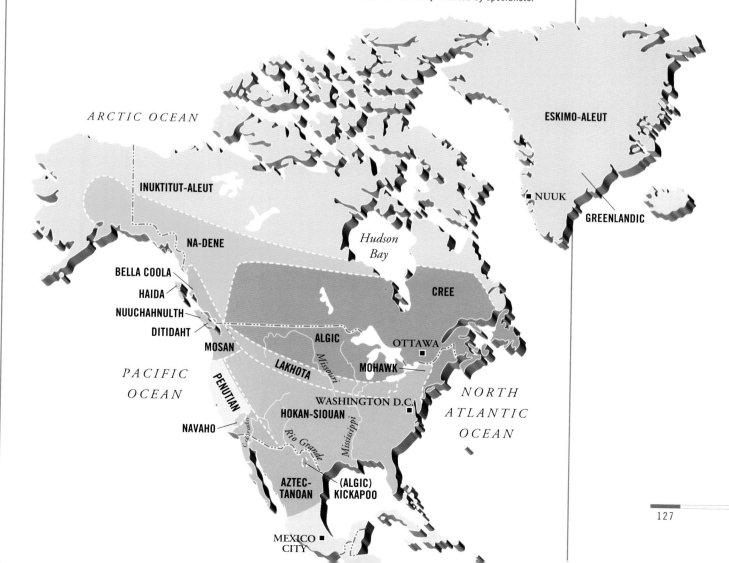

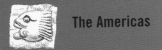

The Americas

LANGUAGE FAMILIES OF NORTH AMERICA

Eskimo-Aleut	Algic	Mosan	Na-Dené	Hokan-Siouan	Penutian	Aztec-Tanoan

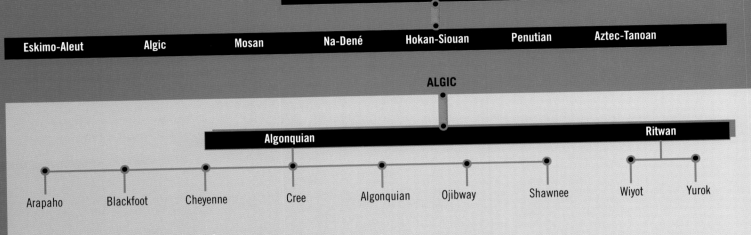

ALGIC

Algonquian

- Arapaho
- Blackfoot
- Cheyenne
- Cree
- Algonquian
- Ojibway
- Shawnee

Ritwan

- Wiyot
- Yurok

The large Algic family, including Algonquian and the Californian Ritwan languages Yurok and Wiyot, spreads across all ten Canadian provinces and over 20 U.S. states as well as to the northeastern corner of Mexico.

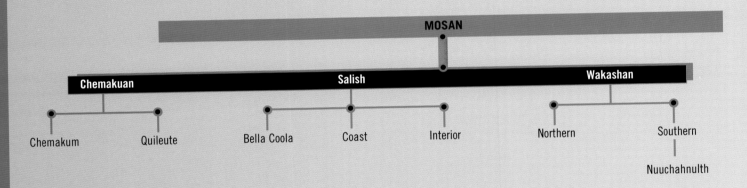

MOSAN

Chemakuan

- Chemakum
- Quileute

Salish

- Bella Coola
- Coast
- Interior

Wakashan

- Northern
- Southern
  - Nuuchahnulth

Mosan is a more contentious classification, first proposed by Sapir in the 1920s. Based on certain similarities, it groups together three distinct language families, Chemakuan, Salish, and Wakashan. The name itself comes from the similar form of the word for "four" in the group which is typically *muu* or *mos* followed by the suffix *-an*.

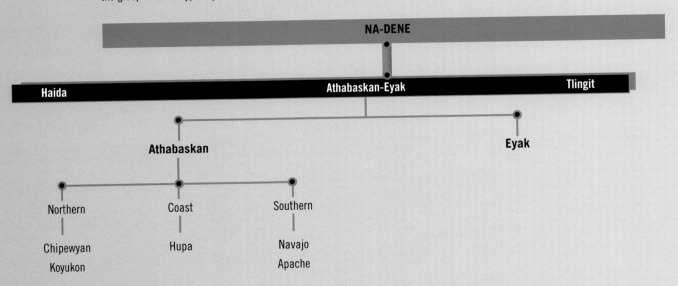

NA-DENE

Haida **Athabaskan-Eyak** **Tlingit**

Athabaskan

- Eyak

Athabaskan
- Northern
  - Chipewyan
  - Koyukon
- Coast
  - Hupa
- Southern
  - Navajo
  - Apache

Na-Dené is a family which groups the Haida and Tlingit languages of the Pacific Northwest together with another extremely widespread group, the Athabaskan languages, spoken from Alaska (Koyukon) to the American Southwest (Navajo and Apache), and from the West Coast (Hupa) to Hudson Bay (Chipewyan), over a thousand miles inland.

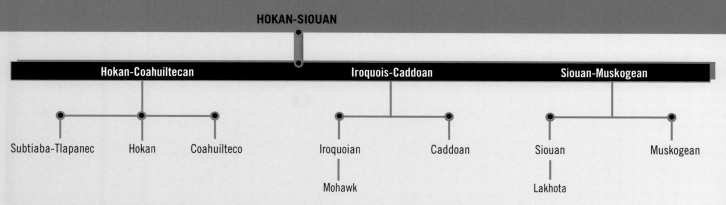

HOKAN-SIOUAN

| Hokan-Coahuiltecan | Iroquois-Caddoan | Siouan-Muskogean |

Subtiaba-Tlapanec   Hokan   Coahuilteco   Iroquoian   Caddoan   Siouan   Muskogean

Mohawk   Lakhota

The Hokan-Siouan family is represented by a number of languages which ranged west from New England over the Canadian and American plains down to Texas, California, and Mexico.

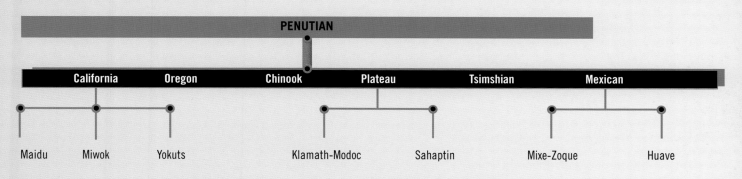

PENUTIAN

| California | Oregon | Chinook | Plateau | Tsimshian | Mexican |

Maidu   Miwok   Yokuts   Klamath-Modoc   Sahaptin   Mixe-Zoque   Huave

The Penutian family is composed of loosely-related sub-families located mainly in California and Oregon State, and also further south in Central America.

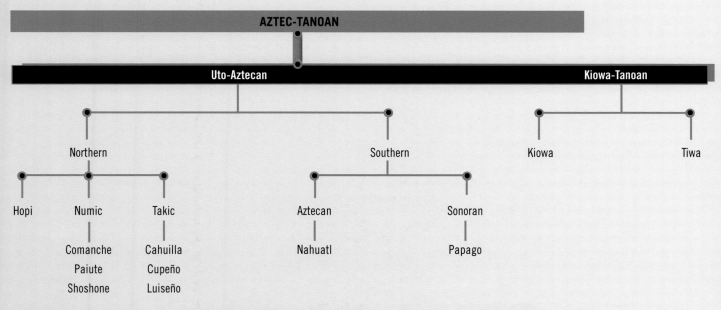

AZTEC-TANOAN

| Uto-Aztecan | Kiowa-Tanoan |

Northern   Southern   Kiowa   Tiwa

Hopi   Numic   Takic   Aztecan   Sonoran

Comanche   Cahuilla   Nahuatl   Papago

Paiute   Cupeño

Shoshone   Luiseño

Finally, the Aztec-Tanoan family is found in Mexico, Central America, and over a large area of the western U.S.A., in the form of languages such as Cahuilla, Cupeño, Kawaiisu, Luiseño, and Serrano (southern California), Comanche and Kiowa (Oklahoma), Paiute (Nevada/Oregon), Papago/Pima and Yaqui (Arizona), Tiwa (New Mexico), and Shoshone (California/Nevada/Idaho/Wyoming/Utah).

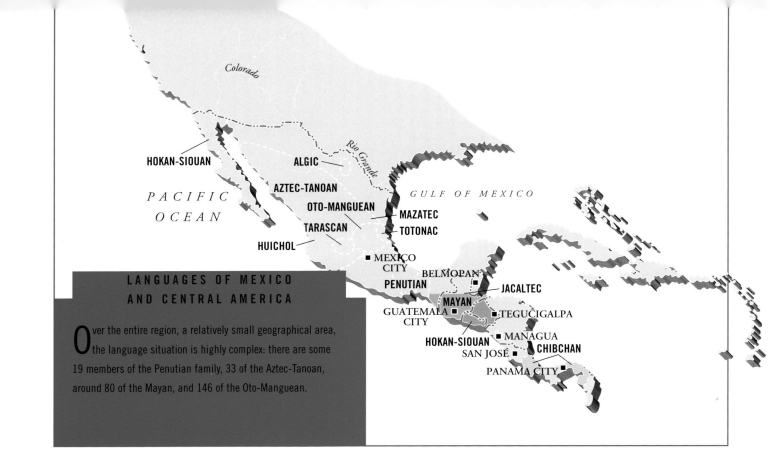

Colorado

HOKAN-SIOUAN

ALGIC

Rio Grande

PACIFIC OCEAN

AZTEC-TANOAN

OTO-MANGUEAN

TARASCAN

HUICHOL

GULF OF MEXICO

MAZATEC

TOTONAC

■ MEXICO CITY

BELMOPAN

PENUTIAN

■ JACALTEC

MAYAN

GUATEMALA CITY

■ TEGUCIGALPA

HOKAN-SIOUAN

■ MANAGUA

CHIBCHAN

SAN JOSÉ

PANAMA CITY

LANGUAGES OF MEXICO AND CENTRAL AMERICA

Over the entire region, a relatively small geographical area, the language situation is highly complex: there are some 19 members of the Penutian family, 33 of the Aztec-Tanoan, around 80 of the Mayan, and 146 of the Oto-Manguean.

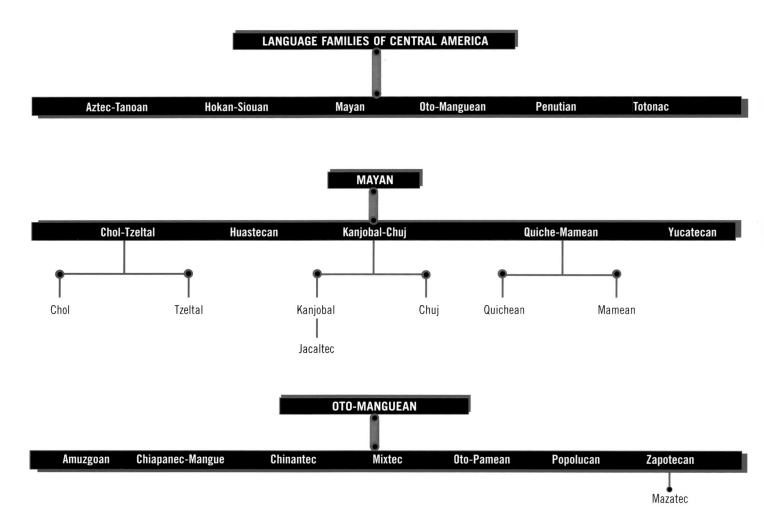

LANGUAGE FAMILIES OF CENTRAL AMERICA

| Aztec-Tanoan | Hokan-Siouan | Mayan | Oto-Manguean | Penutian | Totonac |

MAYAN

| Chol-Tzeltal | Huastecan | Kanjobal-Chuj | Quiche-Mamean | Yucatecan |

Chol — Tzeltal

Kanjobal — Chuj

Quichean — Mamean

Jacaltec

OTO-MANGUEAN

| Amuzgoan | Chiapanec-Mangue | Chinantec | Mixtec | Oto-Pamean | Popolucan | Zapotecan |

Mazatec

The Mayan hieroglyphs present one of the most fascinating puzzles of linguistic analysis since Jean-François Champollion, in the early nineteenth century, began the decipherment of Egyptian hieroglyphics with the aid of the Rosetta Stone. The Mayans had a highly developed system of writing based on hieroglyphics, which can be found on monuments all over the vast Mayan Empire. It is by far the most sophisticated writing system attested in the Pre-Columbian Americas and although linguists have some idea of how Mayan hieroglyphics worked, they are still not fully understood.

The decipherment of the Mayan script was delayed for many years by a common assumption among specialists that the symbols were merely pictographs, that is, pictures representing concepts without any phonetic value. This assumption was made despite early evidence from Spanish missionaries that the system was phonetically based. In fact, the Mayan writing system worked in many respects like Egyptian hieroglyphics. In the example below, there are some clearly picture-like or iconic aspects of the glyphs, but their meanings are in no way transparent to someone unfamiliar with them. Glyphs could stand for their own meaning or could be used only for the sound value that their meaning carried, following the rebus principle (*see chapter 9*); that is, a symbol may be used for its pronunciation alone, for example the use of ◉ to mean "I" or ▱ to mean "be." A specific example of this form of writing is shown below.

The principle seems to have involved taking the first part of one symbol, modifying it with another, and then combining the modified symbol with others. The symbols of the product were not always left separate, but might be merged into a more compressed form.

It is estimated that there were at least 800 distinct hieroglyphs in the Mayan system with which, employing the rebus principle, any word of the spoken language could be represented.

Surviving examples of the Mayan writing system are typically carved on stone monuments. They recount tales of great heroes and battles.

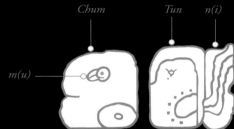

Chum tun *"seating of the tun"* (tun *is a time period in the Mayan calendar)*

A compressed form of the two glyphs left.

LANGUAGES OF SOUTH AMERICA

Less is known about the languages of South America than about those of the remaining western hemisphere, yet there are many important languages in this region, including the Quechua of the Incas, which is spoken over a vast area including Argentina, Chile, Ecuador, and Peru. Guaraní, which along with Spanish is the official language of Paraguay, has 3 million speakers.

In South America the native languages are more widely used than in either of the other two American regions and they have many speakers who may use only one of the local languages throughout their lives. Unfortunately, knowledge of the distribution and family membership of these languages is limited.

Languages within a particular family may have grown as diverse as English and French or, perhaps, as diverse even as English and Russian. That said, a great number of individual languages clearly come from distinctly different origins.

CARACAS

GEORGETOWN   PARAMARIBO

CHIBCHAN
■ BOGOTA

CARIB

BISSAU

ARAWAKAN   YANOMAMAN

PAEZAN   HIXKARYANA

QUECHU-   QUITO
AYMARAN

TUCANOAN   *Amazon*   *Amazon*

JIVAROAN

ZAPAROAN   MURA-PIRAHÃ

WITOTOAN

PANOAN   MACRO-GE

ARAWAKAN   TACANAN   NAMBIQUARAN

São Francisco

■ LIMA

QUECHU-   *Mamoré*
AYMARAN   ■ LA PAZ   ■ BRASILIA

TUPI   GUARANI

*PACIFIC
OCEAN*   ASUNCION ■   MACRO-GE

QUECHU-
AYMARAN   *Paraná*

*SOUTH
ATLANTIC
OCEAN*

Salado

SANTIAGO ■   MONTEVIDEO
BUENOS AIRES ■

Colorado

ARAUCANIAN

LANGUAGE FAMILIES OF SOUTH AMERICA

- Araucanian
- Chibchan
- Macro-Ge
- Paezan
- Quechuan
- Tucanoan
- Carib
- Witotoan
- Arawakan
- Jivaroan
- Nambiquaran
- Panoan
- Yanomaman
- Tacanan
- Tupian
- Zaparoan

LANGUAGES OF SOUTH AMERICA

Over the whole of South America, it is estimated that there are approximately 600 distinct languages, inevitably generating great communication difficulty and much multilingualism. The number of languages spoken in Brazil alone is estimated to be around 250, with 15 language families represented and another 35 or so languages as yet unclassified.

NATIVE AMERICAN ORIGINS

Native American populations certainly came from Asia via the Bering Strait, which at various points in prehistory formed a land bridge, but we do not know when they first reached the New World. The archeological record shows clear traces of human inhabitation from 12,000 and perhaps as far back as 20,000 years ago. Johanna Nichols of the University of California has argued that the diversity of native American languages suggests a much earlier date, perhaps as long as 50,000 years ago.

The first recorded data on any native American language come from the time of Columbus, but they are inadequate, and fail to make important distinctions between sounds. For this and other reasons, most linguists would probably not employ data gathered prior to the twentieth century in their analyses. Native peoples have inhabited the Americas for at least 20,000 years, but knowledge of their languages stems from work gathered only over the course of the last century. By contrast, written records of Indo-European languages date back approximately 3–4,000 years, and yet there is still much disagreement about Proto-Indo-European, which would have preceded the writings by only a thousand years or so. If we consider how much English has changed over the past few hundred years, we cannot push realistic reconstructions of native American languages back more than a few thousand years.

When the comparative method is extended to larger language groupings, the results become less reliable. One controversial proposal for family relationships among the native American languages comes from the late Professor Joseph H. Greenberg of Stanford University, who gathered extensive data from various sources—mostly grammars of individual languages—to argue that all native American languages belong to three "super-families:" Eskimo-Aleut, Na-Dené, and Amerind. Each grouping would correspond

KEY
- LAND TODAY
- ICE AGE GLACIERS
- ICE AGE SHORELINE
- ● PEOPLE LIVED HERE 8,000–10,000 YEARS AGO
- ● PEOPLE LIVED HERE 11,000 YEARS AGO
- ● PEOPLE LIVED HERE 12,500 YEARS AGO

Above: *This map shows the Americas as they appeared 10,000–12,500 years ago, and the land connection—the Bering Strait or Beringia—between Asia and North America.*

to a wave of migration in the settlement of the Americas via the land bridge now covered by the Bering Strait. The Eskimo-Aleut and Na-Dené families are relatively well established and distinctive. The third family, Amerind, would include all the remaining languages of North, Central, and South America—a highly ambitious proposal which many specialists have found unconvincing. The most suggestive evidence for it involves the pronouns "I" and "you" which use *n-* and *m-* respectively in numerous languages of the Americas. This does not seem to be due to chance, since such forms are not common outside the Americas (*m-* is not "you" but "me" in many Eurasian languages), nor to borrowing, since pronouns are rarely borrowed from one language to another. Other items of vocabulary show less persuasive similarities, as in the case of the

THE COMPARATIVE METHOD

The comparative method is used by linguists to determine relationships among languages. The following example is from the Cupan sub-family of Uto-Aztecan:

Cahuilla	Cupeño	Luiseño	
haal	hal	hal	"look for"
silⁱi	silⁱi	siili	"pour"
kiyul	qəyul	kiyuul	"fish"
qasilⁱ	qəsilⁱ	qaasil	"sagebrush"
puul	puul	puula	"doctor"
ʔawal	ʔəwal	ʔawaal	"dog"
mukilⁱ	mukʔilⁱ	muukil	"sore"

By comparing the forms in the three languages, we can conclude that there is far more than chance similarity among them. The correspondences between various sounds are often identical, always phonetically similar. On the principle of "majority wins," a Proto-Cupan language from which all three are descended can be reconstructed along the following lines:

Cahuilla	Cupeño	Luiseño	Proto-Cupan	
haal	hal	hal	*hal	"look for"
silⁱi	silⁱi	siili	*silⁱi	"pour"
kiyul	qəyul	kiyuul	*kiyul	"fish"
qasilⁱ	qəsilⁱ	qaasil	*qasilⁱ	"sagebrush"
puul	puul	puula	*puul	"doctor"
ʔawal	ʔəwal	ʔawaal	*ʔawal	"dog"
mukilⁱ	mukʔilⁱ	muukil	*mukilⁱ	"sore"

etymology for "wood" proposed by Greenberg:

Caddo	nako	"fire"
Pawnee	laktit	"fire"
Arikara	nač	"wood"
Kutenai	łukᵚ	"wood"
Tillamook	-alaq	"wood"
Nuuchahnulth	łoʔok	"board"

Given that *l* and *n* are similar consonants, as are *k*, *kᵚ*, and *q*, there is an initial resemblance between these words, as well as a plausible link between the meanings "wood," "fire," and "board." Since we know that the first three languages all belong to the Caddoan family, the words here can be assumed to derive from a common ancestor. The remaining three are less clearly connected: Tillamook is a Salish language, not known to be related to Caddoan, while Kutenai is considered an isolate, without relatives. The last form, Nuuchahnulth *łoʔok* "board," in fact comes from a different source, which can be seen by comparing it with other Nuuchahnulth words:

łoʔok	"board"
łoʔał	"dish"
łołobiʔs	"halibut"
łoqak	"slanting flatwise"
łoʃa	"plate, tray"

What these items have in common is their flat shape, rather than the connection with wood. Hence the apparent relationship between Nuuchahnulth and Caddoan is probably due to chance—a factor which is notoriously difficult to calculate. This example shows some of the difficulties involved in the investigation of long-distance relationships in general; while the Amerind hypothesis would unify the languages of the Americas, such relationships among the native American languages must await further research.

WORD FORMATION

There is a great deal of variation among the languages of native America in the way in which words are built:

> Mohawk (Iroquoian)
> *wa-hi-'sereht-óhare-'se*
> "he car-washed for me"
> (or "he washed the car for me").

This one-word sentence conveys all the information mentioned in the translation. This is not the only way that a Mohawk speaker may say this sentence, but it is one option which is not usually available to the speaker of English: although we can say either "I sat the baby last night" or "I baby-sat last night," this pattern, called incorporation, is extremely restricted in English, unlike in Mohawk.

Another aspect of word-structure that may appear odd to the English speaker is the possibility in several languages of building words from a single root combined with a fairly large number of suffixes, described by linguists as polysynthesis. This kind of extended word-building also occurs in English, for example in a word such as "antidisestablishmentarianism," but not usually to the extent that we find it in a language such as Nuuchahnulth. The following word, for instance, is nothing out of the ordinary for a Nuuchahnulth speaker, and words may contain up to six or eight suffixes without difficulty:

čuču·kʷaʕinmasitʔi

"those who had gone out to invite"

Again, not all words of Nuuchahnulth are this complex, but it is certainly not uncommon.

NOUNS AND VERBS IN MOSAN

One interesting aspect of the word structure of languages of the Mosan family is their tendency to employ roots which appear not to carry a distinction as to whether they are nouns or verbs, as if it did not matter. An early example of this from one of these languages is from Sapir, who states that the word *ʔinkʷ-it* "fire in the house" in the Nuuchahnulth language is not as clearly a noun as its translation might suggest. He goes on to say that the root *ʔinkʷ-* "fire" is really as much a verbal entity as a nominal one; it may be glossed as "fire" or as "burn," according to the context:

ʔinkʷ-it	=	"fire in the house"
		"burn in the house"
tsʼax	=	"a spear"
		"to spear"
yuxʷ	=	"lungs"
		"to float"
ʔath	=	"night"
		"to become night"
ʔinma	=	"to suck milk"
		"breast"

These examples may be multiplied extensively with the same result; however it is important to note that while the category of the roots may be ambiguous, the final product is not, because context clarifies the meaning.

SOUND SYSTEMS

A further area of distinction among these languages involves the complexity and number of the sounds employed in speaking them. The number of sound distinctions made by the

languages of the world may vary somewhere between 10 and 100, so it is not surprising to learn that the languages of the Americas also vary considerably in the number of distinctive sounds which they employ in constructing their words:

Mura-Pirahā (8 consonants, 3 vowels)
Huichol (13 consonants, 5 vowels)
Nuuchahnulth (29 consonants, 5 vowels)
Navajo (36 consonants, 8 vowels)

In addition to consonants and vowels which are combined to compose words, other factors must be taken into account in a full analysis of the sound system of these languages. One possible contributing factor is the presence of tone, a variation of the pitch at which a word is uttered.

TONE LANGUAGES

A number of languages of the Americas, including the Athabaskan members of the Na-Dené family as well as a number of languages in Central and South America, employ tone as a distinguishing characteristic. The Athabaskan system is typically

TONE IN CHIQUIHUITLAN MAZATEC

Tones are represented in two fashions: first with the traditional numbering system following the word and then in a rough musical notation to represent the relative height of the pitch.

ča¹

"I talk"

ča²

"difficult"

ča³

"his hand"

ča⁴

"he talks"

WORD ORDER

There are many aspects of the grammars of native American languages which help to distinguish them from one another; just a few instances will demonstrate their diversity, beginning with the ordering of words within sentences.

Greenlandic (Eskimo-Aleut)

Greenlandic is a dialect of the Inuit language spoken in Greenland. As can be seen from the example below, Greenlandic syntax is quite different from English, in fact, it is more similar to Japanese, an unrelated language, in which the main verb appears at the end of the sentence. Greenlandic, and Inuktitut more generally, does not make use of prepositions but, rather, marks the object with a suffix, much as in Classical Latin:

Subject	Object	Verb
tigianiaq	*iglu-mut*	*pisug-puq*
"fox"	"house-to"	"go" (past)
	"The fox went to the house"	

	Object	Verb
	tigianiaq	*tukuvaa*
	fox	see-he
	"He saw the fox"	

Such grammatical choices divide the world's languages up into various groups and cut across territorial or familial boundaries.

Ditidaht (Mosan)

Ditidaht is a language spoken along the western coast of Vancouver Island on the West Coast of North America. In this language, unlike Greenlandic or English, the verb appears at the beginning of the sentence:

Verb	Subject	Object
tsasiiks	*be'itlqats*	*hupey'k*
"chase"	"boy"	"ball"
	"The boy chases the ball"	

This is certainly more rare than either the English or the Greenlandic pattern, but is still found in some fairly well-known languages of the world, including Welsh and Irish Gaelic, which are both related to English.

Navajo (Na-Dené)

Navajo (also spelled Navaho) is a language spoken by over 100,000 people in the southwestern U.S.A., particularly Arizona and New Mexico. It is a member of a family of languages which spreads from Northern Alaska to the Mexican-American border. In Navajo, the pattern is similar to Greenlandic, with the verb at the end of the sentence, but in Navajo, prefixes rather than suffixes are used to mark grammatical relationships among words:

Subject	Object	Verb
diné	*ʔàškį́*	*yídĭhltèẹh*
"man"	"boy"	"begin to carry"
	"The man begins to carry the boy"	

In this example the verb is actually just *tèẹh*, and everything in the word before the root belongs to one or another of the numerous grammatical markers used in Navajo. Thus:

yĭ -	*dĭ -*		*hl*	*-tèẹh*
"him"	(future)		Classifier	"carry"
		"begins to carry him"		

Or a more complex example:

ná -	*shi -*	*zh -*	*dĭ -*	*ĭ -*		*hl*	*-tèẹh*
"pick"	"me"	"he"	"up"	(imperfect)		Classifier	"carry"
			"He picks me up"				

There are at least ten distinct prefix positions for the verb and dozens of different prefixes.

Jacaltec (Mayan)

Jacaltec is a language spoken by some 20,000 speakers in the Central American country of Guatemala. Jacaltec, like Ditidaht, places the verb at the beginning of the sentence, but unlike Ditidaht, uses separate words to mark grammatical relations:

Verb	Subject
xb'ey	*heb' naj*
"went"	plural "man"
	"they went"

Verb	Subject	Object
x'il	naj xuwan	ix malin
"saw"	man "John"	woman "Mary"
	"John saw Mary"	

The words *naj* and *ix* are classifiers, serving only to mark the participants in the interaction, "John" as *naj* and "Mary" as *ix*.

Guaraní (Tupi)

The Guaraní language has approximately 3 million speakers in the South American country of Paraguay as well as another 50,000 in surrounding areas. Its word order is surprisingly similar to that of English, as demonstrated by the following sentence:

Subject-Verb	Object
adzupi	petei ivirarakáme
"I climb"	"one" "tree"
	"I climb a tree"

The verb precedes the object in this case, and the subject is marked, as it is in the English "I'll" for "I will," by attachment to the front of the verb.

Mohawk (Iroquoian)

Mohawk is an Iroquoian language spoken in northeastern U.S.A. Word order in Mohawk is actually quite free, as demonstrated by the following sentences, all of which mean:

ieksá:'a	wahonwá:ienhte'	raksá:'a.
"girl"	"hit"	"boy"
	"The girl hit the boy"	

raksá:'a	wahonwá:ienhte'	ieksá:'a.
boy	hit	girl
wahonwá:ienhte'	ieksá:'a	raksá:'a.
hit	girl	boy
ieksá:'a	raksá:'a	wahonwá:ienhte'.
girl	boy	hit

All of these sentences are acceptable to Mohawk speakers and have basically the same meaning although there may be slight nuances which distinguish them. So how do Mohawk speakers know who is doing the hitting and who is being hit? This information is actually encoded on the verb; the presence of the infix -*honwá*- encodes the information that a female is doing something to a male. This type of agreement resembles that found in the Bantu languages of Africa (*see chapter 4*).

Hixkaryana (Carib)

Hixkaryana is a language spoken in the Amazonian rainforest of Brazil by approximately 350 people; it belongs to the Carib family of South American languages. The word order of Hixkaryana, in which the object precedes the verb, is very rare among the languages of the world. It may be interesting to note here that this is apparently the preferred word order in the Klingon language of Star Trek fame, chosen, perhaps, for the exotic "feel" of such a rare word order.

Object	Verb	Subject
kana	yannimno	biryekomo
"fish"	"he-caught-it"	"boy"
	"The boy caught a fish"	

As can be seen from this example, the subject comes at the end of the sentence, the object comes at the beginning, and the verb in the middle, just as if we had rotated an English sentence using the verb as axis. This rare pattern is unattested outside South America, and most languages which exhibit it are members of the Carib family.

Below: *Petroglyphs, such as the so-called "Newspaper rock," have been found in the "petrified forests" of Southwest America. These glyphs were probably carved on the rock some time before* AD 1400 *by peoples, possibly the Hopi and Zuni, who lived settled lives in the pueblos, or villages, of the Southwest.*

MAZATEC WHISTLED SPEECH

This interesting phenomenon, found in the Mazatec language, is fairly rare and yet is found in different parts of the world. It is quite common to encounter it among languages of the same family as Mazatec, but it is also found outside the Americas, in the Canary Islands, France, Africa, Nepal, and elsewhere.

"Whistled speech" is not just a prearranged set of conventions for communications, but rather a well articulated system for representing the Mazatec language by means of whistles made with the mouth. This method of communication is effectively used by speakers of the language over distances which would make normal speech difficult, if not impossible.

In Mazatec, a tone language, the individual tones of the words in a sentence are whistled at an agreed-upon key (the first person usually setting the key) and this mimics the pitch of the tones that would occur in the phrase.

Naturally, some ambiguity may occur, since only the tones are indicated in this fashion, but context and convention help to avoid misunderstanding in most cases. Below are two examples of this phenomenon taken from an early article by George M. Cowan, a specialist in the Mazatec language. Notice how the whistled tones match the tone numbers of the words.

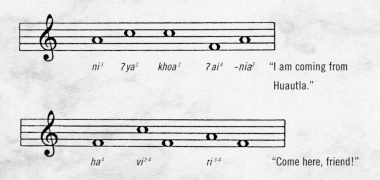

ni³ ʔya² khoa² ʔai⁴ -nia³ "I am coming from Huautla."

ha⁴ vi²⁻⁴ ri³⁻⁴ "Come here, friend!"

quite simple, involving only a high and a low tone, but some of the systems in Central America are quite complex. In the Oto-Manguean language Chiquihuitlan Mazatec, for example, there are four distinct tone levels (*see page 135*).

As can be seen from these examples, changing only the tone will completely change the meaning of the word, just as in the varieties of Chinese and

Right: *The origins of the totem pole are obscure, but they were most fully developed by the Haida. There are four different types: memorial poles, which were the equivalent of a family crest, mortuary poles to contain ashes, house-front poles, and house-posts which were part of the house structure.*

other tone languages found in different parts of the world. So a linguist investigating a language must be very sensitive to the possibility that a language may employ tone to make distinctions in the pronunciation of a word and make careful note of such distinctions.

Words with no Vowels?

In the Bella Coola language (Mosan) spoken in Central British Columbia, there are purported to be a number of words which contain no vowel at all. These words are perfectly acceptable forms in the language and stand alongside words which do contain vowels. This very rare phenomenon has been claimed to exist in other areas of the world, including North Africa where it is found among the Berber languages of Morocco and Algeria. Note that the absence of vowels in these words does not make them impossible to pronounce, as might be the case given a different sequence of sounds, such as "pktgd." Each of the words of Bella Coola (*see opposite*) contains at least one sound which linguists would describe as continuant, such as "m, x̣, ł." Continuant sounds are those that a speaker may "hold" for a period of time before letting go. So in English, when we want someone to be quiet, we will utter the single

BELLA COOLA VOWEL-LESS WORDS

pɬt	"thick"	*kxɬc*	"I looked"
ɬmkmɬp	"jack-pine tree"	*ɬkʼtxʼ*	"make it big"

consonant command "Shhhh." We may hold or continue this sound for an extended period of time, often represented by the addition of further "h's". Such sounds are not impossible for English speakers nor for the speaker of any language, but they are perhaps more productively used by speakers of Bella Coola than by speakers of any other language.

NATIVE AMERICAN WORD-MEANINGS

As can be seen from all of these cases above, there is a great deal of variation among native American languages on all levels of the grammar. One other interesting aspect of language is the area of semantics or the meaning of words. The supposedly enormous treasure trove of words in the Inuit language relating to "snow" is well known, but there are other, less familiar examples. The Nuuchahnulth are a maritime people, living on the western coast of Vancouver Island in the Pacific Northwest. These people have probably always been seafarers and their main staple diet has always been salmon. The average Westerner probably sees little distinction among salmon, only possibly noticing that some salmon is more white while other salmon is more pink. In Nuuchahnulth, the word for "salmon" is *sa:min*, a word borrowed from English.

Why should a maritime people who make their livelihood from fishing for salmon have no word of their own for this fish? For the Nuuchahnulth, "salmon" on its own cannot be spoken of, it must always be referred to as "cohoe salmon" or "spring salmon" or a number of other kinds. The age of the fish is also referred to, as in "young cohoe" or "old spring salmon," because the particular life stage of the fish has a bearing on its availability, edibility, and palatability which could not be described by using just the word "salmon." Instead of one word, we encounter a large number of very different words relating to salmon and to salmon fishing, as befits a culture so heavily imbued with the importance of this staple.

NUUCHAHNULTH SALMON TERMS

The words used by the Nuuchahnulth people of the west coast of Vancouver Island (Canada) in talking about "salmon" are listed below. These are all distinct, individual words with little or no apparent relationship to each other, unlike the English translations of the words, which employ combinations such as "sockeye salmon," "spring salmon," "young salmon," "old salmon," "salmon head," and so on.

Words for Types of Salmon

cuẃit	"cohoe salmon"
ča·p̓i	"humpbacked salmon"
hinku·ʔas	"dog-salmon"
hisit	"sockeye salmon" (when in the ocean or river)
hu·pin	"salmon trout"
kʷiḥnin	"old salmon"
ma·wiɬ	"freshwater salmon"
miʕa·t	"sockeye salmon" (when in the lake)
qiẃaḥ	"steelhead salmon"
saćup	"tyee salmon"
sa·cin	"young spring salmon"
sa·min	"salmon" (from English)
sina·waʔa	"cohoe salmon" (myth name)
su·ha·	"silver spring salmon"
ʕa·k	"dog-salmon" (Northern dialect)

Salmon-related Activities:

caka·št	"dried dog-salmon"
camuqʷa	"salmon roe boiling"
ća·čiqsim	"spear used for tyee salmon"
hu·qʷa·	"salmon going along with dorsal fin out of the water"
ḥuqstim	"salmon-drying pole"
kʷiɬa·	"salmon scraping bottom preparatory to spawning"
qʷ·ḥn	"fishing for tyee or dog salmon with a prong-spear at night"
λiḥata	"salmon jump as in spawning"
ʕaḥa·	"salmon go upstream"
yaḥa·k	"salmon weir"
pišin	"fishing" (from English)
pi·šme·n	"fisherman" (from English)

Words for Salmon Parts

cu·p̓i·	"fat back cut of salmon"
ćipuk	"salmon eggs"
ʕawin	"salmon head"

As can be seen from this example, a culture will elaborate its vocabulary in particular ways which suit the culture at that time and place. English vocabulary lacks equivalents of all of these terms for "salmon" because this area of vocabulary is not particularly meaningful to the average English speaker. The Nuuchahnulth speaker has only a single word for "cow," *mu·smus*, and that is borrowed from another native American language, whereas English has numerous terms, including cow, bull, steer, calf, heifer, bullock, ox, not to mention the names for varieties of cattle, such as Holstein, Jersey, or Longhorn.

EUROPEAN LANGUAGES IN THE AMERICAS

After the arrival of the Europeans following Columbus, the linguistic situation in the Americas changed drastically, along with all other aspects of the cultures that were there before. Today, four major European languages are spoken across most of the continent; they more or less follow political boundaries. Spanish is spoken in most of Central and South America, with the notable exception of Brazil, where Portuguese is spoken. In most of North America English is the main language, with the exception of much of Eastern Canada, where French is spoken.

French was brought to Canada around 1500, and the province of Québec remains largely French-speaking. Its francophone identity is one of the incentives for autonomy, although Québec is known to linguists as a highly successful case of bilingual education. The other North American stronghold of French is in Louisiana, to which French-speakers came from both Canada and the Caribbean during the eighteenth century (Louisiana is named for King Louis XIV). Around New Orleans, the center of Louisiana's French culture, some half a million people still speak a distinct variety of French.

The U.S.A. is also home to numerous minorities and immigrant communities. Most of these have adopted English within two to three generations, leaving traces of their ancestral languages only in their names and in local accents such as the Norwegian intonation in Minnesota.

The exceptions are languages whose use has been preserved for religious reasons, as with Yiddish in New York or Pennsylvania Dutch. Languages whose associated cultures and community ties are especially strong, such as Italian and Chinese, are also used as everyday languages. Continuing immigration, especially from Eastern Europe and East Asia, rejuvenates the minority languages: Russian and Lithuanian communities have received a recent new wave of immigrants, while Cantonese is brought to many cities anew by immigrants from Hong Kong.

Varieties of German are spoken by the Hutterite, Mennonite, and Amish religious sects in the northeast. The most vigorous of these languages, with around 60,000 speakers, is Pennsylvania Dutch. This language is a dialect of German which originated in the Palatinate region, and it is still used in certain sectarian schools. All these varieties of German appear to be in decline, however, with English gradually taking over.

Another language in decline is the Gaelic of Cape Breton, a fishing community in Nova Scotia. Since the 1930s Gaelic has been used less and less, and it is now used for purposes such as greetings, humor, and secrecy.

In Central and South America, the colonial languages Spanish and Portuguese have not asserted themselves as definitively as English in the north. The European settlers mixed with native peoples, as in Colombia where 75 percent of the population is of mixed Hispanic/native descent. Spanish and Portuguese coexist alongside native languages, some of which are used for official purposes. Bolivia has three official languages: Spanish, Quechua, and Aymara. In Peru, Quechua and Aymara are also used for broadcasting, and bilingual education programs have developed. Such retention of indigenous languages alongside Spanish contrasts with North America where only a few of the native languages seem likely to survive, on reservations.

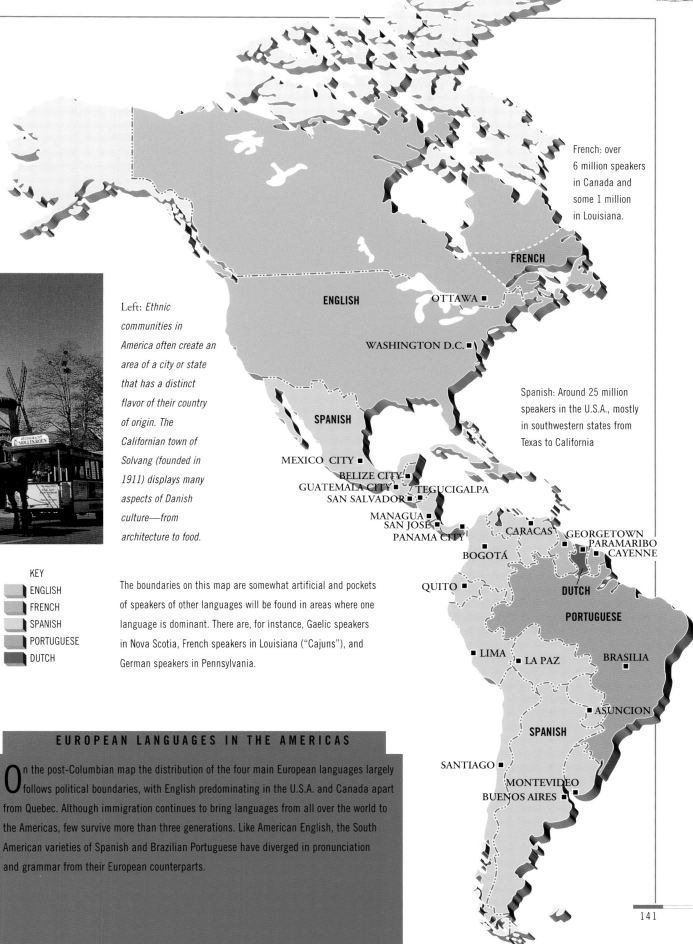

French: over
6 million speakers
in Canada and
some 1 million
in Louisiana.

FRENCH

ENGLISH

OTTAWA ■

WASHINGTON D.C. ■

Left: *Ethnic
communities in
America often create an
area of a city or state
that has a distinct
flavor of their country
of origin. The
Californian town of
Solvang (founded in
1911) displays many
aspects of Danish
culture—from
architecture to food.*

Spanish: Around 25 million
speakers in the U.S.A., mostly
in southwestern states from
Texas to California

SPANISH

MEXICO CITY ■

BELIZE CITY ■
GUATEMALA CITY ■ ■ TEGUCIGALPA
SAN SALVADOR ■

MANAGUA ■
SAN JOSÉ ■
PANAMA CITY ■   CARACAS ■   GEORGETOWN ■
                                           ■ PARAMARIBO
                           BOGOTÁ ■   ■ CAYENNE

KEY

ENGLISH
FRENCH
SPANISH
PORTUGUESE
DUTCH

The boundaries on this map are somewhat artificial and pockets
of speakers of other languages will be found in areas where one
language is dominant. There are, for instance, Gaelic speakers
in Nova Scotia, French speakers in Louisiana ("Cajuns"), and
German speakers in Pennsylvania.

QUITO ■   **DUTCH**

PORTUGUESE

LIMA ■   ■ LA PAZ   ■ BRASILIA

■ ASUNCION

SPANISH

SANTIAGO ■

MONTEVIDEO ■
BUENOS AIRES ■

EUROPEAN LANGUAGES IN THE AMERICAS

On the post-Columbian map the distribution of the four main European languages largely
follows political boundaries, with English predominating in the U.S.A. and Canada apart
from Quebec. Although immigration continues to bring languages from all over the world to
the Americas, few survive more than three generations. Like American English, the South
American varieties of Spanish and Brazilian Portuguese have diverged in pronunciation
and grammar from their European counterparts.

141

Pidgins and Creoles

Pidgins and creoles arose in situations of contact between foreigners where communication was needed but no common language existed, situations created by international trade or the upheavals of colonialism and slavery. Although some simplification is involved in this process, pidgins and creoles are not as crude as often thought, and can have quite complex features. Once considered curiosities, they are now central to the study of linguistic development, and many have now become the languages of independent nations.

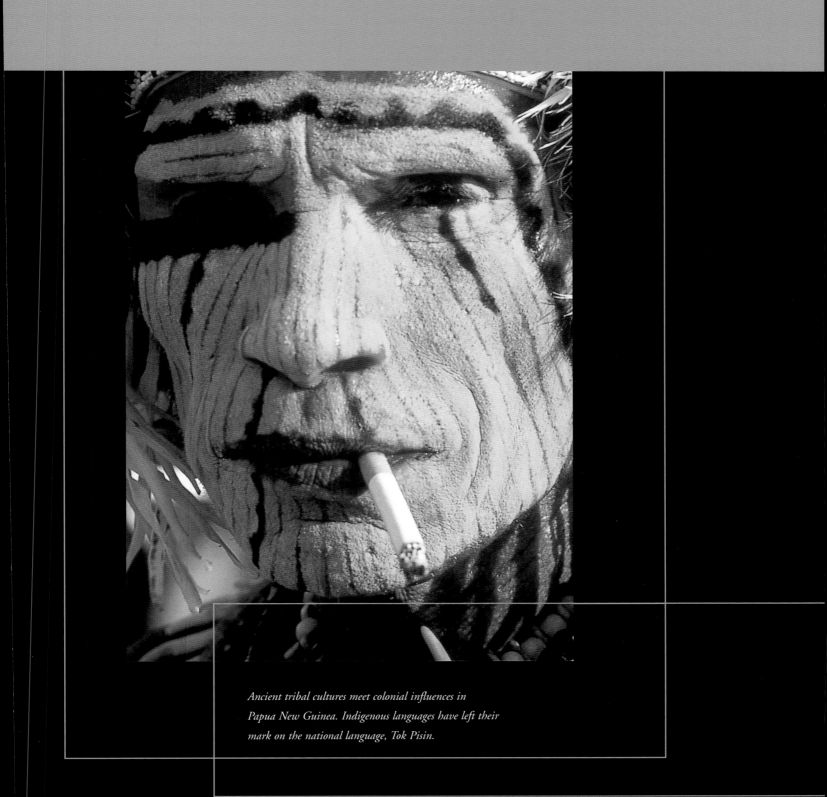

Ancient tribal cultures meet colonial influences in
Papua New Guinea. Indigenous languages have left their
mark on the national language, Tok Pisin.

Nearly everyone has heard of "Pidgin English," but often the phrase is used very loosely to indicate various kinds of non-standard or imperfectly acquired English. Pidgin languages are best thought of as simplified forms which arise in situations where there is a temporary need to communicate among people who lack a common tongue. Usually words from one widely-used language become the basis of an improvised code.

For example, imagine you are a tourist in a foreign country where people are friendly and the markets are crammed with cheap and attractive food and artefacts. You want to buy and the market sellers want to sell, so how is this purpose achieved without a common language? In the beginning there would probably be a good deal of pantomime, such as pointing to objects, displaying money of various denominations, and indicating acceptance or rejection of an offer by whatever body language and facial gestures are available. If you stayed longer you would probably learn some vocabulary, such as the names of particular fruits, words for "buy" and "sell," "yes" and "no," "come" and "go," personal pronouns, numerals, and so on. What would be more difficult would be to acquire the specifics of the language's grammar, its inflections, verb forms, noun cases, or peculiarities of syntax. Because of this, the pidgin languages which emerge in restricted trade settings often show a very simplified structure and minimal vocabulary. An example of this type of trade pidgin is Russenorsk which developed in the nineteenth century between Norwegian fishermen and Russian traders in their border region. This had about 300 words and very limited grammar. Russenorsk was only spoken in the summer, when the two fishing fleets came into contact.

Such trade pidgins have probably been used for millennia by people with limited contact, but a huge increase in their use started at the beginning of the eighteenth century, when some enormous population movements began. The major cause was the rise of the appalling slave trade and of the somewhat less brutal indentured labor schemes for the plantations of the tropics. People from a wide variety of linguistic backgrounds, usually African and Asian, were thrown together, and in the plantation

Above: *A plantation worker in Barbados. Most Barbadians are descendants of African slaves brought to the island after the sixteenth century by the British to work on the sugar plantations. The English language provided the slaves, from different parts of Africa, with a common vocabulary.*

WHERE DID THE WORD PIDGIN COME FROM?

A number of possible origins of the word pidgin have been suggested. Peter Mühlhäusler, one of the leading experts on pidgin languages, has noted at least six different explanations which appear plausible, including words from Portuguese, Hebrew, and South American Indian languages as well as from English. He suggests that they may all have "conspired" to give the term currency. The most commonly suggested etymology is a Chinese rendering of the word "business," but the exact sound changes which would have produced this are hard to demonstrate. If the word did originate on the China Coast in the context of trade conducted in simplified English, a more likely origin might be the common expression *bei chin*, which means "give money" or "pay" in Cantonese. The initial stop in *bei* is unvoiced, making it sound more like a "p" to English-speakers, and adding credence to this explanation.

Speakers of pidgin languages may have their own explanations for the origins of their speech. In Papua New Guinea, the language Tok Pisin can be translated as both "pidgin language" and "bird talk." This fits well with some traditional stories in the country which describe how language was first brought to human beings from birds.

Left: *Gauguin's* The Women of Tahiti *(1891). Paul Gauguin (1848–1903) was fascinated by the islands of the Pacific, and produced the major part of his work on the island of Tahiti. He was one of the many European travelers and artists who were drawn to the islands of the South Seas.*

environment it was often a European language such as English, French, or Dutch which provided them with a common vocabulary.

MELANESIAN PIDGIN ENGLISH

Melanesian Pidgin English, which arose in the Pacific within the last 200 years, is an example of a pidgin language based on English. European languages have actually been in the Pacific for considerably longer than this, as early explorers from Holland, Britain, France, Spain, Portugal, and other countries competed for national honor and wealth. One story tells of the famous Spanish explorer Mendaña, who arrived in the Southwest Pacific in the sixteenth century. He named the islands he surveyed the *Islas de Solomon* (Solomon Islands), in anticipation of the fabulous riches he hoped would be found there. Returning to Spain he announced his discovery and claimed the islands for the Crown. Unfortunately, the Spanish were unable to relocate their discovery, and Britain eventually became the colonizing power. The Pacific has long held a fascination for artists and writers, and romantic stories of a tropical paradise in the South Seas or of adventures amongst head-hunting tribes

Right: *The Solomons archipelago consists of several hundred islands. The population of 326,000 people is spread over 1,000 miles, and over 50 languages are spoken, including the English-based Melanesian pidgin.*

caught the imagination of Victorian Europe.

Much of the early communication between the Europeans and the indigenous peoples probably took place aboard ships or during brief onshore trading encounters. Although a number of European languages were in use, it was English which became the basis of the most widespread pidgin. As communications improved in the nineteenth century, colonies, trading posts, government stations, and missions were established, and Melanesian Pidgin English became stable and widespread. In particular, the development of plantations growing cotton, copra, and sugar in Samoa, Fiji, Queensland, and elsewhere, with Melanesian laborers from the New Hebrides, the Solomon Islands, and New Guinea created an environment where the language thrived. In some cases indentured laborers were recruited for fixed periods under contract, but numerous accounts of "blackbirding" or kidnapping of laborers testify to much brutal abuse.

When the labor trade was abolished early in the twentieth century, Pidgin English served little useful purpose in the largely monolingual communities of Samoa and Fiji and soon died out there. However, in the highly multilingual communities of the New Hebrides, Papua New Guinea, and the Solomon Islands, it became a useful *lingua franca* as these territories were opened up by missionaries and colonizers. Returning laborers were an important factor in the spread of

the language to their home areas and in its subsequent stabilization and development.

SANDALWOOD AND SEA SLUGS

Much of the early trade in the southwest Pacific was concerned with two naturally occurring commodities: sandalwood and sea slugs. Sandalwood trees, which are indigenous to the area, were in great demand for their fragrant wood which was used to construct boxes or to make into incense. "Sea slugs," or *trepang*, which strictly speaking are holothurians or sea cucumbers, were a seafood delicacy sought after in the Far East as much for their alleged medicinal properties as for their taste. Even today they are reputed to promote vitality and virility.

Early traders often spoke a simplified language using words from English, and sometimes known as "Sandalwood English." This nautical jargon was probably in widespread use throughout the vessels and ports of the Pacific in the early decades of the nineteenth century. Dr. T. Crowley, the leading expert on the languages of Vanuatu, traces the complex changes in the word for "sea slug" from the Portuguese *bicho de mar* meaning small sea creature, to the pseudo-French *bêche de mer*, used by English-speakers as *beach-la-mar* with semantic connotations of the English word "beach," eventually to the French reborrowing *biche la mar*. This became the most common name for the pidgin English of the southwestern Pacific, and is now that of Vanuatu's national language, Bislama.

MELANESIAN PIDGIN—SISTER DIALECTS

A number of sister dialects of Melanesian Pidgin English are found in the southwestern Pacific. These dialects developed under the influence of words and grammatical structures from the languages of the region, and today the following are well established:

Tok Pisin is the variety currently spoken in Papua New Guinea. It was widely used by the colonial administration and missions in what was the territory of New Guinea, while a separate pidgin, Hiri Motu, was used in the territory of Papua. Since independence, Tok Pisin has been increasing in all areas of the country, including the Southern Region, formerly Papua.

Bislama is the name of the variety which emerged in the New Hebrides, now the independent state of Vanuatu.

Solomons Pijin developed in the Solomon Islands. Like other dialects of Melanesian Pidgin, it is becoming increasingly used as the first language of a new generation of urban children.

Broken is a variety of pidginized English related to Melanesian Pidgin which has developed in the islands of the Torres Strait between Queensland and Papua New Guinea. Its name, from "broken English," indicates the low status it has been ascribed. Other pidgin and creole languages spoken in Australia include Queensland Plantation English, formerly spoken by indentured Melanesian laborers on the cane fields of Queensland, and Kriol, a creole spoken by aboriginal communities across a wide area of northern Australia (*see chapter* 6).

Left: *The sandalwood is an evergreen tree, native to South Asia and Australia. Its wood contains an aromatic oil, and the trade in sandalwood for incense gave rise to the name Hong Kong ("fragrant harbor" in Cantonese).*

❶ The Portuguese creole which developed in Macau under Malay and Chinese influence, was close to extinction by the time Macau returned to Chinese sovereignty in 1999.

❷ China coast pidgin was spoken in the colonial trading ports of Canton, Hong Kong, and Amoy (today's Xiamen).

❸ Tay Boy, a French-based pidgin, was used in Saigon and the ports of French Indo-China.

❻ Malacca, a trading port established by the Portuguese in 1511, was the birthplace of two creoles, the Portuguese creole Papia Kristang ("Christian speech") and Baba Malay, a hybrid of Hokkien Chinese and Malay.

❺ The creole which developed on Pitcairn in the South Pacific following the mutiny on the *Bounty* is now spoken largely on Norfolk Island, where it is losing ground to English.

❹ Broken, an English-based creole with some 5,000 speakers on the islands of the Torres Strait, is related to Bislama and Kriol. It arose as a *lingua franca* used between the indigenous inhabitants of the islands, who spoke various Australian and Papuan languages, and Pacific islanders from Melanesia and Polynesia who were brought there to harvest pearls and sea slugs.

PIDGINS AND CREOLES OF THE PACIFIC AND SOUTHEAST ASIA

Most of the pidgins and creoles spoken in the Pacific region draw their vocabulary from European languages of colonial powers: English in Melanesia and China, French in Indo-China, Portuguese in Malacca and Macau, and Spanish in the Philippines. Exceptions include Baba Malay and Hiri Motu which have an Austronesian base.

FALSE FRIENDS: FAMILIAR WORDS WITH EXTRA MEANINGS

Many learners of Tok Pisin are fooled by *faux amis* or words which seem straightforward but have extra unexpected meanings. This can lead to much misunderstanding. The following are some examples of words which have an obvious or straightforward meaning plus an extra meaning. They illustrate how the semantic properties of similar words in the languages of the region may persist in the English-based pidgin.

Tok Pisin Term	Predictable Meaning	Additional Unexpected Meaning
gras	grass	hair, feather
karim	carry	give birth
nek	neck	voice
papa	father	owner
tambu	taboo	parents-in-law
bun	bone	strength
inap	enough	capable
lewa	liver	sweetheart
resis	race(s)	compete
laik	like	to be about to
planim	plant	bury
skru	screw	joint, knee
sindaun	sit down	way of life
sapim	sharpen	carve

SIMPLIFYING SOUNDS IN TOK PISIN

English words adopted into Melanesian Pidgin have to fit the phonology of the "host" language. This may result in words which are quite distinct in English converging to become homophones (words which sound alike) in pidgin, as these Tok Pisin examples show:

English	Tok Pisin
shell	*sel*
sail	*sel*
cheese	*sis*
sister (informal)	*sis*
hard	*hat*
hot	*hat*

Potential ambiguity is avoided by added elements:

nail	*nil*
kneel	*nildaun*
ship	*sip*
sheep	*sipsip*
cut	*kat, katim*
cat	*pusi*

Pidgins are often characterized as "simple" languages. However, in expanded pidgins, as in creole languages, the grammar may be quite complex. Among pronouns, for example, there are a number of features not found in English which are important in Tok Pisin.

Firstly, while English has only one form, Tok Pisin has separate second person singular and plural pronouns: *yu* "you" (singular); *yupela* "you" (plural). Similarly, Tok Pisin makes an extra distinction between "inclusive" and "exclusive" first person plural pronouns, depending on whether the person spoken to is included or not: *yumi* "we" (including you); *mipela* "we" (excluding you). A third difference is the existence of forms indicating two or three people: *mitupela* "we" (two); *yumitripela* "we" (three).

Since these features are also found in other languages of the region, it is likely that they were adopted into Tok Pisin by speakers of those languages at the time Tok Pisin was being formed.

HOSTILITY TOWARD PIDGIN LANGUAGES

Pidgin languages have often been subjected to ridicule, abuse, and even hostility. Pidgin English, for example, has been referred to as "broken English" or "bastardized English," and the general assumption has been that it is a poor attempt to speak English properly. Peter Mühlhäusler has cataloged some of the hostile comments directed toward Tok Pisin in Papua New Guinea early in the twentieth century. Comical circumlocutions were ascribed to the language as lexical items, such as "piano" rendered as *bokis i gat waitpela na blakpela tit misis i paitim na em i krai* ("box with black and white teeth the European woman hits and it cries") and "helicopter" as *miksmasta bilong Jisas Krais* ("Holy Mixmaster"). These fanciful inventions no doubt served to hold in contempt the language and, by association, the thought processes of the people who spoke it.

A correspondent, Shelton-Smith, writing in the *Rabaul Times* in 1929, indicates the strength of feeling that could be generated by pidgin languages. He described Tok Pisin as a "tenseless, declensionless, and often obscene jargon that is the only general language of the islands." Another European refers to an "imbecile nursery talk which no German idealist could root out." Even an Australian government report to the League of Nations in 1922 states that Pidgin English "can hardly be dignified by the name of language, as its vocabulary is extremely limited and its construction and mode of expression are of the crudest." Even today, many people ridicule pidgin and creole languages as inferior, and educationalists and policy makers have been slow to accept them as the "real" languages of large communities.

TOK PISIN AS A NATIONAL LANGUAGE

The Papua New Guinea constitution does not bestow official status on any single language, instead recognizing three "national" languages, English, Tok Pisin, and Hiri Motu. English is the major language of education, used in government schools as the medium of instruction from primary level. Hiri Motu was accorded "national" status as the language of the southern provinces of the mainland, formerly Papua, but its use is declining as the reach and importance of Tok Pisin expand.

Tok Pisin is the language used in the majority of speeches and reports in the National Parliament, and in a great deal of verbal communication in government departments. Written communications, however, continue mainly in English, although Father Frank Mihalic, the author of the first dictionary of Tok Pisin, produced a translation of the constitution into Tok Pisin as a gift to the nation. There is a weekly Tok Pisin newspaper, known as *Wantok Niuspepa*, which is increasingly popular with the present generation. Most social interaction between people from different language backgrounds is now conducted in Tok Pisin, especially in urban areas and increasingly in rural communities.

With so many children now speaking Tok Pisin as their first language, the requirement that primary education be in English is coming under increasing scrutiny. Some experimental schools have been set up in the Sepik area in the northwest of the country where initial literacy is taught in Tok Pisin. While many linguists and educationalists applaud these efforts, much

STILMAN HENSAPIM MAN LONG GAN

Ol plisman long Westen Hailans i kis... ripot bilong ol stilman i hensapim ol m... bilong baim kopi na stilim mani bilong o...

Long namba wan ripot, ol plisman i k... ripot i kam long hap bilong Dei Ka... eria.

Dispela ripot i tok olsem ol stilman... bin karamapim pes bilong ol na k... tamiok na tupela sotgan i bin h... wanpela man bilong baim kopi. Pl... tok olsem ol dispela stilman i kisi... mani na kampani ka em dispela... draivim. Ol plisman i wok long... moa long dispela trabel.

...lorg hap bilong Dei Kaunsil...

Above: *A weekly cartoon strip and a news item from the* Wantok Niuspepa. *The first newspaper to be produced in Tok Pisin, its readership is increasing, particularly among younger readers.*

conservative opinion still regards Tok Pisin as an inferior version of English inadequate for "serious" education.

CREOLE: A NEW GENERATION

The name Pidgin is widely used to refer to Tok Pisin, but this is not always strictly accurate. Especially in urban areas, children are growing up speaking Tok Pisin as their first and only language, as a creole. When a pidgin language becomes nativized or creolized in this way, a number of changes typically take place. The speed of speech is greatly increased, which in turn leads to a reduction in the number of syllables and to the dropping of various sounds in the process of streamlining. New morphological and grammatical structures appear, and new words enter the vocabulary from a variety of sources.

The ways in which children "repair" the inherent deficiencies of a pidgin when it becomes their native language have been the subject of a great deal of debate. It has been suggested that language universals are brought into play, and that the resulting creole owes much of its development to the natural instinctive mechanisms of the brain. As noted on page 151, a specific "bioprogram" in the human brain has been suggested as the most likely source of such grammatical innovations.

In the case of creolized Tok Pisin, nativization has proceeded gradually over a number of generations, with innovations produced by children tending to be cancelled out by normative pressure from adults. However, in more extreme circumstances, creoles arise abruptly from the juxtaposition of a diverse mix of languages. In Hawaii, for example, workers were brought from China, Japan, and the Philippines to join native Hawaiians under the control of English-speaking Americans.

Derek Bickerton, whose work has contributed greatly to the recent interest in creoles, has shown how the variable structure of Hawaiian pidgin gave way to a systematic grammar as the language became the mother tongue of the population. The main difference between a pidgin and a creole is that a pidgin is a second or auxiliary language, while a creole is acquired by children as their first language.

Creoles are concentrated in those areas where slave or indentured labor was used: the Caribbean, the Indian Ocean, and Pacific islands where plantations were established. They are largely the products of European colonial expansion, and their vocabulary comes mostly from English,

Left: *Primary school children in Papua New Guinea. For many, Tok Pisin is their first language and the requirement that primary education be in English is coming under increasing scrutiny.*

French, Spanish, or Portuguese. The European element is sometimes sufficient for a speaker of the standard language to understand: for example, *Mi did have a kozin im was a boxer, kom from Panama*, "I had a cousin from Panama who was a boxer" (Costa Rican Creole English), or *Van puasō dā bazar*, "They sell fish in the market" (Mauritian Creole French).

Creoles often resemble European languages spoken badly, and for a long time they were regarded merely as degenerate forms, but while their European words are simplified, creoles do turn out to have their own grammar. For example, "did have," in Costa Rican Creole, is a form of the past tense found in many Caribbean creoles, taking the place of irregular forms such as "had," "was," "came." It is now accepted that far from being poor examples of well-known languages, creoles provide a unique view of how languages develop the structure we recognize as grammar. While the origins of most languages are obscured by successive layers of history, the sources of creoles can be seen clearly. Creoles typically use a verb for "pass" to express comparisons, as in *One pig big pass all we pig come for we yard*, "A pig bigger than all our pigs came into our yard" (Kru English, Nigeria). The fact that such patterns reappear around the world suggests that the same set of concepts underlies all languages which arise in this way.

THE MYSTERY OF CREOLE ORIGINS

The origin of creoles has become one of the most disputed issues in modern linguistics. There are striking similarities between creoles around the world: they have SVO word order, with a basic system of marking tense, mood, and aspect, and several characteristic syntactic patterns. These similarities have prompted a number of explanations. Formerly, the theory of

Above: *A farmer on the Indian Ocean island of Mauritius. The French-based Isle de France creole is spoken in Mauritius and in the Seychelles, having developed in the seventeenth century when Mauritius was a French colony.*

monogenesis proposed that all creoles derive from a single maritime pidgin going back to the ancient Mediterranean *lingua franca*. Certain words of Portuguese origin, such as *savi* meaning "know" and *pickin* "child," do seem to be ubiquitous. A second theory attributes the similarities to a substrate—in the case of Caribbean creoles, the ancestral West African languages of the slaves—and many individual features have been traced in this way. A third, more controversial theory, Bickerton's bioprogram hypothesis, suggests that creoles develop in similar ways because they reflect children's innate ability to construct language. Scholars see elements of truth in each of these theories, so perhaps we should conclude that creoles are true "mixed languages" with substrate, superstrate, and universal features.

GLOBAL DISTRIBUTION OF PIDGINS AND CREOLES

The distribution of pidgins and creoles reflects the colonial expansion of the European powers on whose languages they are based. Many trade routes passed through West Africa which was the main source of slaves in the seventeenth and eighteenth centuries, and the slaves' ancestral languages left their mark on many creoles.

English Based

1 Hawaiian Pidgin / Creole
2 Pitcairnese Creole English
3 Amerindian Pidgin English
4 Gullah
5 Belize Creole English
6 Caribbean Creole English
7 Sranan, Saramaccan
8 English Bush Negro
9 Trinidad and Tobago Creole
10 Guyanese Creole
11 Anglo-Romani
12 Sheldru (Shelta)
13 Inglés de Escalerilla
14 Gambian Krio (Aku)
15 Krio

16 (A) Merico (Settler English)
17 Kru English
18 West African Pidgin English
19 Cameroon Pidgin English
20 St. Helena Creole
21 Madras Pidgin
22 China Coast Pidgin*
23 Japanese Pidgin*
24 Vietnam Pidgin*
25 Tok Pisin
26 Solomon Islands Pidgin
27 Bislama (Beach-la-Mar)
28 Kriol
29 Norfolkese
30 Maori Pidgin

French Based

31 Franco-Amerindian (Michif)
32 Souriquoien
33 Louisiana Creole French
34 Haitan French Creole
35 Antilles Creole
36 French Guyana Creole
37 Franco-Spanish Pidgin
38 North African Pidgin French
39 Sabir*
40 Petit-Négre*
41 Réunionnais

ARCTIC OCEAN   ARCTIC OCEAN

PACIFIC OCEAN

INDIAN OCEAN

42 Mauritian French Creole
43 Rodrigues Creole
44 Seychellois
45 Tay Boy
46 New Caledonia Pidgin

Spanish Based

47 Pachuco (Pochismo)
48 Papiamentu (Papiamento)
49 Pidgin Spanish
50 Spanish Creole
51 Trinidad and Tobago Creole
52 Cocoliche
53 Inglés de Escalerilla
54 Caviteño and Ermitaño
55 Zamboangueño

Portuguese Based

56 Nikari Karu Pidgin*
57 Portuguese Bush Negro*
58 Brazilian Creole Portuguese
59 Cape Verde Creole
60 Kryōl
61 Crioulo
62 Gulf of Guinea Portuguese
63 Sri Lanka Portuguese
64 Goanese
65 Indian Portuguese*
66 Makista (Macanese)
67 Papia Kristang
68 Jakarta Portuguese*

Dutch Based

69 Virgin Islands Dutch Creole*
70 Berbice Dutch
71 Afrikaans Pidgin
72 Cape Dutch (Taal Dutch)

African Based

73 Fanagaló
74 Sango
75 Lingala
76 Kituba

ENGLISH-BASED CREOLES

The major English-based creoles are spoken in the Caribbean, West Africa, and the Pacific, with the best-known examples occurring on the Caribbean islands and along the coast of Central America from Belize to Panama. Many still flourish, and Jamaican, for example, has over 2 million speakers; with the renewed wide dissemination of English, Jamaicans today speak both the creole and standard English, in a continuum of styles from one extreme to the other. This variation can be found in the fiction of the Trinidadian novelist, Samuel Selvon. The following excerpt is taken from *A Brighter Sun*:

"*Urmilla: Girl, I in big trouble. Big, big trouble. If you know what Tiger go and do! He go and invite two Americans he does work with to come for Indian food tonight!*

Rita: Is wat happen to him at all? He crack? He is a damn fool in truth. He bringing wite people to eat in dat hut? Tiger must be really going out of he head, yes. Gul, yuh making joke!

Urmilla: Man, Rita, I tell you is true! My head hot! I don't know what to do!"

Sranan, Saramaccan, and Ndjuka, the creoles of Surinam on the Caribbean coast of mainland South America, are especially interesting. They have been isolated from standard English since the seventeenth century, when the British colonies were ceded to the Dutch. As a result they gained much Dutch vocabulary and retained the very un-European creole grammar, featuring verb combinations known as serial verbs, as in Sranan *mi teki fisi seri*, meaning not "I take fish to sell," but "I sold the fish." Saramaccan and Ndjuka, spoken by the descendants of "maroons" or escaped slaves, have retained distinctively African features, including various distinctions of tone and complex consonants such as kp, mb, and nd (as in the name Ndjuka). Saramaccan also contains numerous Portuguese words whose origin is disputed.

THE *BOUNTY*: AN EXPERIMENT IN CREOLIZATION

There is a unique experiment which some creole scholars would like to conduct: take speakers of half a dozen different languages, put them on a desert island with suitable provisions, and see what language their community develops. Although such an experiment has not been carried out and probably never will be, there are real cases where a comparable situation has arisen; one such resulted from the mutiny of 1789 aboard the *Bounty* in the South Pacific. Having cast off the captain and the remaining crew, the nine English-speaking sailors came to settle on the island of Pitcairn, with 19 Tahitians. A mixed language developed, now spoken on Pitcairn and Norfolk islands. The fact that the history of the speakers and their languages are thoroughly known makes this close to an experimental situation: some of the words can even be traced to individual mutineers, such as *donne* ("don't") from the lone Scotsman. Like many Pacific creoles, Pitcairnese uses dual pronouns as in the phrase *dem tu* ("them two"), which is modeled on a Polynesian pattern.

Above: *Mutineers cast off the captain and remaining crew from* HMS Bounty *during the 1789 mutiny.*

Pacific Ocean

Pitcairn

CARIBBEAN CREOLES

The colonization of the Caribbean by European powers led to creoles based on English (green), French (pink), Spanish (lilac), and Dutch (blue). Most of those spoken on the mainland are dying out, but on the islands many flourish, notably Jamaican and Haitian.

❶ Haitian has more speakers than any other creole—approaching 6 million. It originated with the predominantly French buccaneers who settled on Haiti in the seventeenth century and imported slaves to work on sugar plantations. Since 1987 it has been an official language alongside French.

❷ Berbice Dutch, spoken on the Berbice River in Guyana, is the last surviving Dutch creole of the Caribbean. Its close relative Skepi Dutch is practically extinct, as is the Negerhollands of the Dutch Virgin Islands.

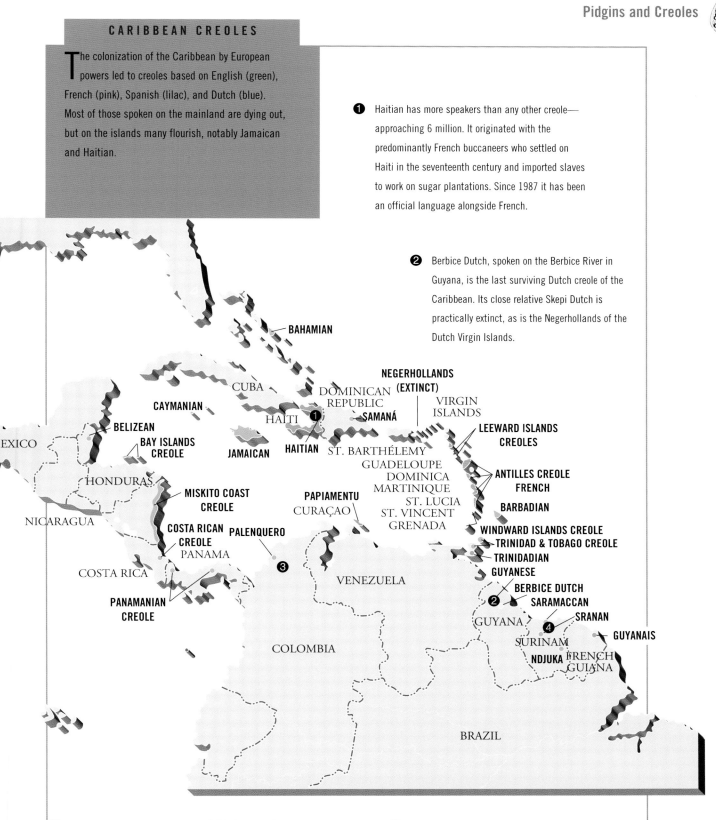

❸ Palenquero is spoken in the town of El Palenque, whose name means a fortified village, and the language is descended from that of the escaped slaves who built the fort as a refuge. The Spanish-based creole includes elements from African languages. It also has some Portuguese vocabulary which may derive from the West African islands through which the slaves passed.

❹ The creoles of Surinam derive from an English base with borrowings from Portuguese and Dutch. Although Dutch remains the official language, in postcolonial times Sranan has become a symbol of national identity and is much used in political discourse.

A CARIBBEAN LULLABY

A lullaby recorded by Nicole Greaux shows some distinctive features of the creole of St. Barthélemy in the French Antilles.

Papa moin y pati en gué	My father has gone to war
Manman moin pati la montagne	My mother has gone to the mountain
Chèché ion ti po lapin	To get a little rabbit skin
Pou fai ion ti emmak pou moin	To make me a little hammock
Ti froué moin y pas vlé domi	My little brother doesn't want to sleep
Hay! Hay! Hay! Sa moin kalé fait?	Oh, oh, oh, what am I going to do?

Most of the vocabulary is recognizably French, but the grammar is quite different. The words appear in a different order (*papa moin* instead of *mon papa*) and "moin" functions, like many creole pronouns, as "I," "me," and "my." The future is expressed by a form *kalé* based on the French *aller* ("go").

FRENCH-BASED CREOLES

French creoles have developed in the Indian Ocean and in the Caribbean, where Haitian is the major example, with some 5 million speakers. Related varieties are spoken in the French Antilles, including Guadeloupe and Martinique, and in declining numbers in the American state of Louisiana.

In the Indian Ocean, the Seychelles, Réunion, and Mauritius were French colonies which produced spices, coffee, and later, cotton. A French-based creole known as Isle de France arose in Mauritius and the Seychelles, while that of Réunion is much closer to standard French and is described as a semi-creole. Mauritian has about a million speakers, with a closely related creole spoken on the small island of Rodrigues.

PORTUGUESE-BASED CREOLES

The Portuguese colonial expansion of the sixteenth century led to creoles in three main areas: West Africa, India and Sri Lanka, and Malaysia and Indonesia. In each case the local languages exerted an influence on the Portuguese base. The use of reduplication, typical of the local Austronesian languages, is found in the Malaysian creoles (for example, *gatu-gatu* "cats" in Papia Kristang). Sri Lankan creole Portuguese, under Sinhalese influence, even allows SOV word order as in: *e:w te:n dizey ta:l pesa:m-pe pe-kaza*, literally, "I have desire such person to marry."

Left: *A French map from the colonial era shows the Isle de France, as Mauritius was known before it came under British rule in 1810. Isle de France creole takes most of its vocabulary from French.*

The Portuguese colonies in the East Indies included Malacca and Macao. Here the Portuguese traders mixed with local populations, and creoles with largely Portuguese vocabulary resulted. The creole of Malacca in Malaysia, since it was spoken by a Catholic community, is known as Papia Kristang, "Christian Speech." In Macao, founded in 1555, Portuguese settlers and Malay women mixed with local Chinese, resulting in a Portuguese-based creole with Malay and Cantonese influences.

SPANISH-BASED CREOLES

Spanish colonization left two creoles in the Caribbean. Palenquero, the language of a colony of runaway slaves near the coast of Colombia, was only recognized as a creole in the 1960s and is rapidly dying out. Papiamentu, spoken on the islands of Curaçao, Aruba, and Bonaire, is unusual in also containing Portuguese elements, as well as Spanish, reflected in the very name of the language and of the island Curaçao.

MAURITIAN CREOLE

In Mauritius, speakers of Malagasy and Tamil as well as African languages contributed to the developing creole. Although much of the vocabulary is recognizably French, the grammar is not. Many nouns begin with a French definite article attached to them, as in *lagazet* "(a) newspaper," but Mauritian has developed a new article from the French demonstrative forms (*lagazet-la* "the newspaper").

The prefix *ti-* comes from French *petit*, but is used as a diminutive prefix in the manner of the Bantu languages (*en ti-lakaz* "a little house"). A reduplicated adjective after the noun has an attenuated meaning, as in *en rob ruz-ruz*, "a reddish dress"; this usage seems to derive from Malagasy (*see chapter 5*).

The folk song below shows how the future tense is expressed by *pou* (from the French *pour*) and the past by *ti*, instead of the endings characteristic of French verbs.

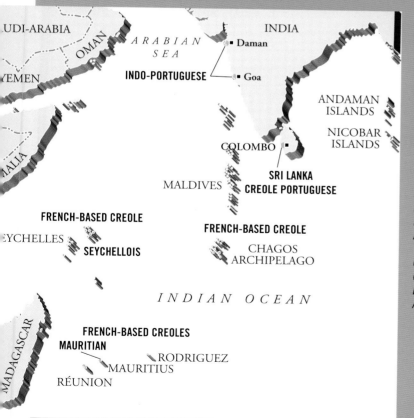

Sega folk song

Moi, mo ène debutante	Me, I am a debutante
Oui mo pou sorte ek mo matante	Yes I will go out with my aunt
Li invite moi pou alle danser	He invites me to go dancing
Oui li ti croire mo pou sorte tousle	Yes he thought I would go out alone
No man, mo p'esperer guetter	No man, I'm hoping to see
Kot li pou decourazer	How he will be discouraged
Lère li trouve moi debarké	When he sees me turn up
Ek matante Dédé	With my aunt Dede
Li crier, mo tire	He shouts, I pull
Lere li trouve moi debarké	When he sees me turn up
Ek matante Dédé	With my aunt Dede
Ala li galopé	There he'll go running away
Qui coté, qui cote linne passé	Which way, which way did he take?
Qui coté, qui cote linne allé	Which way, which way did he go?
Dégazé, dégazé nu alle guetter	Hurry, hurry let's go and see
Ala li p'allé	There he goes!

The vocabulary of Zamboanga's thriving creole is a mixture of Spanish and local Philippine languages. Curiously, adjectives with a positive meaning tend to be Spanish-derived, while their negative counterparts are of Philippine origin:

Spanish	Philippine
gránde "big"	*dyútay* "small"
buníto "pretty"	*ʔumálin* "ugly"
dulse "sweet"	*mapaʔit* "bitter"
sabróso "tasty"	*mataʔbang* "tasteless"
líso "smooth"	*makasap* "rough"

This distribution of vocabulary reflects the perception of Spanish terms as relatively formal or polite in the colonial context in which the creole arose.

The creole Spanish of the Philippines, known as Chavacano, developed as a result of the construction of Spanish garrisons to protect the spice islands of the southern Philippines. It contains numerous elements of Tagalog and Cebuano vocabulary, and grammatical features such as reduplicated plural forms (*cosa-cosa* "things"), which are typical of the local Austronesian languages.

BERBICE: A DUTCH-BASED CREOLE

Berbice Dutch is the only surviving creole to derive from the Dutch colonies in the Caribbean; the Negerhollands creole of the Virgin Islands died with its last speaker in 1987. Now also dying out, Berbice Dutch is spoken on the Berbice River in coastal Guyana. Its African substrate which clearly derives from Ijo, a Nigerian language spoken by the slaves, makes it especially interesting. For example, in the sentence *da di toko di kujara* ("That's the child's canoe"), the words *da* and *di* are Dutch, *toko* ("child") is from Ijo, and *kujara* ("canoe") is from Arawak, a local native American language.

SEMI-CREOLES

Languages with some creole features are known as semi-creoles. Some varieties of Afrikaans and Brazilian Portuguese, which have undergone grammatical change in the course of mixture, are examples. African-American English, while moving progressively closer to mainstream American English, has some features which resemble the Caribbean creoles. It has even been suggested that Middle English underwent partial creolization under Norse and French influences. Although some of the simplification in word forms between Old and Middle English could be attributed to the mixture, English retained an essentially Germanic grammatical structure, making the idea of English as even a semi-creole rather far-fetched.

CREOLES TODAY

Creoles were largely the product of the colonial era, and the post-colonial period has

Below: *Many Mauritians work in the sugar industry. Mauritian creole includes Malagasy and Bantu elements, the legacy of slaves who worked the plantations until emancipation in 1835.*

sometimes raised their status and sometimes eclipsed them. Several creoles, such as Mauritian and Papiamentu, have become national languages, developing their own written forms. Others have come under renewed influence from standard European languages, leading to gradual decreolization, whereby the differences between creole and standard language become eroded. The Jamaican and Guyanese creoles, for example, have moved closer to standard English, while Macanese has given way to standard Portuguese. Many creoles of smaller communities such as Berbice Dutch and Palenquero are dying out, often leaving only cultural traditions such as "creole" cooking, as in the case of Louisiana's cajun French.

Above: *Outside restaurants on a Singapore street—the popular "Peranakan" cuisine reflects the mixing of Malay and Chinese cultures.*

BABA MALAY

While most of the creoles that have been studied are based on European languages, Baba Malay is especially interesting as it derives from Malay and Hokkien, a Chinese dialect. It has its origins in the fifteenth century when migrants from China's Fukien province began to settle in the trading port of Malacca, on the Malay peninsula. The Chinese married local women and the "baba" or "Nyonya" culture developed, speaking a creole combining Hokkien elements with mostly Malay vocabulary. The pronouns illustrate how this mixture took shape:

"I"	gua	"we"	gua orang, kita orang
"you"	lu	"you"	lu orang, lu samua
"he/she"	dia	"they"	dia orang

The pronouns *gua* "I" and *lu* "you" are from Hokkien, while the third person *dia* "he/she" is Malay. The two forms for "we" use the Hokkien *gua* (excluding the person spoken to) and the Malay *kita* (including the person spoken to). This distinction is made in both Malay and Hokkien. All the plural pronouns add the Malay word *orang* "person" (as in *orang-utan*, the "man of the jungle"), but use it in a way based on Hokkien forms such as *lu nang* "you people." The plural of "you" is *lu orang* "you people," or *lu samua* "you all." These two alternative forms may be compared to "you guys" and "y'all" respectively in U.S. English.

Baba Malay is still spoken in Malacca and Singapore, but by dwindling numbers, threatened by Bahasa Malaysia and by Chinese. Perhaps the best known legacy of the Nyonya culture is the "Peranakan" cuisine, a blend of Chinese and Malay cooking popular in Singapore.

Writing Systems

Spoken language and written language are not to be confused: it is probable that this book will fall into the hands of people who through familiarity with its Latin script are able to give its letter symbols their approximate sound values, but who may not recognize what language they record. Almost everyone with certain basic cognitive abilities knows one language, but many are unable to read or write. Human language may have existed for one hundred millennia, but writing systems have developed in only the last five.

ALPHABETS

An alphabet is a phonetic writing system (unlike a logographic script) which consists of symbols representing individual consonant and vowel sounds (unlike a syllabic script). In this book, the term *alphabet* is reserved for phonetic writing systems which possess both consonant and vowel symbols. Phonetic writing systems, such as Phoenician, which have only consonant characters are identified as *consonantal scripts*.

Sequoya, a Cherokee from North Carolina, created a phonetic writing system for his Iroquoian tribe in 1821. In a very short time, most Cherokees had a high degree of literacy.

The following pages examine writing around the globe—its origins, its spread, its diversification. "Writing" means the graphic representation or recording of language and excludes such things as prehistoric cave paintings, and the knotted string messages of the Yoruba. Our focus is on the attempts to record with symbols actual human speech, and the scope of our discussion includes most of the known writing systems, both ancient and modern.

MESOPOTAMIA

When the first humans began to write, they may have done so by building upon a system already in use for the recording of concepts, but not for the recording of speech. Professor D. Schmandt-Besserat (University of Texas) has argued that as early as c. 8000 BC, small clay tokens were in use at various sites in Mesopotamia for recording quantities of grain, and that the appearance of such tokens was occasioned by the advent of agriculture. These so-called plain tokens, normally smooth in finish, survive in various shapes—spherical, discoid,

conical, cylindrical—but give no indication of the commodities which they quantified.

From a much later archeological period, tokens of a different sort emerge alongside plain tokens, apparently with the advent of the first cities on the Sumerian plain of southern Mesopotamia (in modern Iraq). Many of the earliest examples of these complex tokens have been recovered from the remains of the ancient Sumerian city of Uruk and are dated to approximately 3400 BC. Unlike all but a few plain tokens, these have a surface which had been marked with a stylus while the clay was still damp, and exhibit a great variety of shapes. In some cases their shape mimics that of the commodity which they recorded, resembling miniature tools and vessels. The early complex tokens at Uruk are found in and around the temple of the goddess Inanna, and Schmandt-Besserat has proposed that they were used to keep account of commodities entering as tax revenue.

Plain tokens were usually stored by the Sumerians in hollow, opaque clay envelopes; the tokens would be pressed into the envelope's moist surface and then sealed within. As a consequence, the persons responsible for cataloging and archiving tokens could readily determine the contents of any envelope. From the perspective of record-keeping, impressing a token into the surface of an envelope and then sealing it within is clearly redundant—the quantity is being recorded twice.

Such redundancy was eliminated in the second half of the fourth millennium BC when hollow envelopes containing plain tokens began to be replaced by small solid clay tablets whose surface was marked with impressions of plain tokens. Plain tokens were beginning to serve essentially as stamps.

Unlike plain tokens, it appears that complex tokens were usually stored by being threaded onto

Above: *Small clay tokens from Choga Mish, Iran. They date from c. 8000 BC and are believed to have been used to record quantities of commodities such as grain.*

strings. These complex tokens also began to be reproduced in the surface of clay tablets, but rather than being impressed, complex tokens were inscribed free-hand into the surface with a stylus. With their etched surfaces, complex tokens perhaps produced a less acceptable facsimile when impressed.

The plain and complex tokens of ancient Mesopotamia may form the immediate precursor of humankind's earliest writing system, the pictographic script of the Sumerians. The earliest Sumerian writing occurs on clay tablets excavated from the remains of the city of Uruk and is dated to approximately 3400 BC, though a few scholars have proposed that tablets from Tell Brak in northern Mesopotamia are older. Tablets from Susa, written in an early form of the language called Elamite, are slightly later than the Uruk Sumerian tablets. Sumerian writing in its earliest form is pictographic in nature; that is, the symbols of the writing system resemble miniature pictures. However, the meaning-shape relationship of certain symbols is more transparent than that of others, perhaps suggesting some period of development and standardization of the symbols prior to the earliest attested examples.

Early Sumerian writing was nonphonetic. Unlike the Latin alphabetic writing system used for writing English and many of the other languages of the world, the symbols of the early Sumerian script do not reveal the individual phonetic components (consonants and vowels) from which Sumerian words are built; instead, each symbol represents a single word in its entirety. Compare the two "spellings" three and 3: both represent the same English word, but only the former is phonetically revealing. A reader of English who knows the phonetic values assigned to alphabetic characters and who has

CUNEIFORM SIGNS

Sumerian transliteration	Sumerian meaning	Sumerian	Old Babylonian	Neo-Assyrian
DINGIR	god			
NAG	drink			
TÙR	animal pen			
DUB	tablet			
IZI	fire			
ANŠE	donkey			
GU₄	ox			
ŠÚR	angry			
GIŠIMMAR	date palm			
KUR	mountain			
MUŠ	serpent			
ŠÀ	heart			
GE₆	black			
KI	land			
KU₆	fish			

Above: *Mesopotamian cuneiform symbols at various stages in their development. To the left of each set is the early Sumerian pictogram (late fourth millennium BC); in the* *middle is the more stylized form typical of the Old Babylonian period (early second millennium BC); on the right is the classical Neo-Assyrian form (seventh century BC).*

Right: *A reconstruction of the Shamash Gate at Nineveh, built during Sennacherib's reign (705–681 BC).*

UKRAINE

Dniepe **Don**

Volga

■ Tartaria

■ Odesa

SEA OF ASOV

KUBAN

Danube

■ Maikop

ARAL SEA

Laxartes

BLACK SEA

C a u c a s u s

CASPIAN SEA

Oxus

BALKANS

■ Karanovo

■ Istanbul

■ Troy

ANATOLIA

■ Hattusha

ARMENIA

Lake Sevan

Araxes

TURKMENISTAN

Karakorum Desert

■ Dashliji Tepe

■ Kanesh

Lake Van

■ Tushpa

Lake Urmiah

■ Anau

■ Namazga

■ Balkh

■ Athens

■ Beycesultan

Carchemish

■ Nineveh

■ Nimrud

■ Turang Tepe

Iranian Plateau

Hindu-Kush

■ Aleppo

■ Ebla

■ Assur

■ Tepe Hissar

■ Knossos

Ugarit

Ganj Dareh

■ Ecbatana

■ Kition

■ Byblos

■ Mari

■ Tepe Giyan

IRAN

AFGHANISTAN

CRETE

CYPRUS

■ Damascus

MESOPOTAMIA

■ Tepe Sialk

PAKISTAN

M E D I T E R R A N E A N   S E A

Euphrates

■ Babylon

Tigis

■ Harappa

■ Jerusalem

■ Jerico

ELAM

■ Susa

ANSHAN

Dashi-i-Kevir Desert

MELUHHA

■ Ur

■ Persepolis

■ Shiraz

■ Memphis

MOAB

EDOM

Sinia

■ Teima

BALUCHISTAN

■ Tepe Yahya

■ Mohenjo-Daro

■ Nal

■ Amri

Indus

EGYPT

ARABIA

Fars Mountain

■ Kulli

■ Chanhu-Daro

■ El-Amarna

ARABO-PERSIAN GULF

SHERIHUM

■ Bahrain

■ Thebes

■ Medina

DELMUN

QATAR

Jabal Akhdhar

■ Lothal

RED SEA

Nile

HEJAZ

MAGAN

NUBIA

■ Mecca

Arabian Desert

OMAN

INDIAN OCEAN

THE NEAR EAST IN ANTIQUITY

The ancient Near East was home to humankind's earliest known writing systems. The Sumerians of the southern Mesopotamian cities such as Ur (in modern Iraq) appear to be the first people to have written. The use of their cuneiform writing system was continued and further developed by the Assyrians and Babylonians of Mesopotamia and spread to the Elamites (western Iran), Hurrians (northern Syria), Urartians (around Lake Van), and Hittites (Anatolia). The Sumerian script probably provided the inspiration for the development of writing in Egypt, which in turn gave rise to scripts of the Levant and Arabia.

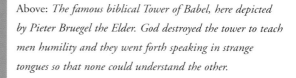

Above: *The famous biblical Tower of Babel, here depicted by Pieter Bruegel the Elder. God destroyed the tower to teach men humility and they went forth speaking in strange tongues so that none could understand the other.*

never before read this word could, upon first encountering it in writing, determine its pronunciation with accuracy. The single symbol 3, however, gives no clue to its pronunciation. Conversely, in the proper context, the symbol 3 could represent several different phonetic realities: three or *trois* or *tres* and so forth. Writing systems which consist of characters that represent words in their entirety rather than their phonetic components are called logographic, and the symbols of such a system are called logograms. The logographic (and pictographic) inscriptions of early Sumerian are often poorly understood.

Toward the end of the fourth millennium BC, the logographic Sumerian script had begun to develop into a partially phonetic writing system. This transition occurred as Sumerian scribes began to exploit phonetic similarities between words. Every child who has solved a rebus puzzle is familiar with the principle involved. Consider a rebus such as the following: 👁 want a 🔔 of 🔧 + 🔑 shoes (meaning "I want a pair of tacky shoes"). As English possesses a pair of homophones (words which sound alike but which have different meanings) "I" and "eye," a pictographic symbol for the latter (👁) can be used to represent "I." The same holds for "pair" and "pear"—the former can be written as 🔔. Furthermore, since the sequence of words "tack" and "key" is phonetically quite similar to the single two-syllable word "tacky", we can represent "tacky" as 🔧 + 🔑

Homophony is a property of all natural languages, including Sumerian. Because the Sumerian word meaning "arrow," TI (Sumerian logograms are usually transcribed in capital letters), is a homophone of the word meaning "life," the Sumerian logogram for "arrow" came to be used to represent the word "life." Further, the logographic symbol for "arrow" also began to be used to spell the syllable -*ti* (much as the pictograph 🔑 represents the second syllable of "tacky" in the rebus above). Once symbols

representing syllables (syllabograms) were introduced into the writing system, it became partially phonetic; in other words symbols began to spell particular sequences of consonants and vowels.

Why were syllabic symbols ever introduced into Sumerian logography? If a writing system is capable of representing an entire word with a single character, what is the advantage of introducing symbols which can spell only individual syllables? Syllabograms were utilized in several ways by the Sumerian scribes. They distinguished, for example, between ambiguous logographic spellings. In some instances, a single logogram had acquired two or more word-values (a condition known as polyphony); for instance, the logogram transcribed as DU, meaning "leg," was also used for GIN, meaning "go." In order to distinguish DU from GIN, the latter was written with the aid of a syllabogram -*na* as GIN-*na*, with the -*n* of -*na* representing the final consonant of the word and so providing a phonetic clue to the proper reading of the logogram. A syllabic symbol used in this way is called a phonetic complement.

Another clue-providing feature of the Sumerian writing system is the determinative. While a phonetic complement offers overt phonetic information, a determinative provides semantic guidance. A determinative is a logographic symbol written either before or after another word symbol to reveal to what "class" the word belongs. For example, the Sumerian logogram GIŠ, meaning "wood," is written alongside logograms for objects made of wood; KI, "place," was written beside placenames; MUŠEN, "bird," beside names of birds; DINGIR, "god," alongside names of deities, and so forth.

Like phonetic complements, determinatives could distinguish between ambiguous

Below: A cuneiform legal document from Syria. The tablet was sealed within a clay envelope, as such documents often were. At several places the scribe's finger prints can be seen frozen in the hardened clay envelope (as on the bulbous projection by the top right corner of the tablet).

PERSIAN SYLLABARY

a	i	u	ka	ku	xa	ga	gu	ca	ja	ji	ta
tu	θa	ça	da	di	du	na	nu	pa	fa	ba	ma
mi	mu	ya	ra	ru	la	va	vi	sa	ša	za	ha

LOGOGRAMS

xšāyaθiya (king)

dahyāuš (country)

būmiš (earth)

baga (god)

Auramazdā (Ahuramazda)

NUMBERS

⊤	1
⊤	2
⊤⊤	3
⟨	10
⟨⟨	20
⟨⟨⟨⟨	40
⟨⊤	100

Above and Left: The Old Persian syllabary was inspired by the cuneiform script of Mesopotamia but is quite distinct from it. Some scholars believe that the Persian king Darius I (521–486 BC) commissioned the creation of the script. In contrast to the complex Mesopotamian script, the Persian system contains only 36 syllabic symbols and five logograms.

Above: Stele bearing the Law Code of Hammurabi. The cuneiform inscription on this pillar preserves the lengthiest of the early Mesopotamian law codes, attributed to the eighteenth-century BC Babylonian ruler.

logograms. Both the name of the goddess Nanše and that of the city Sirara were spelled with the same single logogram. When it was to be read as the divine name *Nanše*, it was preceded by the determinative DINGIR; when it was to be read as *Sirara*, it was followed by the determinative KI. At an early period, the determinative's position relative to its modified logogram was variable. Determinatives were merely text markers providing for the reader a key to the value of a logographic symbol, and as such would not have been read as words of the text; a Sumerian scribe would have read DINGIR NANŠE simply as *Nanše*.

Sumerian scribes used a stylus, or, as they called it, a "tablet-reed," to write on the wet clay tablets. The stylus of the earliest periods was probably sharply pointed at one end for drawing pictographic characters and blunt at the other for making circular impressions. Eventually the sharp end was modified to allow the scribe to write faster by simply impressing the tip of the stylus into the clay. The symbols produced in this way became progressively conventionalized and are distinguished by a characteristic wedge-shape; such characters are called cuneiform, after the Latin *cuneus*, meaning "wedge."

With the waning of the Sumerian civilization early in the second millennium BC, the Babylonians and the Assyrians came to prominence in Mesopotamia. Cultural heirs to the

Sumerians, the Babylonians and Assyrians continued the practice of recording their language on clay, and on other materials such as stone, using cuneiform script.

The Assyro-Babylonian writing system is heterogeneous in nature, as the Sumerian system had come to be, utilizing logograms, syllabograms, and determinatives. Assyrian and Babylonian scribes extensively developed the syllabic symbols, the phonetic component of the script. While Sumerian logograms continued to be used, the phonetic reading of them naturally changed, as the Assyrians and Babylonians were speakers of various forms of East Semitic Akkadian, a language unrelated to and structurally quite unlike Sumerian. Sumerian logograms in Akkadian texts were often accompanied by a phonetic complement reproducing the final sounds of the Akkadian word represented. For example, the Sumerian word for "king" is *lugal*; in Akkadian the word is *šarrum*. When the logogram LUGAL occurs in Akkadian texts, it is frequently written as LUGAL-*um* or LUGAL-*rum*.

The Akkadian writing system possesses syllabic symbols which represent simple vowels (V symbols); consonant plus vowel sequences (CV symbols); vowel plus consonant sequences (VC symbols) and consonant plus vowel plus consonant sequences (CVC symbols). Variation occurs in the types of symbols used for spelling any given word. Just to take one example: *šarrum* ("king") could be written as *šar-rum* (with two CVC symbols), as *šar-ru-um* (CVC-CV-VC), as *ša-ar-rum* (CV-VC-CVC), or as *ša-ar-ru-um* (CV-VC-CV-VC).

The Babylonians in turn gave way to the Persians as the dominant power in Mesopotamia. Inscriptions written in a cuneiform script have survived from the Achaemenid dynasty of Persia (550–331 BC). Unlike the writing systems of the Sumerians, Babylonians, and Assyrians, which possessed hundreds of symbols (including determinative, logographic, and syllabic, and many characterized by polyphony and homophony), the Persian cuneiform script contains only 41 characters. As shown in the table opposite, the Persian system includes three V symbols, 33 CV symbols, five logograms, and a word-divider. Though a cuneiform script, Persian writing appears not to have been based directly upon any of the earlier known cuneiform systems; although inspired by them, it is of largely original design.

Perhaps the most famous monument bearing an inscription in the Persian syllabary is the massive Behistun Stone. Carved into living rock, it depicts the Persian king Darius (521–486 BC) with two of his attendants facing captured enemy kings. Around the figures are inscriptions written in three different languages, each using its own cuneiform script: Old Persian, Babylonian, and Elamite. This trilingual inscription was instrumental in the decipherment of these three languages. A principal figure in the decipherment of Old Persian and Babylonian was the nineteenth-century British scholar, Sir Henry Rawlinson.

EGYPT

Writing appears securely in the archeological record of ancient Egypt by about 3100 BC, slightly later than its first attestation in Mesopotamia. Recently discovered bone and ivory tags, however, may preserve a form of the Egyptian hieroglyphic script which dates to as early as 3400 BC. Although the Egyptian hieroglyphic script is clearly not a direct borrowing of the Sumerian script, it appears probable that the Egyptian writing system developed under Sumerian influence. Each of the character-types found in the Sumerian system—logograms, phonetic symbols, and determinatives—also appears in Egyptian writing.

Below: *For writing on their moist clay tablets, Sumerian scribes used a stylus of reed (or, far less commonly, bone or metal.)*

Right: *A limestone statue of an Egyptian scribe of the Fifth Dynasty (c. 2498–2345 BC), from Saqqara in Lower Egypt (site of the earliest Egyptian pyramids). As in Mesopotamia, the scribes of Egypt occupied a position of prestige, if not wealth.*

While phonetic characters occur in both the Mesopotamian and the Egyptian writing systems, the nature of the phonetic symbols in the two scripts is markedly different: the Sumerian and Assyro-Babylonian phonetic symbols are syllabic in value, representing a single vowel or a vowel plus consonant(s); Egyptian phonetic characters represent not vowels, but either one, two, or three consonants (*see page 170*). Altogether, the Egyptians used about one hundred biconsonantal characters and half as many triconsonantal signs. The 24

monoconsonantal symbols can be used to spell out entire words one consonant at a time, but are more commonly employed in conjunction with other types of symbols: Egyptian logograms, as well as biconsonantal and triconsonantal signs, are often accompanied by monoconsonantal symbols used as phonetic complements.

The curious inclusion of phonetic characters representing only consonants may be a reflection of the structure of Egyptian words. Egyptian, like the Semitic languages to which it is related, is characterized by a word-structure in which the consonantal component is quite stable. The Egyptian word root contains, most often, three consonants; while these consonants usually remain unchanged, the vowels associated with them will vary with the grammatical usage of the word. Some scholars believe that this conspicuous consonantal skeleton led the Egyptian scribes to develop phonetic characters from which specific vowel values were absent.

One of the notable elements of Egyptian orthography is the cartouche. By the time of the Fifth Dynasty of the Egyptian Old Kingdom (about 2400 BC), the ruler of Egypt, the Pharaoh, was using five names. Two of these names,

EGYPT

Perhaps the most recognizable of all ancient writing systems is the monumental hieroglyphic script of the Egyptians, with its elegant and intricate symbols. The idea of writing was probably introduced into Egypt from Sumeria during a period of Mesopotamian cultural influence. The earliest examples of Egyptian writing, such as that on the Palette of Narmer (*see opposite*), are dated to the end of the fourth millennium BC. At this earliest known phase, however, the writing system already appears to be relatively sophisticated, suggesting an earlier period of development and use. During its long history of recorded use (from c. 3100 BC to the present-day liturgical use of Coptic), the Egyptian language was written with a variety of scripts: hieroglyphic, hieratic, demotic, and alphabetic Coptic.

Left: *The Rosetta Stone, a monument from Ptolemaic Egypt (dated to 196 BC), was crucial in the modern decipherment of Egyptian writing. It bears an inscription recorded with three scripts: Egyptian hieroglyphic, demotic, and the Greek alphabet (from top to bottom).*

designated the *praenomen* and *nomen* by Egyptologists, were written within an ovoid outline called a cartouche, or, by the ancient Egyptians, a *shenu*. The outline was probably meant to represent the path of the sun and to suggest that the Pharaoh whose name appeared therein was ruler of all the lands lying within the sun's circuit.

The monumental hieroglyphic script, with its meticulous pictographic symbols, is probably the Egyptian script with which most readers are familiar; it is not, however, the only one. From an early period there also existed a cursive variant called hieratic, normally written with ink and a reed brush. An additional cursive script, demotic, having characters which are quite different from both the hieroglyphic and hieratic, had been introduced before the end of the seventh century BC. Demotic supplanted hieratic and remained in use until about the middle of the fifth century AD. The latest known hieroglyphic inscriptions are dated to the end of the fourth century AD.

In 1799, soldiers of Napoleon Bonaparte digging fortifications in the Nile delta uncovered a large black basalt stele at the site of ancient Rosetta. The discovery was of crucial importance in the decipherment of Egyptian writing, for the Rosetta Stone bears an inscription commemorating the accession of Ptolemy V Epiphanes (205–180 BC) written in both Egyptian and Greek; furthermore, the Egyptian lines appear not only in hieroglyphic script but also in demotic. Ancient Greek was well known at the time of the discovery and so provided scholars with a key that unlocked the language and scripts of the Egyptians. The single most significant figure in the decipherment was the young French scholar Jean-François Champollion (1790–1832), who demonstrated the phonetic nature of much of Egyptian writing.

Below right: *The names of each of seven Egyptian monarchs, framed within a cartouche, appear on this limestone slab from the temple of Ramses II (c. 1279–1213 BC) at Abydos: (from left to right) Amenhotep II, Thutmose IV, Amenhotep III, Horemheb, Ramses I, Sety I, and Ramses II.*

Above right: *The Palette of Narmer. A slate palette from Predynastic Egypt preserving early hieroglyphic writing. On the front, or obverse, of the palette (right), King Narmer (c. 3100 BC) is depicted vanquishing one of his enemies; the king's name appears directly above his head.*

SYMBOLS IN EGYPTIAN WRITING

Like the Sumerian script, the Egyptian writing system is internally heterogeneous, employing various types of symbols: logograms, determinatives, and phonetic signs. Unlike the Mesopotamian system, however, the Egyptian phonetic component consists not of syllabic symbols but of characters which represent only consonants. This hallmark of Egyptian writing would be exploited in the next important step in the history of Near Eastern writing—the development of the Semitic consonantal script.

Right:

A monoconsonantal symbol existed for each of the 24 consonantal sounds of the spoken language. These symbols could be used to spell a word one consonant at a time, but were more frequently employed in conjunction with other types of symbols.

MONOCONSONANTAL SIGNS

Symbol	Transliteration	Sound Value
	3	glottal stop
	i	y
	y	y
	‘	guttural
	w	w
	b	b
	p	p
	f	f
	m	m
	n	n
	r	r
	h	h
	ḥ	emphatic h
	ḫ	ch as in Scottish loch
	ẖ	ch as in German ich
	z	z
	s	s
	š	sh
	ḳ	q
	k	k
	g	g
	t	t
	ṱ	ty
	d	d
	ḏ	dy

BICONSONANTAL SIGNS

Symbol	Transliteration
	ir
	pr
	mi
	mr
	ms
	ḥ3
	ḥr
	s3
	sw
	š3
	k3

TRICONSONANTAL SIGNS

Symbol	Transliteration
	‘nḫ
	n’r
	nfr
	ḫpr
	ḫnt
	s3ḥ
	stp

Below left: *A few of the c. 100 hieroglyphic symbols which represent two consonants in sequence. Multiconsonantal characters are used early in the history of Egyptian writing.*

SYRIA-PALESTINE AND ARABIA

In 1904–1905, while digging at Serabit al-Khadim in the west of the Sinai Peninsula, the British archeologist Sir Flinders Petrie discovered several inscriptions written in a pictographic script previously unknown to modern scholars. These inscriptions, found by Petrie and others, appear to be the handiwork of speakers of a Canaanite dialect of West Semitic who were mining the region's copper and turquoise deposits. At the end of the twentieth century, inscriptions written with the same script, which scholars call Proto-Sinaitic, were found in the Egyptian desert, north of the Valley of the Kings. West Semitic speakers in Egypt may have been writing with Proto-Sinaitic by as early as 1900 BC.

The Proto-Sinaitic script is a phonetic writing system which appears to have been inspired by the ancient Egyptian system of writing and derived from it in a quite deliberate fashion. Like the phonetic component of the Egyptian system, the Proto-Sinaitic script has symbols (probably at least 23) only for consonants. The British Egyptologist Sir Alan Gardiner proposed that these were derived from Egyptian characters on the acrophonic principle, according to which the Canaanite value assigned to an adopted pictographic Egyptian symbol is the value of the first consonant in the Canaanite word for the object which the symbol resembles. For example, the Egyptian hieroglyphic symbol which looks

like a cobra has the consonantal value transcribed as [dj] (similar to the consonant at the beginning and end of the English word "judge"). This symbol was adopted for use in the Proto-Sinaitic script but given the value [n]. According to Gardiner's acrophonic principle, this is because the Canaanite word for "snake" began with [n]: *naḥašu.*

It is now known that the Proto-Sinaitic script is just one form of a consonantal writing system in use throughout Syria-Palestine and the Sinai which is called Proto-Canaanite. The script perhaps had its origin during the period of the Hyksos Dynasty of Lower (northern) Egypt (c. 1700–1550 BC), a time when Lower Egypt was ruled by an Asian people, among whom are attested Semitic names. The Proto-Canaanite script progressively lost its pictographic character, and by the eleventh century BC had evolved into the Linear Phoenician script.

From the remains of the ancient city of Ugarit (modern Ras Shamrah on the coast of Lebanon), which was a thriving center of international commerce in the second half of the first millennium BC, yet another phonetic script used for writing a West Semitic language has come to light. As in Proto-Canaanite, 27 of the Ugaritic characters are purely consonantal, but they are

Left: *Symbols representing three consonants in sequence also occurred in the phonetic component of the Egyptian writing system.*

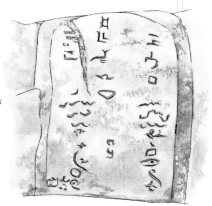

Below: *Semitic-speaking laborers, digging for turquoise and copper in the Egyptian mines of the Sinai Peninsula, left behind inscriptions written in the script now called Proto-Sinaitic (c. 1600–1500 BC). A consonantal writing system, the Proto-Sinaitic script was probably inspired by Egyptian phonetic spelling.*

UGARITIC CONSONANTAL SCRIPT

'a	b	g	ḫ	d	h	w	z	ḥ	ṭ	y
k	s	l	m	ḏ	n	ẓ	s	ʿ	p	ṣ
q	r	ṯ	ġ	t	ʾi	ʾu	ś	word divider		

Left: *With its roots in the Proto-Canaanite writing tradition, the Ugaritic script is a predominantly consonantal writing system, though it possesses three characters with syllabic values ('a, 'i, and 'u). The Ugaritic script was inspired by a cuneiform writing system, but some scholars contend that the Ugaritic symbol-shapes are derived from the Proto-Canaanite pictographic characters.*

cuneiform, and thus appear quite unlike those of Proto-Canaanite. However, three of the symbols are syllabic, as in the cuneiform scripts of Mesopotamia: *'a*, *'i*, and *'u* are characters representing the glottal stop [ʔ] plus each of three vowels. The character transcribed as *ś* was used only in the spelling of words from the Hurrian language of ancient Anatolia. In spite of the differences between the Ugaritic and Proto-Canaanite scripts, it is highly probable that the two scripts are historically linked. The ancient Semitic language of South Arabia was written in a script which evolved from the Proto-Canaanite system, a development which perhaps had occurred by about 1300 BC. The earliest attested form of this script is found on documents dated as early as the eighth century BC. South Arabian was the writing system of the wealthy kingdoms of the southwest Arabian peninsula; the scripts of the kingdoms of Saba (Biblical Sheba) and Ma'in are dated to about the sixth century BC. South Arabian script, like its Proto-Canaanite ancestor, is one which has symbols only for consonants, and is striking in its elegant simplicity.

The South Arabian system was transported northward along the trade routes, and spawned consonantal scripts which were used to record pre-Arabic North Arabian languages. The Thamudic script is attested from about the sixth century BC, as is the Lihyanic, while the Safaitic script is known extensively from the first century BC.

The South Arabian script was exported not only to the north, but also into Africa. Here it evolved into the writing system used to record the Semitic language of Ethiopic. The earliest Ethiopic script, like its South Arabian ancestor, has symbols only for consonants. By the fifth century AD, however, this script has developed into a syllabary and its original consonantal symbols have acquired the CV value of *consonant* + the vowel *a*. Each of these is further modified in

Above: *Sir Flinders Petrie (1853–1942) initiated the practice of excavating all objects from a site, not just those of artistic value. His careful fieldwork greatly extended knowledge of Ancient Egypt, as well as having a marked impact on archeological methods.*

ETHIOPIC

ሀ ha	ሁ hū	ሂ hī	ሃ hā	ሄ hē	ህ he	ሆ hō
ለ la	ሉ lū	ሊ lī	ላ lā	ሌ lē	ል le	ሎ lō
ሐ ḥa	ሑ ḥū	ሒ ḥī	ሓ ḥā	ሔ ḥē	ሕ ḥe	ሖ ḥō
መ ma	ሙ mū	ሚ mī	ማ mā	ሜ mē	ም me	ሞ mō
ሠ ša	ሡ šū	ሢ šī	ሣ šā	ሤ šē	ሥ še	ሦ šō
ረ ra	ሩ rū	ሪ rī	ራ rā	ሬ rē	ር re	ሮ rō
ሰ sa	ሱ sū	ሲ sī	ሳ sā	ሴ sē	ስ se	ሶ sō
ቀ qa	ቁ qū	ቂ qī	ቃ qā	ቄ qē	ቅ qe	ቆ qō
በ ba	ቡ bū	ቢ bī	ባ bā	ቤ bē	ብ be	ቦ bō
ተ ta	ቱ tū	ቲ tī	ታ tā	ቴ tē	ት te	ቶ tō
ኀ ḫa	ኁ ḫū	ኂ ḫī	ኃ ḫā	ኄ ḫē	ኅ ḫe	ኆ ḫō
ነ na	ኑ nū	ኒ nī	ና nā	ኔ nē	ን ne	ኖ nō
አ 'a	ኡ 'ū	ኢ 'ī	ኣ ā	ኤ 'ē	እ 'e	ኦ 'ō
ከ ka	ኩ kū	ኪ kī	ካ kā	ኬ kē	ክ ke	ኮ kō
ወ wa	ዉ wū	ዊ wī	ዋ wā	ዌ wē	ው we	ዎ wō
ዐ 'a	ዑ 'ū	ዒ 'ī	ዓ 'ā	ዔ 'ē	ዕ 'e	ዖ 'ō
ዘ za	ዙ zū	ዚ zī	ዛ zā	ዜ zē	ዝ ze	ዞ zō
የ ya	ዩ yū	ዪ yī	ያ yā	ዬ yē	ይ ye	ዮ yō
ደ da	ዱ dū	ዲ dī	ዳ dā	ዴ dē	ድ de	ዶ dō
ገ ga	ጉ gū	ጊ gī	ጋ gā	ጌ gē	ግ ge	ጎ gō
ጠ ṭa	ጡ ṭū	ጢ ṭī	ጣ ṭā	ጤ ṭē	ጥ ṭe	ጦ ṭō
ጰ p̣a	ጱ p̣ū	ጲ p̣ī	ጳ p̣ā	ጴ p̣ē	ጵ p̣e	ጶ p̣ō
ጸ ṣa	ጹ ṣū	ጺ ṣī	ጻ ṣā	ጼ ṣē	ጽ ṣe	ጾ ṣō
ዐ ḍa	ዑ ḍū	ዒ ḍī	ዓ ḍā	ዔ ḍē	ዕ ḍe	ዖ ḍō
ፈ fa	ፉ fū	ፊ fī	ፋ fā	ፌ fē	ፍ fe	ፎ fō
ፐ pa	ፑ pū	ፒ pī	ፓ pā	ፔ pē	ፕ pe	ፖ pō

Above: The basic Ethiopic syllabary consists of 182 CV (consonant + vowel) characters. Each CV symbol represents a distinct combination of one of 26 consonants and one of seven vowels. Consonant + e syllabic symbols also serve to represent individual consonant sounds (without an ensuing vowel). The syllabary was originally a consonantal script derived from the South Arabian writing system.

some way, often by the use of a diacritic, to produce CV symbols with the vowel values $\bar{u}$, $\bar{\imath}$, $\bar{a}$, $\bar{e}$, e, and $\bar{o}$. This is only one of several examples from the history of the world's writing systems of a script which represents individual sounds developing into a syllabary. Unlike the South Arabian script, which is last attested in the sixth century AD, the Ethiopic syllabary has remained in use to the present day.

As was noted earlier, the Proto-Canaanite script evolved into the Linear Phoenician script by about the eleventh century BC. Several inscribed arrowheads found at 'El-Khadr, a village west of Bethlehem, are dated to 1100 BC and bear witness to the transitional phase. The Phoenician writing system contains 22 characters, representing consonant sounds only. The language of the Phoenicians is West Semitic, closely related to Hebrew.

Plying the waves of the Mediterranean and beyond, the Phoenicians were the pre-eminent maritime culture of the Near East during the first millennium BC. Important Phoenician colonies appeared in Cyprus, Sicily, Sardinia, North Africa, and the western Mediterranean. The Phoenician script was thus introduced to new places and people, setting the stage for the next significant development in the history of writing. Beyond this, however, the Phoenician script would spawn further offspring in Palestine.

The Phoenician script was used in writing the earliest known Hebrew inscriptions, such as the tenth-century BC Gezer Calendar, the oldest known Hebrew document. Curiously, the earliest extensively attested use of a distinct Hebrew script occurs on a tablet bearing an inscription, not in Hebrew, but in Moabite, a Canaanite Semitic language closely related to Hebrew; the Moabite Stone is dated to the ninth century BC. The Hebrew script was employed less

and less after the Babylonian Exile of the sixth century BC, and eventually fell into disuse except among the sect of the Samaritans, who have continued to use it as a liturgical script until the present day.

The Arameans of Syria were writing their West Semitic language with the Phoenician script by approximately the eleventh century BC, and by about the eighth century BC, a distinctive Aramaic script had evolved. Owing to the status of Aramaic as a *lingua franca* and an official language of the Persian empire spoken in Anatolia, the Levant, Egypt, and Mesopotamia, the Aramaic script enjoyed widespread use. With the ascendancy of Persia and the return to Palestine of the deported Jews of the Babylonian Exile, it was the Aramaic script which replaced the old Hebrew system. The modern Hebrew square print and its cursive variant are descended from the Aramaic and were in use by the Roman period of Palestine's history.

The Aramaic script, like its Phoenician parent, possessed only consonantal symbols. However, particular consonant letters came to be used for signaling the presence of long vowels: at the end of the word, w (*waw*) could represent $\bar{u}$, y (*yod*) could represent $\bar{\imath}$, and h (*he*) could represent $\bar{e}$, $\bar{a}$, and even $\bar{o}$. These characters are the so-called *matres lectionis*, "the mothers of reading." By the ninth century BC, this aspect of Aramaic spelling had been adopted into the Hebrew writing system. Eventually, a variable use of the *matres lectionis* was extended to the interior of words.

In order to represent Hebrew vowels and so preserve the correct reading of the text of the Hebrew Bible, systems of vowel diacritics or vowel points were developed by the Jewish scholars known as the Massoretes. In about the eighth century AD, the Massoretes of the Babylonian school developed one such system,

PHOENICIAN

Symbol	Transliteration
𐤀	'
𐤁	b
𐤂	g
𐤃	d
𐤄	h
𐤅	w
𐤆	z
𐤇	ḥ
𐤈	ṭ
𐤉	y
𐤊	k
𐤋	l
𐤌	m
𐤍	n
𐤎	s
𐤏	'
𐤐	p
𐤑	ṣ
𐤒	q
𐤓	r
𐤔	š
𐤕	t

Above: *The Phoenicians recorded their Northwest Semitic language with a consonantal script, the direct descendant of the Proto-Canaanite writing system. The earliest inscriptions which can be identified as distinctly Phoenician appear in the eleventh century BC.*

Below: *The tomb inscription of a woman named Mishta, daughter of David (c. AD 717). The Square Hebrew script is clearly quite close to the Modern Hebrew script illustrated right.*

SAMARITAN

Symbol	Transliteration
ࠀ	'
ࠁ	b
ࠂ	g
ࠃ	d
ࠄ	h
ࠅ	w
ࠆ	z
ࠇ	ḥ
ࠈ	ṭ
ࠉ	y
ࠊ	k
ࠋ	l
ࠌ	m
ࠍ	n
ࠎ	s
ࠏ	c
ࠐ	f
ࠑ	ṣ
ࠒ	q
ࠓ	r
ࠔ	š
ࠕ	t

HEBREW

Old Hebrew	Modern Hebrew	Name	Transliteration
𐤀	א	aleph	'
𐤁	ב	beth	b
𐤂	ג	gimel	g
𐤃	ד	daleth	d
𐤄	ה	he	h
𐤅	ו	waw	w
𐤆	ז	zayin	z
𐤇	ח	ḥeth	ḥ
𐤈	ט	ṭeth	ṭ
𐤉	י	yod	y
𐤊	כ (ך)	kaph	k
𐤋	ל	lamed	l
𐤌	מ (ם)	mem	m
𐤍	נ (ן)	nun	n
𐤎	ס	samekh	s
𐤏	ע	ayin	'
𐤐	פ (ף)	pe	p
𐤑	צ (ץ)	ṣade	ṣ
𐤒	ק	qoph	q
𐤓	ר	reš	r
𐤔	ש	šin	š/s
𐤕	ת	taw	t

Above: *Modern Hebrew square characters have their origin in the Aramaic script. The characters* kaph, mem, nun, pe, *and* ṣade *have variant forms which are used at the ends of words.*

Left: *Following the sixth-century Babylonian Exile of the Jews, the Old Hebrew script gradually gave way to Aramaic. The old characters are, however, still used as a liturgical script by the Samaritans.*

while two appeared at the hands of the Palestinian Massoretes. One of these latter systems, the Tiberian, eventually became standard. In modern Hebrew writing, vowel points are used in only a few contexts: for example, in the text of the Bible, in children's literature, and in poetry.

The Aramaic script was also utilized by an Arab people called the Nabateans. In the second century BC, the Nabateans established a prosperous kingdom extending from Transjordan into the Sinai, with their capital at the city of Petra. Though speakers of the Semitic language of Arabic, the Nabateans wrote in Aramaic, developing their own distinct variety of the script, which existed in both a monumental and a cursive form. There are also a few examples of it being used to record the Arabic language, and it was probably this Nabatean Aramaic script which later evolved into the Arabic writing system.

The earliest Arabic inscription in a distinctive, though perhaps transitional, Arabic script appears in about the fourth century AD. This is one of only a very few examples of Arabic script attested prior to the advent of Islam in the seventh century AD, when there is a marked increase in examples; it was in the middle of the seventh century that the Koran was compiled and published. Two principal varieties of Arabic script developed early in the Islamic period: Naskhi and Kufic. The former tends to be cursive and slanting, the latter beautifully thick. The modern Arabic script is a descendant of Naskhi. Vowels are marked by three vowel points and by the consonantal characters *alif*, *ya*, and *waw*.

ARABIC

| Symbol | | | | Transliteration |
Final	Medial	Initial	Independent	
ا			ا	ā
ب	ـبـ	بـ	ب	b
ت	ـتـ	تـ	ت	t
ث	ـثـ	ثـ	ث	θ
ج	ـجـ	جـ	ج	ǰ
ح	ـحـ	حـ	ح	ħ
خ	ـخـ	خـ	خ	x
ـد			د	d
ـذ			ذ	ð
ـر			ر	r
ـز			ز	z
س	ـسـ	سـ	س	s
ش	ـشـ	شـ	ش	š
ص	ـصـ	صـ	ص	ṣ
ض	ـضـ	ضـ	ض	ḍ
ط	ـطـ	طـ	ط	ṭ
ظ	ـظـ	ظـ	ظ	ẓ
ع	ـعـ	عـ	ع	ʕ
غ	ـغـ	غـ	غ	ɣ
ف	ـفـ	فـ	ف	f
ق	ـقـ	قـ	ق	q
ك	ـكـ	كـ	ك	k
ل	ـلـ	لـ	ل	l
م	ـمـ	مـ	م	m
ن	ـنـ	نـ	ن	n
ه	ـهـ	هـ	ه	h
ـو			و	w
ى	ـيـ	يـ	ي	y

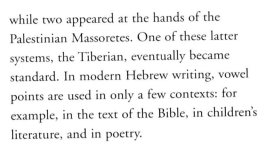

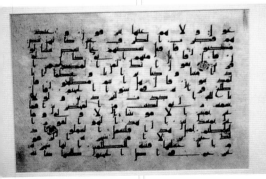

Above: *An early form of Arabic script called Kufic existed in addition to Nashki. As can be seen from this page of a manuscript of the Koran (c. ninth or tenth century), Kufic is a bold and thick script.*

Above: *The modern Arabic script, with its delicately cursive consonantal symbols, is a descendant of the earlier Nashki script. All but six of the characters of the modern system have positional variants for use at the beginning, in the middle, and at the end of a word, as well as having independent forms.*

Yet another writing system to evolve from the Aramaic is that of Syriac. The Syriac language was the dialect of Aramaic spoken in Edessa (now Urfa, Turkey) and its surrounding areas. Owing to the city's position as a center of Christianity, the Bible was translated into Syriac, a large corpus of Christian Syriac writings appeared, and Syriac became widely used as a literary and liturgical language. The earliest known text in the Syriac script is dated to the first century AD. The Syriac system, being descended from Aramaic, is consonantal, but developed various means for marking vowels. The early, Nestorian system used diacritic vowel points together with the consonantal symbols *waw* and *yod*, while the Jacobite system of the eighth century used small subscript and superscript Greek vowel letters. The Syriac use of vowel points is likely to be the source of the Arabic and Hebrew practice of so representing vowel sounds.

There is another possible descendant of the Phoenician script; in the North African Phoenician colony of Carthage, established in the late ninth century BC, a dialect of Phoenician developed known as Punic. In antiquity, the Libyan peoples of North Africa used a writing system which has survived in the form of the modern script called Tifinagh used by some Berber-speakers. Perhaps, at least in part, the ancestor of Tifinagh developed from the Punic system.

SYRIAC			
Estrangelā	Nestorian	Jacobite	Transliteration
			'
			b
			g
			d
			h
			w
			z
			ḥ
			ṭ
			y
			k
			l
			m
			n
			s
			ʻ
			p
			ṣ
			q
			r
			š
			t

Above: *Three varieties of the consonantal Syriac script are illustrated here. The earliest of these is Estrangelā (first century AD). The later Nestorian and Jacobite scripts were used by the eastern and western Syriac churches respectively.*

Left: *Petra, in modern Jordan, the "rose red city, half as old as time," was capital of the wealthy Nabatean kingdom (second century BC to 106 AD). The Nabateans spoke an early form of Arabic but wrote in the Aramaic language, using their own Nabatean variety of the Aramaic consonantal script.*

TIFINAGH

Name	Symbol	Transliteration
tar'erit	•	'
leb	⊞ ⊕	b
let	+	t
led	⊓ ∧ ⊔	d
lej	⊥	j
lez	⧣	z
lez'	⚡ ⚡	z'
ler	□ ○	r
les	⊡ ⊙	s
leg	⸪ ⸫	g
leg'	⋈	g'
lef	⊐⊏ ⊐⊏	f
lel	‖	l
lem	⊐	m
len			n
lek	∴	k
lak'	∴∴	q
ler'	⦂	ɣ
lech	Ɔ	š
lah	⦂	h
ladh	∃	d,t
lakh	∷	χ
laou	⦂	w
léy	⩶	y
lebt	⊞	bt
lezt	⩲	zt
lert	⊞	rt
lest	⊞	st
legt	⸬	gt
leg't	⋈	g't
lelt	⩏	lt
lemt	⊞	mt
lent	+	nt
lecht	⊖	št
lenk	⸬	nk

Right: Tifinagh, descended from a Libyan script of antiquity, is a writing system used by the Tuareg, a pastoralist people of North Africa, for recording their dialect of Berber.

ANATOLIA

During the second millennium BC, several Indo-European languages were being spoken and written in Anatolia. Of these, the best known is Hittite, with texts dating to perhaps the seventeenth century BC. The scribes of the Hittite empire kept their records utilizing Babylonian cuneiform. The Hittites introduced an additional complication into the already complex Babylonian system of Sumerian logograms, syllabic symbols, and determinatives by retaining certain Akkadian phonetic spellings, so-called akkadograms. The cuneiform documents excavated at Bogazköy, site of the ancient Hittite capital, also preserve texts written in the Indo-European languages Palaic and Luvian, and the non-Indo-European Hattic.

The Luvian language of Anatolia was also recorded using a highly pictographic writing system called Hieroglyphic Luvian (formerly erroneously labeled Hieroglyphic Hittite), attested from approximately 1500 BC to 700 BC. Like the cuneiform script of Anatolia, the Hieroglyphic Luvian system contains logograms, syllabograms, and determinatives; it also existed in a cursive form.

BRONZE AGE AEGEAN

Between 2000 BC and 1450 BC, the Minoan civilization flourished on the Aegean island of Crete. Within their brilliantly colored palace complexes decorated with marvelous frescoes of dolphins and acrobats, Minoan scribes used a variety of scripts. Throughout much of their history the Minoans used a pictographic script classified, by the British archeologist Sir Arthur Evans, as Cretan Hieroglyphic. Some scholars have conjectured that this still-undeciphered script may possibly be linked to Hieroglyphic Luvian.

A second pictographic script from Minoan Crete, dated to approximately 1700 BC, appears only on a single double-sided document, a clay disk recovered from the ruins of the palace at Phaistos. Each of the 45 symbols appearing on the Phaistos Disk was produced by impressing a stamp into the moist clay medium. The script of the disk probably has the distinction of being the world's most frequently deciphered writing system. It seems likely that the script is syllabic in nature, though none of the decipherments so far proposed carries conviction.

From about the middle of the eighteenth century BC, yet another writing system was employed by the Minoans, the much more stylized, linear script called Linear A. Though the exact nature of the process is unclear, Linear A almost certainly evolved out of Cretan Hieroglyphic, which continued to be used alongside Linear A. Both syllabograms and logograms occur within the symbol inventory of Linear A, the decipherment of which is ongoing. Various attempts have been made to match it with known languages of antiquity; the one which seems perhaps to hold some promise is that which sees behind the script an Indo-European language of the Anatolian sub-family—a language such as Luvian.

During the mid-fifteenth century BC, the Minoans were superseded in Crete by the Mycenaeans, a Greek people whose culture first appears in the archeological record of the Greek mainland at about 1600 BC. In AD 1877, the Spanish consul in Crete reported finding an inscribed clay tablet at the site of the ruined Mycenaean palace at Knossos. Since that time, many such clay documents have been unearthed at Knossos and other Mycenaean palace sites both on Crete and on the Greek mainland. These documents remained unreadable until 1952, when a young British architect named Michael Ventris deciphered their script. This, the earliest known writing system of the Greeks, is Linear B, so named by Sir Arthur Evans long before its decipherment.

The Linear B script, descended from Minoan Linear A, is a syllabic system. Logograms also occur but are usually used only in conjunction with numerals to specify a quantity of some commodity—olive oil, grain, chariots, swords, and so on—which is often also spelled out using syllabic symbols; most of the Linear B tablets are palace business records.

Linear B syllabograms, with only a few exceptions, are of the V and CV type; thus the spelling of two or more consonants in sequence and of consonants occurring at the end of a word is problematic. Linear B scribes responded to this problem by developing a spelling strategy which involves, in some cases, simply not writing the consonant and, in other cases, writing a vowel which does not actually occur in the spoken form of the word being written. Thus Greek *sperma* ("seed") is spelled *pe-ma*, while *tektones* ("carpenters") is spelled *te-ke-to-ne*. As a rule, the script does not distinguish voiced, voiceless, and voiceless aspirated consonants which are produced at a single point in the vocal tract; and so, for example, the phonetic CV sequences [ba], [pa], and [pʰa] are all written as the same syllabic symbol. Also not distinguished are the liquid consonants [l] and [r]. Exceptionally, however, [d] is distinguished from [t] and [tʰ]. The use of the Linear B script disappears from the archeological

THE WRITING OF BRONZE AGE GREECE

The Minoan civilization of Bronze Age Crete has left evidence of three different writing systems: Cretan Hieroglyphic, the Phaistos Disk script, and Linear A. At the same time that the Minoans flourished in Crete, mainland Greece was home to the Mycenaeans, whose era is remembered in Homer's *Iliad* and *Odyssey*. From the Minoans, the Mycenaean Greeks acquired a writing system, now called Linear B. Most of the surviving Linear A and Linear B inscriptions are found on clay tablets. The scripts' symbols, which are curvilinear, are not easily incised in wet clay, however, perhaps suggesting the scripts were designed for and most often written on some other, perishable medium.

LINEAR A

Sym.	Translit.	Sym.	Translit.	Sym.	Translit.	Sym.	Translit.	Sym.	Translit
	AB(01)		AB(22)		AB(41)		AB(66)		AB(120)
	AB(02)		AB(22ʲ)		AB(44)		AB(67)		A(120b)
	AB(03)		AB(22ᵐ)		AB(45)		AB(69)		AB(122)
	AB(04)		AB(23)		AB(46)		AB(70)		AB(123)
	AB(05)		AB(23ᵐ)		AB(47)		AB(73)		AB(131a)
	AB(06)		AB(24)		AB(49)		AB(74)		AB(131b)
	AB(07)		AB(26)		AB(50)		AB(76)		A(131c)
	AB(08)		AB(27)		AB(51)		AB(77)		AB(164)
	AB(09)		AB(28)		AB(53)		AB(78)		AB(171)
	AB(10)		A(28b)		AB(54)		AB(79)		AB(180)
	AB(11)		AB(29)		AB(55)		AB(80)		AB(188)
	AB(13)		AB(30)		AB(56)		AB(81)		AB(191)
	AB(16)		AB(31)		AB(57)		AB(82)		A(301)
	AB(17)		AB(34)		AB(58)		AB(85)		A(302)
	AB(20)		AB(37)		AB(59)		AB(86)		A(303)
	AB(21)		AB(38)		AB(60)		AB(87)		A(304)
	AB(21ʲ)		AB(39)		AB(61)		A(100/102)		A(305)
	AB(21ᵐ)		AB(40)		AB(65)		AB(118)		A(306)

Above: *Linear A is the name given by the British archeologist, Sir Arthur Evans, to this Bronze Age Minoan script, descended from the Cretan Hieroglyphic writing system. The symbols illustrated here are known to have syllabic value, though the script is still being deciphered.*

LINEAR B

Symbol	Translit.	Symbol	Translit.	Symbol	Translit.	Symbol	Translit.	Symbol	Translit.
	a		e		i		u		o
	pa		pe		pi		pu		po
	ta		te		ti		tu		to
	da		de		di		du		do
	ka		ke		ki		ku		ko
	kwa		kwe		kwi		kwo		
	sa		se		si		su		so
	za		ze				zo		
	ma		me		mi		mu		mo
	na		ne		ni		nu		no
	wa		we		wi		wo		
	ya		ye				yu		yo
	ra		re		ri		ru		ro
	a₂		a₃		au				
	pa₃		pu₂		pte				
	ta₂		two						
	dwe		dwo						
	swa		swi						
	nwa								
	ra₂		ra₃		ro₂				

LINEAR B

The Unidentified Signs

Left: *The descendant of Linear A script, Linear B, has been deciphered. In 1952 Michael Ventris, a British architect who in boyhood had encountered an aged Sir Arthur Evans and his Linear B tablets, succeeded in deciphering the script and discovered that the language behind this syllabic writing system is an early dialect of Greek. Only a few signs (below left) are still unknown.*

Left: *This clay tablet, bearing an inscription in Linear B, was recovered from the remains of the Mycenaean palace at Pylos, home of the Homeric hero Nestor.*

record at about 1200 BC as the Mycenaean civilization comes to an end, victim of a great conflagration which swept across the Aegean and eastern Mediterranean at the close of the Bronze Age.

CYPRUS

With the collapse of the Mycenaean civilization, large numbers of Greeks left their homeland for other regions, including the island of Cyprus. The earlier Cypriot writing dates to about 1500 BC, and is attested in a set of scripts called Cypro-Minoan. As the name implies, these evolved from a Minoan system, probably Linear A. Traditionally, three separate Cypro-Minoan scripts, designated simply as Cypro-Minoan I, II, and III have been identified, the last found at Ugarit rather than on Cyprus. All remain undeciphered, though it has been conjectured that each writes a different language. Recently,

however, some authorities have begun to question this three-way division.

The Mycenaean Greek settlers of Cyprus adapted one of the Cypro-Minoan scripts for their own use by at least the mid-eleventh century BC, thus creating the second (known) Greek writing system, the Cypriot syllabary. This syllabic script consists, much in the manner of the earlier Mycenaean system, of only V and CV symbols, plus a very few CCV symbols. The strategy of Linear B scribes for spelling sequences of consonants was employed by the Cypriot Greek scribes, though with one fundamental and significant modification: those very consonants occurring in sequence which had not been spelled within the Linear B system are now represented in the Cypriot syllabary by using a CV symbol whose vowel component matches the first vowel preceding the consonant sequence. *Artemidi* ("for Artemis"), for example, is written *a-ra-te-mi-ti*.

CYPRIOT

Symbol	Translit.	Symbol	Translit.	Symbol	Translit.	Symbol	Translit.	Symbol	Translit.
✳	a	✳	e	✗	i	≚	o	⋎	u
‡	pa	ϟ	pe	↟	pi	ς	po	⋓	pu
⊢	ta	⋡	te	↑	ti	F	to	冚	tu
⇑	ka	⋨	ke	⋔	ki	∩	ko	✳	ku
∨	sa	⊢	se	⇑	si	≚	so	⊃木	su
						⅙	zo		
⋊	ma	⋇	me	⋎	mi	⊕	mo	⋈	mu
⊤	na	⎰⎱	ne	⋡	ni	⫫	no	⋋	nu
⋊	wa	ⲓ	we	⋌	wi	⌒	wo		
φ	ya					⤳	yo		
Ω	ra	⏶	re	϶	ri	𝄴	ro	⋉	ru
⋎	la	𝟪	le	≤	li	+	lo	⋒	lu
⊃⊂	ksa	⏀	kse						

Above: *The syllabic Cypriot script was probably devised by descendants of émigrés from Mycenaean Greece. A comparison of this Greek script with Linear B reveals similarities between the two; these were utilized by Michael Ventris in his decipherment of Linear B.*

GREEK

Euboea	Ionia	Athens	Corinth	Modern Capitals	Modern Lower Case	Transliteration	Name
ΑΛ	ΑΛ	ΑΛ	ΑΛ	Α	α	a	alpha
Β	Β	Β	Ⴖ	Β	β	b	beta
‹C	Γ	Λ	CС	Γ	γ	g	gamma
DD	Δ	Δ	Δ	Δ	δ	d	delta
ᚠΕ	ᚠΕ	ᚠΕ	Β	Ε	ε	e	epsilon
Ϝ	—	Ϝ	Ϝ	Ϝ	Ϝ	w	digamma
Ι	Ι	Ι	Ι	Ζ	ζ	zd	zeta
—	ΘΗ	—	—	Η	η	ē	eta
ΘΗ	—	ΘΗ	ΘΗ	—	—	h	
⊗⊕⊙	⊗⊕⊙	⊗⊕⊙	⊗⊕⊙	Θ	θ	th	theta
Ι	Ι	Ι	⸙	Ι	ι	i	iota
Κ	Κ	Κ	Κ	Κ	κ	k	kappa
Ʌ	ΓΛ	Ʌ	ΓΛ	Λ	λ	l	lambda
ᛘᛟΜ	ᛟΜ	ᛟΜ	ᛟΜ	Μ	μ	m	mu
ᛁΝ	ᛁΝ	ᛁΝ	ᛁΝ	Ν	ν	n	nu
Χ	‡	(ΧϚ)	‡	Ξ	ξ	ks	xi
Ο	Ο	Ο	Ο	Ο	ο	o	omicron
ΓΓ	Γ	Γ	ΓΓ	Π	π	p	pi
Μ(?)	—	—	Μ	Μ	—	s	san
Ϙ	Ϙ	Ϙ	Ϙ	Ϙ	ϙ	k	qoppa
Ρ	ΡD	ΡR	ΡR	Ρ	ρ	r	rho
Ϛ	ξ	Ϛ	—	Σ	ςϛ	s	sigma
Τ	Τ	Τ	Τ	Τ	τ	t	tau
ΥϒV	VΥ	ΥϒV	ΥϒV	Υ	υ	u	upsilon
ΦⱰ	Φ	ΦⱰ	ΦⱰ	Φ	φ	ph	phi
ΨV	Χ	Χ	Χ	Χ	χ	kh	chi
(ΦϚ)	ΥV	(ΦϚ)	ΥΨ	Ψ	ψ	ps	psi
—	ՈΩ	—	—	Ω	ω	ō	omega

Above: *The first writing system to contain symbols for individual consonant sounds (as in Proto-Canaanite) and for individual vowel sounds (as in the various Near Eastern and Greek syllabaries) was the Greek alphabet. There were many local varieties of the Greek alphabet, such as the four illustrated here.*

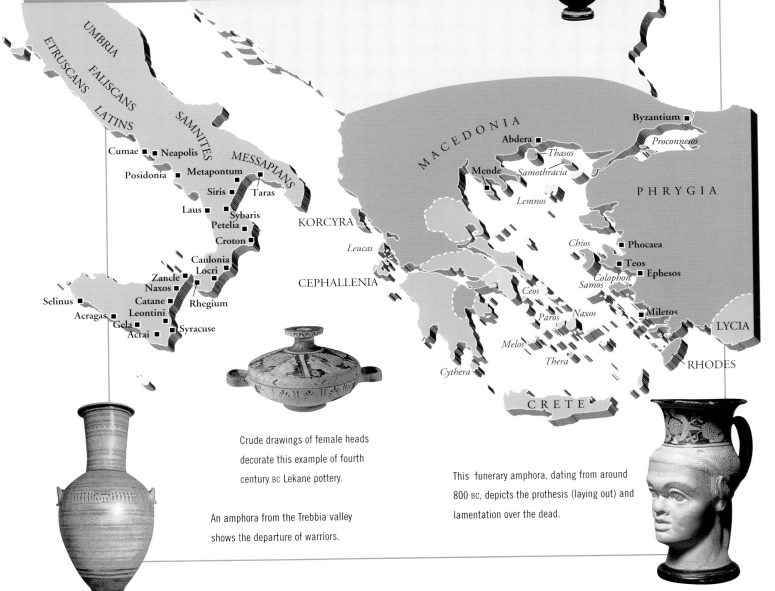

LOCAL GREEK

The local, or *epichoric*, alphabets of the ancient Greeks can be divided into four different types according to the manner in which they represent certain consonant sounds. In 1887 the German scholar Kirchhoff published a study of the Greek alphabets in which he included a map showing the distribution of the alphabet types. The four types were color-coded as green, red, blue, and light blue; the practice of identifying the alphabets in this way has persisted.

This Greek canthare, from about 540 BC, has a double head of one white and one black or negro woman.

The head of a satyr is depicted on a fourth century BC painted pottery Rhyton, also from the Trebbia valley.

UMBRIA
ETRUSCANS
FALISCANS
LATINS
SAMNITES
Cumae ■ ■ Neapolis
Posidonia ■ ■ Metapontum
MESSAPIANS
Siris ■ ■ Taras
Laus ■ ■ Sybaris
Petelia ■
Croton ■
Caulonia ■
Zancle ■ Locri ■
Naxos ■
Selinus ■ Catane ■ ■ Rhegium
Acragas ■ Leontini ■
Gela ■ ■ Acrai ■ Syracuse

KORCYRA
Leucas
CEPHALLENIA

MACEDONIA
Abdera ■
Mende ■ Thasos
Samothracia
Lemnos
Byzantium ■
Proconnesos

PHRYGIA

Chios ■ Phocaea
Teos ■
Colophon ■ Ephesos
Ceos Samos
Paros Naxos
Melos Miletos
Thera LYCIA
Cythera RHODES

CRETE

Crude drawings of female heads decorate this example of fourth century BC Lekane pottery.

An amphora from the Trebbia valley shows the departure of warriors.

This funerary amphora, dating from around 800 BC, depicts the prothesis (laying out) and lamentation over the dead.

Voiced, voiceless, and voiceless aspirated consonants which are produced at a single point in the vocal tract are not distinguished from one another, including dentals, as can be seen by the example cited above. In contrast to the Linear B practice, [l] and [r] are distinguished in the Cypriot system. Also, special mechanisms are devised for spelling both word-final consonants and the first consonant occurring in word-initial consonant sequences.

GREECE

The Greek alphabet is yet a third Greek writing system. Though much earlier dates have been proposed, the most widely accepted for the first appearance of the Greek alphabet is the eighth century BC.

As with the two earlier Greek scripts, the alphabet was based upon a writing system already used by a people with whom the Greeks came into contact, in this instance the Phoenicians. Various places have been suggested for the Greek adaptation of the Phoenician consonantal script, including Cyprus, Crete, Rhodes, and the Syrian coastal town of Al Mina. Wherever this adaptation occurred, it must have been carried out within a bilingual Phoenician-Greek context. In the view of the author, the evidence points overwhelmingly to Cyprus, on which there had been a significant Phoenician presence since the middle of the ninth century BC. Certain peculiarities of the Greek alphabet suggest that the Greeks who adapted the Phoenician writing system were accustomed to spelling their language with the Cypriot syllabary. For example, the Greek alphabet contains a symbol with the value [k] + [s] (the progenitor of the x symbol used in spelling English); with both a symbol for [k] and one for [s], the alphabet has no need at all for such a double consonant character. Within the Cypriot syllabary, however, *ksV* syllabic characters

Left: This funerary inscription on the gravestone of M. Domitius Pyrilampes from Dion, Greece is written in both Latin and Greek. The main text is in Greek, while the name and age of the deceased appears horizontally in Latin at the top.

ETRUSCAN

Archaic Etruscan	Neo-Etruscan	Transliteration
A	A	a
Ɔ	Ɔ	c
Ⅎ	Ⅎ	e
ꟻ	ꟻ	v
I	ꟷ	ts
B	⊖	h
⊗ O	⊙ O	th
I	I	i
K		k
ꟼ	ꟼ	l
M	M	m
ꟺ	ꟺ	n
ꟷ	ꟷ	p
M	M	ś
Q		k
ꟼ	Ɑ	r
Ƨ	Ƨ	s
T	ꟷꟷ	t
Y	V	u
X		s
Φ	Φ	ph
Ψ	Ψ	kh
ꟻ	8	f

Left: The Etruscans, a non-Indo-European people from Italy, acquired a variety of the red alphabet type from the Greeks who settled in the area of Pithekoussae and Cumae in southern Italy (modern Naples). The approximate values of individual symbols are known, but much remains a mystery.

are needed as a consequence of the peculiar strategy used for spelling consonant sequences. Provision was made in the new alphabetic script for a [k] + [s] character because the adapters were already familiar and writing with a system in which [k] + [s] symbols occurred.

The Greek alphabet was unlike any earlier writing system. As with the Phoenician and Aramaic scripts and their descendants, it is a phonetic script, representing individual sounds; but unlike these, the Greek script employs not only consonant symbols but vowel symbols as well. *Matres lectionis* were used at the end of words in the Aramaic script prior to the advent of the Greek alphabet, but their use is sporadic and limited. Moreover, the *matres lectionis* are consonant symbols which are at times employed to signal the presence of vowel sounds; they are not distinct vowel characters. Owing to phonetic differences between the Greek and Phoenician languages, the

Greek adapters of the Phoenician script had at their disposal more consonant symbols than were required for spelling Greek. To these extra consonant characters, the Greeks assigned vowel values, and so was born the first alphabet.

Many local varieties of the Greek alphabet developed as the script spread across the Greek-speaking world. These local alphabets have traditionally been classified into three major groups and named after the colors used to encode their distribution on the map which appeared in A. Kirchhoff's 1887 *Studien zur Geschichte des Griechischen Alphabets* (*see map page 184*). The green alphabets were used on Crete and certain neighboring islands, and were characterized by the absence of so-called supplemental characters, consonantal symbols appended to the end of the adapted Phoenician script; a vowel symbol for ō, called *omega*, would also sometimes be added. The red alphabets, such

Above: *The Tomb of the Leopards, Tarquinia. An underground Etruscan chamber tomb dating from c. 550–520 BC, it takes its name from the leopards above the festive scene depicted.*

as those of Euboea and Laconia, have the supplemental characters Φ and Ψ, with the respective values [pʰ] and [kʰ]. The blue alphabets are of two subtypes: dark blue, used in Corinth and Rhodes, with supplementals Φ, X, and Ψ, representing [pʰ], [kʰ], and [pˢ] respectively; light blue from Attica, with only Φ and X, taking the same values as in the dark blue subtypes. The form of the Greek alphabet that survives today is Ionic (dark blue).

Much of Sicily and the south of Italy was colonized by the Greeks. One of the oldest known examples of Greek alphabetic writing comes from the ruins of the Greek colony on the island of Pithekoussae in the bay of Naples. These letters comprise a verse inscription on the so-called Cup of Nestor, dated to approximately 725 BC.

ITALY

In the seventh century BC, a non-Indo-European people called the Etruscans lived in western central Italy. The southern reaches of Etruscan settlement neighbored upon the Euboean Greek colonies of Pithekoussae and Cumae. From the Greeks of southern Italy, the Etruscans learned to write. As the sounds of the Etruscan language differed from those of Greek, the Etruscans introduced certain changes into the red Greek alphabet which they acquired. Etruscan lacked voiced stops (sounds such as [b], [d], and [g]), and although the earliest Etruscan alphabets retained the Greek letters for such consonants, eventually the Greek symbols B and Δ representing [b] and [d], were dropped. The Greek letter Γ, for [g], was, however, retained to represent the voiceless stop [k] when it occurred before the vowels e and i. The Etruscans used the Greek K to spell [k] before the vowel a, and the Greek symbol Q (called *qoppa*) to spell [k] before *u*; the Greeks had used *qoppa* for representing a *k*-sound produced a bit further back in the oral cavity than [k].

The longest single Etruscan document yet discovered was found not in Italy but in Egypt. A Croatian traveling in Egypt in the nineteenth century acquired for the Zagreb National Museum a mummy which was entombed in linen bandages with an inscription of about 1,200 words detailing a sacred Etruscan calendar. Why and how such a document came to wrap an Egyptian mummy is unknown.

Also coming to light in the nineteenth century was a stele on the island of Lemnos in the Aegean.

Below: *Oscan and Umbrian were two of the several Italic (Indo-European) languages of ancient Italy. Each used an alphabet derived from the Etruscan script. Within the last three centuries BC, these languages and their alphabets fell victim to the spread of Latin and its script throughout Italy.*

OSCAN		UMBRIAN	
Symbol	**Translit.**	**Symbol**	**Translit.**
Я	a	Я	a
ᗺ	b	ᗺ	b
ᐳ	g	ᑫ	ř
Я	d	Ⴒ	e
Ⴍ	e	ᒥ	v
ᒧ	v	Ⳏ	ts
I	ts	Ⴛ	h
ᗺ	h	I	i
I	i	ᛕ	k
ᛕ	k	ᒐ	l
ᒐ	l	ᛖ(ᐱ)	m
ᛖ	m	Ⴈ	n
Ⴈ	n	ᒊ	p
ᑭ	p	ᑫ	r
ᑫ	r	ⰶ	s
ᙇ	s	✝(Ⴍ)	t
Ⴒ	t	ᐁ	u
ᐁ	u	४	f
४	f	ᑫ	ç
Ⴑ(ᚲ↑)	í		
ᐱ	ú		

The Lemnian Stone, dated to the sixth century BC, bears an inscription in a script which is quite similar to the Etruscan alphabet. This inscription is not yet understood, though it has been conjectured that it writes a language similar to Etruscan.

The Etruscan alphabet was introduced to the region of Latium and its Latin-speaking inhabitants in the seventh century BC. Again, because of consonant and vowel differences between their own Indo-European language and Etruscan, the Latin-speaking users of the Etruscan script made certain modifications. While early Latin writers continued the Etruscan practice of using three different characters to represent the voiceless stop [k], the third letter of the adapted Etruscan script, C (which was Greek γ in origin) was eventually generalized for spelling Latin [k] in all contexts. A modified form of this C, designed G, was used for spelling the Latin voiced stop [g], and placed seventh in the Latin alphabet, replacing an unneeded Etruscan character, the Greek *zeta* in origin. Latin Q, from Etruscan (and earlier Greek) *qoppa*, came to represent the voiceless labiovelar stop [kʷ]. The early form of the Etruscan alphabet acquired in Latium retained the Greek symbols for [b] and [d], but the Etruscan letters which continued the Greek symbols for the voiceless aspirated stops [pʰ], [tʰ], and [kʰ] (Φ, θ, and Ψ in the red alphabet of the Euboean colonies) were not required for spelling Latin and so were deleted. The letters Y and Z were appended in the first century BC in order to spell more accurately the many Greek loan words entering the Roman language.

Latin was only one of several Indo-European languages of the Italic subfamily spoken in Italy when the Latin alphabet appeared. Oscan and Umbrian, for example, both developed their own Etruscan-based alphabets. With Rome's highly effective colonization of the Italian peninsula, these languages and their scripts were supplanted by Latin and its alphabet. The pre-eminent status of the Latin alphabet would in time be extended considerably beyond Italy.

Right: One of the more unusual alphabetic scripts of early Europe is Ogham, the writing system of the Celts of Britain and Ireland.

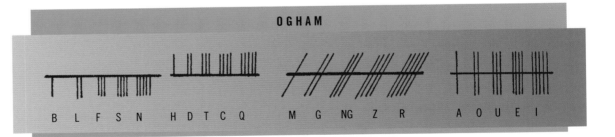

OGHAM

B L F S N   H D T C Q   M G NG Z R   A O U E I

Below: Runes were the alphabetic symbols used by the various Germanic peoples of Europe, known from at least the third century AD. The runic system, or futhark, of the Anglo-Saxons contains 31 characters. Runes were commonly inscribed on wood, metal, and stone.

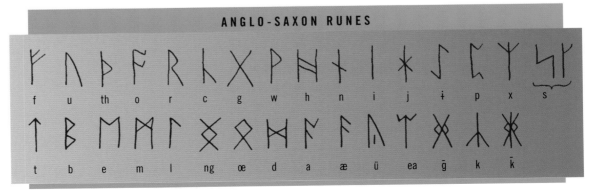

ANGLO-SAXON RUNES

f u th o r c g w h n i j ï p x s

t b e m l ng œ d a æ ü ea ḡ k k̄

NORTHERN EUROPE

The Celts of the European continent were writing with both the Greek and Latin alphabets by the first two centuries BC. In Britain and Ireland a rather unusual script was in use among the Celts by the second century AD; this is the alphabetic script called Ogham, perhaps named after Oghma, the divine Celtic strong man. The Ogham inscriptions are seen principally, though not exclusively, on boundary or grave stones. The 20 characters of the script consist of short lines of one to five strokes, touching or crossing a horizontal or vertical reference line at right angles or diagonally. Vowel characters sometimes consist of one to five dots, rather than lines. The origin of the script is uncertain. Some scholars have speculated that Ogham is based upon a secret finger-language of the Druidic priests, citing a medieval Irish manuscript in which such a finger-code is described. It has also been proposed that the script developed under the influence of the Latin or Greek alphabets and the Germanic runes.

The runic script of the Germanic peoples first appears in the archeological record in the third century AD (though a date of the second century AD has been proposed for certain recent finds). The runic symbols, with their characteristic vertical and diagonal lines, are arranged in an alphabetic order which scholars call a *futhark* (or *futhork*), after the value of the first six characters (f, u, th, a, r, and k). The earliest *futharks* consist of 24 symbols, and it was perhaps the Latin alphabet which provided the inspiration for their development. By the fifth century AD, a *futhark* of 31 symbols had evolved for writing Anglo-Saxon.

During the fourth century AD, the Visigothic bishop Wulfila who translated the Bible into

Gothic did not simply appropriate a runic script, but designed his own alphabet for the translation. The symbols of his Gothic writing system were based upon Greek and Latin alphabetic characters with the exception of *u* and *o*, which appear to be of runic origin.

The non-Latin scripts of much of Europe gave way as the Latin alphabet advanced. Roman armies had already transported their system across the European continent and Britain, but it was the spread of Christianity and the concomitant status of the Latin language and writing which would in the end be the undoing of runes and oghams. In the Christian monasteries of Europe, many distinct styles of Latin script evolved—Irish, Anglo-Saxon, Carolingian, Gothic (not to be confused with Wulfila's script), Italic, and Roman. Medieval monks not only filled pages of

Left: *Rome not only gave its version of the alphabet to Italy, Europe, and much of the world but is the source of the elegantly sublime lapidary letter-style, as used on this monument from Grado, Italy.*

Right: *The Gothic alphabet, not to be confused with the Gothic script of the Roman alphabet, was invented for the purpose of translating the Bible into the East Germanic language of Gothic.*

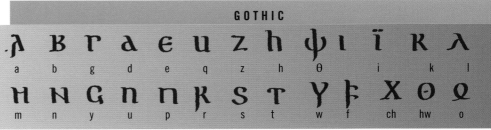

GOTHIC

Ʌ	B	Γ	ᴆ	E	U	Z	ħ	ψ	ι	ī	K	Λ
a	b	g	d	e	q	z	h	θ	i		k	l

Ƕ	N	G	ᴨ	ᴨ	R	S	T	Y	F	X	Θ	Ω
m	n	y	u	p	r	s	t	w	f	ch	hw	o

COPTIC

Name	Letter	Transliteration	Name	Letter	Transliteration
Alfa	Ⲁ ⲁ	a	Ro	Ⲣ ⲣ	r
Vida	Ⲃ ⲃ	v [b]	Sīma	Ⲥ ⲥ	s
Gamma	Ⲅ ⲅ	g	Dau	Ⲧ ⲧ	t
Dalda	Ⲇ ⲇ	d	He	Ⲩ ⲩ	y, u
Ei	Ⲉ ⲉ	ĕ	Phi	Ⲫ ⲫ	ph
Sīta	Ⲍ ⲍ	z	Chi	Ⲭ ⲭ	kh
Hīda	Ⲏ ⲏ	i, é	Epsi	Ⲯ ⲯ	ps
Tīda	Ⲑ ⲑ	th	O	Ⲱ ⲱ	ō
Jōda	Ⲓ ⲓ	i	Shāi	Ϣ ϣ	š
Kappa	Ⲕ ⲕ	k	Fāi	Ϥ ϥ	f
Lōla	Ⲗ ⲗ	l	Chāi	Ϧ ϧ	ḫ
Mi	Ⲙ ⲙ	m	Hori	Ϩ ϩ	h
Ni	Ⲛ ⲛ	n	Džandža	Ϫ ϫ	j
Exi	Ⲝ ⲝ	ks	Schima	Ϭ ϭ	č
O	Ⲟ ⲟ	ŏ	Di	Ϯ ϯ	ti
Bi	Ⲡ ⲡ	p			

Left: *The demotic script of Egyptian was supplanted by a new writing system based on the Greek alphabet, Coptic (the Bohairic version is shown here). The ancient writing system of the Egyptians would not, however, disappear without a trace—the last seven characters of this Coptic alphabet were furnished by demotic.*

LYCIAN

Letter	Transliteration
𐊀	a
𐊁	e
𐊂	b
𐊃	β
𐊄	g
𐊅	d
𐊆	i
𐊇	w
𐊈	z
𐊉	θ
𐊊	j
𐊋	k
𐊌	q
𐊍	l
𐊎	m
𐊏	n
𐊐	m̃
𐊑	ñ
𐊒	u
𐊓	p
𐊕	r
𐊖	s
𐊗	t
𐊘	τ
𐊙	ã
𐊚	ẽ
𐊛	h
𐊜	χ

Left: *In southwest Asia Minor, speakers of Lycian (an Indo-European language) were writing with their own script, derived from a Greek alphabet of the red type, by the fifth century* BC.

Right: *Old Church Slavonic, or Old Bulgarian, is the south Slavic language into which the Bible was translated by the ninth-century Greek missionaries St. Cyril and St. Methodius. The Cyrillic alphabet script which was devised for recording this language bears the name of one of the Greek brothers.*

OLD CHURCH SLAVONIC

Symbol	Transliteration	Symbol	Transliteration
А а	a	Х х	ch
Б б	b	Ѡ ѡ	o
В в	v	Ц ц	ts
Г г	g	Ч ч	č
Д д	d	Ш ш	š
Є є	e	Щ щ	št
Ж ж	ž	Ъ ъ	ŭ
Ѕ ѕ	dz	Ꙑ ꙑ	y
З з	z	Ь ь	ĭ
И и	i	Ѣ ѣ	ĕ
І ı і	i	Ю ю	ju
К к	k	Ꙗ ꙗ	ja
Л л	l	Ѥ ѥ	je
М м	m	Ѧ ѧ	ę
Н н	n	Ѫ ѫ	ą
О о	o	Ѩ ѩ	ję
П п	p	Ѭ ѭ	ją
Р р	r	Ѯ ѯ	ks
С с	s	Ѱ ѱ	ps
Т т	t	Ѳ ѳ	θ
Ѹ ѹ	u	Ѵ ѵ	ü
Ф ф	f		

books with sacred words written in these styles, but transformed them into magnificent works of art, producing lavish illuminated manuscripts. Then, with the ensuing age of global European exploration and colonization, the Latin script was spread around the world.

Non-Latin scripts in Europe

The Etruscan writing system was by no means the only offspring of the Greek alphabet. In Asia Minor, the Phrygians had adopted the Greek system in the eighth century BC, and distinct Lydian and Lycian alphabets, based upon the Greek, were in use in the fifth and fourth centuries BC. The Greek script had also been adapted for the alphabetic spelling of the Egyptian language by as early as the first century AD, the standard form of this Coptic alphabet being built from 24 Greek characters plus seven symbols from demotic, which Coptic supplanted.

In the ninth century AD, a group of Greek missionaries led by St. Cyril and St. Methodius went to spread their faith among the Slavs of southern Europe. The Slavs were converted to Christianity, and Cyril and Methodius prepared a translation of the Bible in the language now called Old Church Slavonic. Two alphabetic scripts were used by the early Slavic Christians, Cyrillic and Glagolitic. Early Slavic tradition credits St. Cyril with the development of a Slavic alphabet, and Cyrillic bears his name. The tradition is ambiguous, however, and there is disagreement among scholars as to which of the scripts was the creation of Cyril. With its 43 characters, the Cyrillic script was clearly based upon the Greek alphabet, but with many supplementary symbols added.

The early Cyrillic script evolved into the alphabets of many of the modern Slavic languages, such as Russian, Ukrainian, Bulgarian, and Serbian, while in those Slavic areas in which the leading sect of Christianity is the Roman Catholic Church, such as the Czech Republic,

RUSSIAN		
Capitals	**Lower Case**	**Transliteration**
А	а	a
Б	б	b
В	в	v
Г	г	g
Д	д	d
Е	е	e
Ё	ё	ë
Ж	ж	ž
З	з	z
И	и	i
Й	й	j
К	к	k
Л	л	l
М	м	m
Н	н	n
О	о	o
П	п	p
Р	р	r
С	с	s
Т	т	t
У	у	u
Ф	ф	f
Х	х	x
Ц	ц	c
Ч	ч	č
Ш	ш	
Щ	щ	
Ь	ь	"
Ы	ы	y
Ь	ь	'
Э	э	e
Ю	ю	ju
Я	я	ja

Left: The form of the Cyrillic script which is now used for recording Russian is a descendant of the Old Church Slavonic writing system. Russian Cyrillic has been and is still used for spelling various non-Slavic languages which were drawn into the realm of Soviet influence.

ARMENIAN

Symbol		Transliteration
Ա	ա	a
Բ	բ	b
Գ	գ	g
Դ	դ	d
Ե	ե	e
Զ	զ	z
Է	է	ē
Ը	ը	ə
Թ	թ	t'
Ժ	ժ	ž
Ի	ի	i
Լ	լ	l
Խ	խ	ch
Ծ	ծ	ts
Կ	կ	k
Հ	հ	h
Ձ	ձ	j
Ղ	ղ	ł
Ճ	ճ	č
Մ	մ	m
Յ	յ	y
Ն	ն	n
Շ	շ	š
Ո	ո	o
Չ	չ	č'
Պ	պ	p
Ջ	ջ	ǰ
Ռ	ռ	ř
Ս	ս	s
Վ	վ	v
Տ	տ	t
Ր	ր	r
Ց	ց	ts'
Ւ	ւ	w
Փ	փ	p'
Ք	ք	k'

GEORGIAN

Symbol	Transliteration
ა	a
ბ	b
გ	g
დ	d
ე	e
ვ	v
ზ	z
თ	t
ი	i
კ	ḳ
ლ	l
მ	m
ნ	n
ო	o
პ	ṗ
ჟ	ž
რ	r
ს	s
ტ	ṭ
უ	u
ფ	p
ქ	k
ღ	γ
ყ	q
შ	š
ჩ	č
ც	ts
ძ	dz
წ	ṭs
ჭ	č
ხ	χ
ჯ	j
ჰ	h

Far left: *The origin of the Armenian alphabet is traditionally assigned to the early fifth century AD and its inventor is identified as St. Mesrop, who is said to have been assisted by St. Sahak.*

Left: *St. Mesrop is also credited with designing the Georgian writing system. An alternative tradition attributes this version of the script called Mkhedruli to the Georgian king, P'arnavaz.*

Above: *St. Luke is portrayed penning his Gospel in this illumination from an eleventh-century Biblical manuscript produced at the monastery of Echternach (Luxembourg). The Gospel writer holds a quill and a penknife, tools of the medieval scribe.*

Slovakia, Poland, and Croatia, the Latin alphabet is used. Before the dissolution of the Soviet Union, when the influence of Russian language and culture was widespread, the Russian variety of Cyrillic was adapted for writing many non-Slavic, and even non-Indo-European languages, including Kurdish, Chechen (Caucasian), Chuvash, Mongolian, and Yuit (an Eskimo language).

The characters of the Glagolitic script are not so easily matched with those of a pre-existing writing system. Many scholars believe Glagolitic to have been developed prior to Cyrillic and contend that, as with Cyrillic, the Greek alphabet provided the model. The Georgian and various Semitic scripts are among other writing systems which have been conjectured to have exerted influence in the development of this Slavic alphabet. Glagolitic has survived in modern times only as the liturgical script of a very few Roman Catholic Slavs in southern Europe.

Two other alphabets used to record languages of Europe are attributed to a saint: St. Mesrop is traditionally identified as the inventor of both the Armenian and Georgian scripts (*see left*). He is said to have begun designing a writing system for the Armenian Christians in 406 AD. The source of this script is uncertain, with the Aramaic and Iranian Pahlavi systems proposed as candidates, and the presence of vowel characters suggesting a Greek derivation.

If St. Mesrop did invent the Georgian alphabet, he was perhaps responsible only for Khutsuri, the ecclesiastical script. Some scholars detect similarities between Khutsuri and Armenian

script, though the former preserves an Aramaic letter-order not found in the latter, which clearly suggests that Aramaic, or Syriac, played some role. Again, vowel characters also betray a Greek template. The Georgian script commonly used today developed from the earlier Mkhedruli system, the so-called script of warriors. The chronology of its development relative to Khutsuri is another matter of disagreement.

INDIA

The earliest writing of India was left by the people of the Indus Valley civilization (2500–1750 BC); their script is poorly understood, though recent advances have been claimed. From the third century BC, however, Indic writing of a quite different sort is well attested. There were two writing systems in use by this period: Kharoshthi and Brahmī. The Kharoshthi, or Bactrian, is believed to have developed from the Aramaic consonantal script of the Persian Empire. The origin of Brahmī is probably the same, though on

Right: *The earliest Indus Valley settlements were agricultural, but from 2500–1750 BC the Indus Valley was the focus of a flourishing civilization.*

DEVANAGARI

Vowel Symbols

अ	आ	इ	ई	उ	ऊ	ऋ	ॠ	ऌ	ए	ऐ	ओ	औ
a	ā	i	ī	u	ū	ŕ	ȓ	ḷ	e	ai	o	au

Consonant + Vowel Symbols

क	ख	ग	घ	ङ			ह	:
ka	kha	ga	gha	nga			ha	ḥ
च	छ	ज	झ	ञ	य		श	
ca	cha	ja	jha	ña	ya		śa	
ट	ठ	ड	ढ	ण	र		ष	
ṭa	ṭha	ḍa	ḍha	ṇa	ra	ḷa	ṣa	
त	थ	द	ध	न	ल		स	
ta	tha	da	dha	na	la		sa	
प	फ	ब	भ	म	व			
pa	pha	ba	bha	ma	va			

Sample Vowel Diacritics

का	की	कु
kā	kī	ku

Left: *Sanskrit, one of the earliest recorded Indo-European languages, is written with the syllabic script called Devanagari (meaning "script of the city of the gods"). Each of the basic consonant + vowel symbols has the value of consonant + a. The vowel value of basic CV symbols can be modified by the addition of a diacritic stroke.*

Below: *A women's cooperative in Sri Lanka producing a newspaper. Sinhalese script appears to have been influenced by both North and South Indian writing systems.*

this point there is less agreement; it is undoubtedly of Semitic origin, however. Both of these scripts were used for recording the edicts of the Maurya prince Ashoka between approximately 257 and 235 BC. The Kharoshthi system remained in use until about the fifth century AD. Brahmī appears to be the parent of all of the many modern scripts of India, recording both Indo-Aryan and Dravidian languages. Roughly following this linguistic bifurcation, the writing systems of India are divided into a North and a South branch. Among the North Indian group are the scripts of Devanagari, Bengali, Gujarati, Gurmukhi, and Oriya. The unusual, distinctive appearance of the characters of the Oriya script, reminiscent of so many melted light bulbs, is said to be a consequence of the material on which the script was written during an early period. The

ORIYA

Vowel Symbols

ଅ	ଆ	ଇ	ଈ	ଉ	ଊ	ଋ	ଌ
a	ā	i	ī	u	ū	ru	rū

ୠ	ଏ	ଐ	ଓ	ଔ	ଂ	ଃ
lu	ē	ai	ō	au	an	a'

Consonant + Vowel Symbols

କ	ଖ	ଗ	ଘ	ଙ
ka	kha	ga	gha	nga

ଚ	ଛ	ଜ	ଝ	ଞ
ca	cha	ja	jha	ña

ଟ	ଠ	ଡ	ଢ	ଣ
ṭa	ṭha	ḍa	ḍha	ṇa

ତ	ଥ	ଦ	ଧ	ନ
ta	tha	da	dha	na

ପ	ଫ	ବ	ଭ	ମ
pa	pha	ba	bha	ma

ଯ	ର	ଲ	ଳ	ଵ
(ja)	ra	la	ḷa	wa

ଶ	ଷ	ସ	ହ	କ୍ଷ
śa	ṣa	sa	ha	khya

KANNADA

Vowel Symbols

ಅ	ಆ	ಇ	ಈ	ಉ	ಊ	ಋ
a	ā	i	ī	u	ū	ru

ಎ	ಏ	ಐ	ಒ	ಓ	ಔ
e	ē	ai	o	ō	au

Consonant + Vowel Symbols

ಕ	ಖ	ಗ	ಘ	ಙ
ka	kha	ga	gha	nga

ಚ	ಛ	ಜ	ಝ	ಞ
ca	cha	ja	jha	nya

ಟ	ಠ	ಡ	ಢ	ಣ
ṭa	ṭha	ḍa	ḍha	ṇa

ತ	ಥ	ದ	ಧ	ನ
ta	tha	da	dha	na

ಪ	ಫ	ಬ	ಭ	ಮ
pa	pha	ba	bha	ma

ಯ	ರ	ಲ	ವ
ya	ra	la	va

ಶ	ಷ	ಸ	ಹ	ಳ
śa	ṣa	sa	ha	la

Far left: Oriya is an Indo-Aryan language of eastern India, closely related to Bengali. The symbols of this script have a conspicuously curved dome, a feature which is attributed to the early practice of writing Oriya on palm leaves which were easily split by horizontal scoring.

Left: While the syllabic writing system of Kannada shares common roots with the Devanagari and Oriya scripts, the language of Kannada, spoken in southwestern India, belongs to the Dravidian family.

long slender palm leaves used were easily split by horizontal strokes, so rounded characters were more generally favored. The South Indian group of writing systems includes those of Tamil, Kannada, Telugu, and Malayalam. On the island nation of Sri Lanka, the Sinhalese script appears to have developed under the influence of both North and South Indian groups.

Kharoshthi, Brahmī, and its offspring are syllabic writing systems. Devanagari is the script of Sanskrit, the ancient and sacred language of India, and is also used for various modern languages such as Hindi. Its fundamental

characters are of two types, V and CV. The value of CV characters alone is always consonant + *a*. In order to mark a CV symbol as representing some vowel other than a, a diacritic is added, as illustrated by the characters for *kā*, *kī*, *ku* in the table (*left*). To represent a sequence of two or more consonants, ligatures are used, that is, composite symbols created by actually combining various CV characters into a single form, usually with modification of the appearance of some of the characters being combined. In this way, symbols become available of the type CCV (such as *kra* and *dya*), CCCV and so on—even

Writing Systems

SINHALESE

Vowel Symbols

අ	ආ	ඇ	ඈ	ඉ	ඊ	උ	ඌ
a	ā	æ	ǣ	i	ī	u	ū

ඍ	එ	ඒ	ඓ	ඔ	ඕ	ඖ
ri	e	ē	ai	o	ō	au

Consonant and Vowel Symbols

ක	ඛ	ග	ඝ	ඞ
ka	kha	ga	gha	nga

ච	ඡ	ජ	ඣ	ඤ
ca	cha	ja	jha	ña

ට	ඨ	ඩ	ඪ	ණ
ṭa	ṭha	ḍa	ḍha	ṇa

ත	ථ	ද	ධ	න
ta	tha	da	dha	na

ප	ඵ	බ	භ	ම
pa	pha	ba	bha	ma

ය	ර	ල	ව
ya	ra	la	va

ශ	ෂ	ස	හ	ළ
śa	ṣa	sa	ha	la

TIBETAN

Consonant and Vowel Symbols

ka	kha	ga	nga
ca	cha	ja	ña
ṭa	ṭha	ḍa	ṇa
ta	tha	da	na
pa	pha	ba	ma
tsa	tsha	dsa	
ya	ra	la	wa
ša	sa	ṣa	ža
ha	'a	a	za

Ligatured Symbols

| kra |
| lca |
| nra |
| sba |
| rtsva |
| bya |
| hra |

Vowel Diacritics

| ki | ku |
| ke | ko |

The Tibetan script is of Indic origin and, like Indic scripts, has basic symbols representing consonant + vowel sequences. The Tibetan system, however, has only a single vowel character, a. Other individual vowels are indicated by the use of diacritics with the a symbol.

Above: *Sinhalese is the Indo-Aryan language of the island of Sri Lanka. A script was probably introduced into Sri Lanka from northern India by the third century BC but was subsequently influenced by South Indian writing.*

CCCCCV as in *rtsnya*. A consonant occurring at the end of a word is written using the appropriate consonant + *a* symbol, accompanied by a sublinear diacritic called a *virama* which indicates that the *a* of the CV symbol is not to be read. Some scholars have suggested that Devanagari and other Indian scripts are not truly syllabic because they possess a means for adjusting both the consonant and vowel values of the basic CV symbols. The value of the fundamental symbols of these scripts (including those symbols which are compounded to produce ligatures) is, however, plainly syllabic; they are better seen as syllabaries which operate more economically than those with distinct symbols for all expressed combinations of consonants and vowels.

CENTRAL AND EAST ASIA

The writing systems of India, like their Semitic predecessor, were exported far from home. Tibetan script, which had its origin in the seventh century AD, is based upon an early North Indian writing system. The spelling practices are similar to those described above for Devanagari, one difference being that Tibetan has only a single V character, which represents *a*. Several symbols

196

CAMBODIAN

Vowel Symbols

ā	i	ī	u	ū	ri	rī

lī	e	ai	o	ao	au

Consonant and Vowel Symbols

ka	kha	ko	kho	ngo
ca	cha	co	cho	ño
da	tha	do	tho	no
ta	tha	to	tho	no
ba	pha	po	pho	mo
yo	ro	lo	wo	
sa	ha	la		

Vowel Diacritics

Symbol	Transliteration	
	1st Series	2nd Series
CV	ā	ie
CV	e	i
CV	ei	ī
CV	e	i
CV	ei	ī
CV	o	u
CV	ou	ū
CV	ue	ue
CV	ae	ē
CV	ie	ie
CV	ie	ie
CV	ei	i
CV	ae	ē
CV	ai	ī
CV	ao	ō
CV	au	iu

Above: *Cambodian, or Khmer, belongs to the Austro-Asiatic family of languages. The Cambodian writing system, developed from a Brahmī script. Like other writing systems derived from Brahmī, the Cambodian system is a syllabary with basic consonant + vowel symbols. However, in the case of the Cambodian script, the vowel value of the basic CV symbols shows variation: some symbols have an a vowel (as in Devanagari, Sinhalese, Tibetan, and so forth), but others have an o vowel. The former symbols are said to belong to the "first series," the latter to the "second series." To indicate that a consonant + vowel symbol has a vowel value other than a or o, diacritic strokes are used in conjunction with the symbol.*

Right: *The writing system of Lao descends from Indic Brahmī. The vowel of the basic consonant + vowel symbols of Lao is o and the script has no independent vowel symbols. To write individual vowels, diacritics are used in conjunction with the symbol 'o.*

LAO

Consonant and Vowel Symbols

ko	kho	kho	ngo	cho	so	so
nyo	do	to	tho	tho	no	bo
po	pho	fo	pho	fo	mo	yo
ro	lo	wo	ho	'o	ho	

THAI

Consonants

Mid	High		Low			
ก	บ	ข	ค	ฅ	ฆ	ง
ko	kho	kho	kho	kho	kho	ngo
จ	ฉ		ซ	ฌ	ฌ	ญ
co	cho		so	cho	cho	yo
ฎ ฏ	ฐ		ฑ		ฒ	ณ
do to	tho		tho		tho	no
ด ต	ถ		ท		ธ	น
do to	tho		tho		tho	no
บ ป	ผ	ฝ	พ	ฟ	ภ	ม
bo po	pho	fo	pho	fo	pho	mo

Low

ย	ร	ล	ว
yo	ro	lo	wo

High

ศ	ษ	ส
so	so	so

High	Low	Mid	Low
ห	ฬ	อ	ฮ
ho	lo	'o	ho

Vowel Diacritics

cv	cv ะ	cv	cv า	cv
	a	a	ā	i
cv	cv	cv	cv	cv
ī	u	ū	u	ū
เ cv ะ	เ cv	เ cv	แ cv ะ	แ cv
e	ē	e	e	ē
โ cv ะ	โ cv	เ cv าะ	cv อ
o	ō	o	am
เ cv	ไ cv	เ cv า
ai	ai	au

Above: Thai script was probably based upon that of Cambodian, and so is ultimately also of Brahm origin. As with the script of Lao, the basic consonant + vowel symbols have an o vowel value, and there are no independent vowel symbols (to write a single vowel, as in Lao, vowel diacritics are used together with the symbol 'o), Thai is a tone language and the variant forms of the basic consonant + vowel symbols are used to distinguish mid, high, and low tone classes.

were added for sounds not occurring in Indic, and superfluous ones were omitted. While Tibetan spelling has remained quite conservative, the sounds of Tibetan have changed considerably since the script's inception; consequently, its spelling no longer closely fits its pronunciation.

Also descended from Indian scripts are the writing systems of Cambodian (Khmer), Lao, Thai, and Burmese. In both the Thai and Burmese systems, means have been devised for representing tones; Tibetan is also a tone language, but the variety of Tibetan represented by the writing system is probably not tonal. The traditional writing system of the Javanese is descended from the early Kavi script of Java, known from at least the eighth century AD and itself developed from an Indic script. The Javanese script, in turn, is the likely source of the Batak system of Sumatra and the Buginese of Celebes.

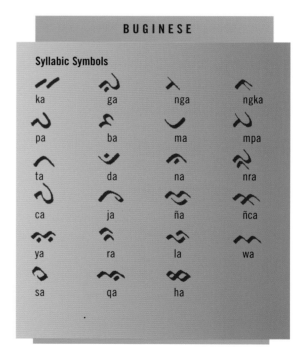

BUGINESE

Syllabic Symbols

ka	ga	nga	ngka
pa	ba	ma	mpa
ta	da	na	nra
ca	ja	ña	ñca
ya	ra	la	wa
sa	qa	ha	

JAVANESE

Consonant and Vowel Symbols

Aksara Jawa	Aksara Pasangan	Transliteration
		ha
		na
		ča
		ra
		ka
		da
		ta
		sa
		wa
		la
		pa
		da
		ja
		ja
		ña
		ma
		ga
		ba
		ta
		nga

Left: *The Javanese syllabic script, with its roots in Indic writing, consists of basic consonant + a-vowel symbols. These are the characters listed beneath the heading Aksara Jawa. The corresponding Aksara Pasangan characters are used in conjunction with the basic CV symbols to spell consonant sequences.*

BATAK

Vowel Symbols

Symbol	Transliteration
	a
	i
	u

Consonant and Vowel Symbols

Symbol	Transliteration	Symbol	Transliteration
	ha		ga
	ma		dya
	na		da
	ra		nga
	ta		ba
	sa		wa
	pa		ya
	la		ña

Vowel Diacritics

Symbol	Transliteration
	i
	u
	o
	e

Right: *The Batak script of Sumatra is believed to have developed from the early Kavi writing system. The script has vowel and consonant + a symbols. The vowel value of the basic CV characters can be adjusted with vowel "diacritics."*

Left: *The writing system of the Buginese language of Celebes is probably likewise descended from Kavi. The CV symbol qa is also used for writing the vowel a at the beginning of a word. Vowel diacritics are used in conjunction with this symbol for writing other word-initial vowels and for changing the vowel value of the basic syllabic symbols.*

EVOLUTION OF CHINESE WRITING

Modern Pronunciation/ Meaning	Oracle bone form (Shang Dynasty)	Greater Seal (W. Chou)	Lesser Seal (E. Chou-Han)	Modern Form (3rd century AD onwards)
Objects				
jen / man				
nü / woman				
erh / ear				
yü / fish				
jih / sun				
yueh / moon				
yü / rain				
ting / cauldron				
ching / well				
Relationships				
shang / above				
hsia / below				

CHINESE SCRIPT

Eight full-form printed characters

中	海	茶	飯
zhōng	hǎi	chá	fàn
middle	sea	tea	food

錢	龍	聞	識
qián	lóng	wén	shí
money	dragon	hear	know

The same characters in standard written form

中	海	茶	飯
zhōng	hǎi	chá	fàn

錢	龍	聞	識
qián	lóng	wén	shí

CHINA

Linear etchings occur on Chinese pots dated to the fifth millennium BC. There is no indication, however, that such marks are symbols of a script. The advent of Chinese writing can be dated to the early second millennium BC, and it appears to have developed independently, without influence from a Near Eastern or Indus Valley system.

The earliest known form of Chinese writing occurs on oracle bones which have survived

Left: A typical Chinese character combines a radical, indicating some aspect of the word's meaning, with a phonetic clue to the pronunciation of the word. Thus the character for "hear" incorporates the "ear" as a radical, the rest of the character serving as a phonetic cue. Handwritten characters may be written in more or less cursive fashion, reaching an extreme in calligraphy where impressionistic distortions of the printed forms are appreciated as art.

Left: *Chinese characters began as pictograms, gradually becoming logograms as they became more stylized and lost their pictorial element. Four stages of this development are shown here. Whereas the oracle bone symbols for "fish" and "moon" are easily recognized, few if any of the modern forms are so transparent that their meaning can be guessed without knowledge of the language.*

Below: *Among the earliest examples of Chinese writing are the oracle bone inscriptions. Dating from the early Shang dynasty (1240-1181 BC), this example lists a number of animals to be sacrificed as part of a divination rite.*

from the Shang dynasty of the mid to late second millennium BC. These are usually tortoise shells or bovine scapulas bearing carved inscriptions which were sometimes then painted. The oracle bones were heated until they cracked, and the cracks then used to determine the divination.

The fundamental principles of the Chinese writing system are already displayed in these the earliest of Chinese documents. Chinese writing, like the early Sumerian script, is logographic and pictographic. Homophonous logographic characters (symbols for words which sound alike but have different meanings) were derived by application of the rebus principle. As homophonous words are particularly common in the Chinese language, this rebus technique enjoyed extensive use. In early Chinese writing, rebus spelling was not systematic, resulting in various spellings of a single word, but in time such homophonous spellings were regularized. However, even in the writing of the Shang dynasty, a means had already been developed for making certain homophonous spellings less ambiguous; as in both Mesopotamia and Egypt, a semantic tag was used to mark the meaning of a logographic character. Unlike the determinatives of both Mesopotamian and Egyptian, the semantic tags of the early Chinese scribes were actually integrated into the character with which they were used, producing a compound character or *xie-sheng*. Such compound logograms thus consist of a phonetic component and a semantic component; this became a highly productive method of character formation, with 90 percent of modern Chinese characters being of this type. Another method of producing compound characters, also in use during the Shang dynasty, involved simply the writing together of individual logograms (that is, the combining of semantic components); these are called *hui yi* characters. For example, the symbols for "sun" and "moon" were compounded to produce the character meaning "bright."

JAPANESE AND KOREAN

The Chinese script was adapted by Japanese-speakers for writing their own language. Japanese tradition preserves accounts of Korean scholars

JAPANESE

Hiragana

あ	か	さ	た	な	は	ま	や	ら	わ	ん
a	ka	sa	ta	na	ha	ma	ya	ra	wa	n
い	き	し	ち	に	ひ	み		り		
i	ki	shi	chi	ni	hi	mi		ri		
う	く	す	つ	ぬ	ふ	む		る		
u	ku	su	tsu	nu	fu	mu		ru		
え	け	せ	て	ね	へ	め	ゆ	れ		
e	ke	se	te	ne	he	me	yu	re		
お	こ	そ	と	の	ほ	も	よ	ろ	を	
o	ko	so	to	no	ho	mo	yo	ro	wo	

Katakana

ア	カ	サ	タ	ナ	ハ	マ	ヤ	ラ	ワ	ン
a	ka	sa	ta	na	ha	ma	ya	ra	wa	n
イ	キ	シ	チ	ニ	ヒ	ミ		リ		
i	ki	shi	chi	ni	hi	mi		ri		
ウ	ク	ス	ツ	ヌ	フ	ム		ル		
u	ku	su	tsu	nu	fu	mu		ru		
エ	ケ	セ	テ	ネ	ヘ	メ	ユ	レ		
e	ke	se	te	ne	he	me	yu	re		
オ	コ	ソ	ト	ノ	ホ	モ	ヨ	ロ	ヲ	
o	ko	so	to	no	ho	mo	yo	ro	wo	

ここは
不忍通り
Shinobazu dōri Ave.
千駄木2-42

Below: *A little more than 150 years after Ramkhamhaeng is said to have devised the Thai script, yet another East Asian king developed a system for recording his language. The Korean king Sejong is credited with designing what has been called the world's most perfect writing system. The Han'gul script is fundamentally alphabetic, but consonant and vowel characters are typically written together as a syllabic unit.*

Below: *Not all the scripts of East Asia are derived from Chinese and Indic writing systems. The Mongolian script traces its roots to the Syriac form of Aramaic. Symbols take different forms, depending upon whether they occur at the beginning of a word, in the middle, or at the end.*

KOREAN

Symbol	Translit.	Symbol	Translit.
	i		k
	e		n
	æ		t
	ü		l
	ö		m
	ŭ		p
	ə		s
	a		ng
	u		č
	o		čh
	ya		kh
	yæ		th
	yə		ph
	ye		h
	yo		k'
	yu		t'
	wa		p'
	wæ		s'
	wə		c'
	we		
	ŭi		

MONGOLIAN

Initial symbol	Medial symbol	Final symbol	Translit.
			a
			e
			i
			o
			u
			ö
			ü
			n
			q
			g
			k
			g
			p
			b
			m
			l
			r
			t
			d
			y
			j
			č
			s
			š
			w

introducing Chinese script to the island of Japan in the third or fifth century AD. The earliest Japanese writing now known is dated to the eighth century. In the earliest materials, the writing consists solely of Chinese logographic symbols, though perhaps they were read as Japanese words. Owing to significant grammatical differences between the two languages (such as the occurrence in Japanese of many suffixes and grammatical particles), some Chinese logograms came to be used phonetically to represent individual Japanese syllables—a process similar to the one displayed in the development of Sumerian writing.

By the ninth century, two Japanese syllabaries had developed: *kata-kana* was devised for use alongside Chinese characters (the name means "side-*kana*"); *hira-gana*, with a notably more cursive appearance, could be used without accompanying Chinese symbols. In modern Japanese writing, these two syllabic scripts continue to be employed, as do Chinese logograms, called *kanji*. *Kanji* are normally used for writing nouns, verbs, and adjectives, *hira-gana* for spelling suffixes and grammatical particles, and *kata-kana* for foreign loan words and emphasis. Japanese writing is commonly cited as the most complex of all current writing systems across the world.

Japanese is sometimes also written in the Latin alphabet with the system called *romaji*. *Romaji* is used, for example, for writing acronyms and in public areas (on maps, signposts, and information boards) for the assistance of tourists. In the nineteenth and twentieth centuries, there have been unsuccessful attempts to institute *romaji* as the regular form of Japanese writing.

According to Korean tradition, the Chinese writing system was brought to Korea in the third century AD. As with Japanese, the writing of Korean with the Chinese script is problematic, given the appreciable grammatical differences between the two languages; nevertheless, Korean was written in this way for hundreds of years. This situation was remedied from the early fifteenth century with the creation of the Korean alphabet, *Han'gul*, traditionally credited to the Korean king Sejong. *Han'gul* consists of 40 characters and has been claimed to be the most phonetically efficient of the world's writing systems. Chinese characters, however, are still used in South Korean script to spell Chinese loan words.

The Mongolian writing system, which is written in left-to-right vertical columns, appears to have developed in the fourteenth century AD. It was derived from the Uighur script, the system of the Turkic people of that name, which in turn has its roots in Aramaic. Still earlier, by the seventh century AD, an early Turkic language of central Asia was being written in Turkic runic script, the origin of which is still uncertain.

THE NEW WORLD

Various scripts developed among the native peoples of the New World. In Mesoamerica, the Maya people independently developed a system which is strikingly reminiscent of the scripts of ancient Mesopotamia, Egypt, and China, and is attested to about AD 300 (*see table opposite*).

The Mayan script is still in the process of being deciphered, although important gains have been made in recent years. It is now clear that it uses more than a single type of character. Many of the Mayan symbols, or glyphs, are logographic. As in other systems, a single logogram came to be used to represent homophonous words by application of the rebus principle. Syllabic symbols also make up part of the glyph inventory. These phonetic symbols are used to spell individual words and affixes (prefixes and suffixes) syllabically, and are also conjoined with logograms as phonetic complements, just as syllabic symbols are in Mesopotamia and Egypt. In addition, glyphs are similarly used as determinatives, semantic tags which help clarify ambiguous readings.

Among later writing systems used by native peoples of North America, one of the most important is the Cherokee syllabary, appearing in the 1820s (*see page 206*). The inventor of this script, a Cherokee by the name of Sequoya, had encountered English writing and originally decided to devise a logographic script for the spelling of his own language. This enterprise was jettisoned, however, in favor of a syllabic script. The resulting writing system consisted of 85 syllabic symbols, many of which are based on Latin letters, but with entirely different values.

Another syllabic script devised for spelling a native American language is the Cree syllabary (*see page 207*). In this case, however, the designer of the script was not native American, but an English missionary named James Evans. By 1833 Biblical texts were translated using this script into the Algonquian language of Cree. The script consists fundamentally of 12 sets of characters, the syllabic symbols which compose each set varying from one another by spatial orientation. Somewhat different forms are used in final position (at the end of a word).

Right: *This table displays consonant + vowel symbols of the Mayan script. This script, developed independently by the Maya people in Mesoamerica in about AD 300, is still in the process of being deciphered.*

MAYAN

Translit.	a	e	i	o	u
b					
ch					
ch'					
h					
c					
k					
l					
m					
n					
p					
s					
t					
tz					
dz					
u					
x					
y					

DIRECTION OF WRITING

It is usually the case that at any given time a writing system will be characterized by a particular direction of writing, though variability does occur, and within the history of a script the direction of writing may change. Early Sumerian writing shows a somewhat random distribution of symbols, with, however, a general right-to-left progression across the tablet. By the beginning of the second millennium BC the direction of writing had shifted and Sumerian scribes were writing in horizontal lines running left-to-right. In addition, the orientation of Sumerian symbols had rotated 90 degrees counterclockwise. Later Mesopotamian cuneiform scripts maintained the left-to-right direction.

The overall direction of Egyptian hieroglyphic writing was commonly right-to-left, though the reverse order did also occur. Writing may proceed in vertical columns from top to bottom, with columns progressing to the left (and less commonly to the right), or in horizontal rows. For example, Egyptian demotic script is written from right-to-left in horizontal rows.

The Proto-Canaanite script, which had its roots in the Egyptian system, used a variety of directions: vertical, horizontal, right-to-left, left-to-right, and boustrophedon. The latter term (meaning "as the ox turns," referring to

Right: In 1821 Sequoya, a Cherokee from North Carolina created a phonetic writing system for his Iroquoian language. The system is primarily a syllabry, though symbols with consonantal value also occur. Within a few years after its invention, a high level of literacy had been achieved within the Cherokee community.

CHEROKEE

Syllabary

a	e	i	o	u	v
ga	ge	gi	go	gu	gv
ka					
ha	he	hi	ho	hu	hv
la	le	li	lo	lu	lv
ma	me	mi	mo	mu	
na	ne	ni	no	nu	nv
hna					
nah					
qua	que	qui	quo	quu	quv
sa	se	si	so	su	sv
s					
da	de	di	do	du	dv
ta	te	ti			
tla	tle	tli	tlo	tlu	tlv
dla					
tsa	tse	tsi	tso	tsu	tsv
wa	we	wi	wo	wu	wv
ya	ye	yi	yo	yu	yv

plowing) describes written lines which alternate in direction—for example, right-to-left, left-to-right, right-to-left, and so on. Boustrophedon direction occurs among other scripts as well, such as Hieroglyphic Luvian, the Cypriot syllabary, and the Greek alphabet. The offspring of Proto-Canaanite, Phoenician and Aramaic, and many of the scripts descended from them, are written horizontally from right-to-left.

Greek scripts display a variety of directions. The Mycenaean Linear B is left-to-right. The Greek Cypriot syllabary scripts are mostly right-to-left, with some left-to-right, and others boustrophedon. Early Greek alphabetic writing also shows all three patterns, but left-to-right predominates and continues in its descendants: Etruscan, Latin, Coptic, Cyrillic, and so forth.

Writing in vertical columns is not unique to Egyptian and Proto-Canaanite. Chinese is traditionally written in columns from top-to-bottom, with columns proceeding right-to-left. Mongolian writing is also from top-to-bottom, but with the columns left-to-right. The Batak script is vertical but from bottom-to-top with columns proceeding left-to-right.

Right: In the early nineteenth century James Evans designed a script for writing a Cree dialect of western Canada. This was adapted for other native languages of North America including Choctaw, Chippewa, and Slave. Fundamentally a syllabary, the script is also able to spell single consonants at the end of a word.

CREE

Vowel Symbols

ē	i	o	a

Consonant and Vowel Symbols				**Final Consonant Symbols**
pē	pi	po	pa	p
tē	ti	to	ta	t
čē	či	čo	ča	č
kē	ki	ko	ka	k
mē	mi	mo	ma	m
nē	ni	no	na	n
lē	li	lo	la	l
sē	si	so	sa	s
yē	yi	yo	ya	y
rē	ri	ro	ra	r
vē	vi	vo	va	v
zē	zi	zo	za	z
fē	fi	fo	fa	f

Epilogue: Language Loss and Revival

The diversity of the world's languages is at least as threatened as that of its plant and animal species. The passing of traditional ways of life and the economic lure of major languages is driving local tongues toward extinction. But today dying languages are at least being recorded for posterity, and much work is underway to reverse their decline; the revival of Hebrew offers an inspiring success story.

Red Thundercloud, who died in January 1996, was the last speaker of the Sioux language, Catawba. He recorded examples of the language for the Simithsonian Museum.

As the twentieth century drew to a close it became commonplace to hear of the extinction of yet another language. When Red Thundercloud, the last speaker of Catawba, died in January 1996, the world heard, and the *Times* of London took note, because he had consciously made himself the last representative of this particular Siouxan language, recording hunting songs and hymns for posterity. He became something of a celebrity, like Ishi, the last speaker of Yahi, who had lived in hiding in northern California after the destruction of his tribe. Edward Sapir, the leading specialist in native American languages of the time, elicited aspects of his language and myths, but contact with American society led to Ishi's death from tuberculosis. More often the last speakers die in obscurity, and the languages with them.

The loss of languages parallels the extinction of animal and plant species in many respects. In many parts of the world, such as the Amazon region, destruction and industrial exploitation of the natural habitat lead to a breakdown of the communities in which minority languages survive. Just as we do not know what natural medicines lie within vanishing rainforests, we do not know what wisdom is recorded in the grammar and vocabulary, poetry and stories of dying languages, many of which have vanished without being studied in depth. At the current rate of extinction, it has been estimated that the current century will see as many as 90 percent of the world's languages become extinct or moribund (the estimate for plant and animal species is 50 percent). The environmental problem is now widely seen as urgent, and the loss of language diversity is increasingly seen in the same light.

HOW AND WHY LANGUAGES DIE

Languages have always been eclipsed and extinguished, but recent centuries have seen an acceleration of the process. Between 1490 and 2000 around half the world's languages died out. Allowing for the problems involved in distinguishing languages from dialects, a maximum of 10–15,000 languages would have been spoken at the point of greatest linguistic diversity.

There are several ways in which languages become extinct; the native Tasmanians were hunted and removed from their habitat, while some native American tribes suffered a similar fate as the West was settled. More often, tribes have succumbed to disease and western plagues— alcoholism is endemic in some North American Indian populations and cocaine addiction is now spreading in Amazonian villages. As tribal groups disappear or are wiped out, their languages naturally disappear with them.

The main cause of extinction, however, is less dramatic and perhaps more insidious. Language shift occurs where speakers adopt the language of the majority, of prestige, or of wealth. Hispanic and other immigrants to the United States

Left: Some two million native people once occupied the vast area of the Amazonian rainforest; today only about 50,000 survive. With the disappearance of traditional communities, languages, folklore, and an unrivaled knowledge of the potential of the rainforest are also irretrievably lost.

exemplify this process, which takes place over only three generations. The first generation is monolingual and learns little of the dominant language. The second generation becomes bilingual, learning the ancestral language from their parents and the dominant language from the surrounding community. The third generation learns only the dominant language both at home and in the community. It may be that in some such cases loss is inevitable, but languages at least deserve a dignified death. In some Asian American families children cannot communicate with their grandparents, because they know only English and their grandparents only Chinese, Korean, or Vietnamese. Amy Tan's novel, *The Joy Luck Club*, turns on the clash of generations and failure of understanding between Chinese mothers and their Chinese-American daughters. Equally sad is the case of grown-up third generation children who blame their parents for not transmitting their ancestral language to them: if they begin re-learning such languages in adulthood, they will at best become second-language speakers.

In the later stages of shift we find "semi-speakers," who may understand the language well but do not speak it, or speak it in a way which mixes it with the dominant language, and which the older generation finds imperfect. As one of the last speakers of the Australian language Dyirbal commented: "That Phyllis, she don't talk Guwal right. She mixes up the English. She got it wrong." Many children of Cantonese parents raised in Canada speak Cantonese without the tones. Their vocabulary is replaced by words from the dominant language, and their grammar becomes simplified. As the vocabulary becomes impoverished, the meanings of words become generalized. Hungarian, for example, like many languages, distinguishes between old

Above: *Like the Chinese, Korean immigrants to the United States have formed close-knit communities where their language, food, and other aspects of their culture can be preserved. Thriving Koreatowns have developed in cities such as New York and Los Angeles.*

people (*öreg*) and old things (*régi*), but to shifting semi-speakers both are "*öreg*"—a simplification which reflects English usage.

REVERSING LANGUAGE SHIFT

When a language ceases to be transmitted to children, it is considered moribund and on the way to extinction unless intervention can stop the decline in its use. This process can be reversed; in Wales, bilingual schooling means that many children speak Welsh more fluently than their parents. Perceptions of the language's worth have shifted, and the decline has been reversed. In Brittany, on the other hand, no such policy supports Breton, whose status and rate of transmission to children are low. Welsh is now the only Celtic language whose future seems secure.

The will to reverse a language's shift is inevitably associated with the assertion of the distinct cultural identity of its speakers. Sometimes this involves the desire for greater political status or autonomy, as in the cases of

MINORITY LANGUAGES IN EUROPE

In an increasingly federal Europe, a new awareness of local languages and cultures has fueled campaigns to promote the use of minority languages, and even to revive extinct ones, for use alongside national languages.

1 Scots Gaelic: 88,000 speakers, mainly on Hebridean islands.

2 Manx: extinct in 1974, retrieved in the 1980s.

3 Irish: declining use in western counties. Known by 900,000, but used regularly by 120,000.

4 Welsh: widely taught in bilingual schools. 590,000 speakers.

5 Cornish: extinct in 19th century, revived in 20th century and now taught in a few schools.

6 Breton: 600,000 speakers but in daily use by only 250,000.

7 Occitan: descended from the Provençal of medieval poets. Spoken by 2 million in rural communities in southern France.

8 Gascon: a distinctive variety of Occitan with 250,000 speakers.

9 Catalan: 10.7 million speakers in eastern Spain and the Balearic islands. Now used in several universities.

10 Galician: some 2.5 million speakers in northwestern Spain. Now used in broadcast media, higher education, and in literature.

11 Basque: growing recognition, including university devoted to Basque studies, with teaching in Basque. 800,000 speakers.

12 Romantsch: Fourth language of Switzerland. 65,000 speakers.

13 Ladin: 35,000 speakers in four mountain valleys.

14 Friulan: 600,000 speakers, under strong Italian influence.

15 Istro-Rumanian: c.1000 speakers, mainly on Istrian peninsula in former Yugoslavia.

16 Arumanian: related to Romanian, spoken in northern Greece. Estimated 50,000 speakers.

17 Macedonian: Slavic language related to Bulgarian. Around 2 million speakers in south of former Yugoslavia and northern Greece.

18 Upper and Lower Sorbian: isolated Slavic languages surrounded by German-speaking territory, with fewer than 70,000 speakers.

19 Frisian: 20,000 speakers on islands off German coast; 700,000 speakers in Friesland, Netherlands. Losing ground to Dutch, despite bilingual education.

20 Faroese (not shown): relative of Icelandic, with 47,000 speakers.

21 Letzebuergisch: German dialect of Luxembourg; 335,000 speakers.

Right: *A signpost in both Welsh and English. Bilingual schooling in Wales has ensured that the future of the Welsh language is secure.*

Basque and Catalan in Spain, so that there are likely to be political aspects to the question. Some fear that the preservation of distinct identities will lead to discord. Others argue that speakers of a minority language would do better to shift to a major one; while this may be true in short-term material terms, the abandonment of a language on these grounds may be cause for regret in the longer term. These concerns can be countered by promoting bilingualism, which serves as a bridge to the dominant language and culture without abandoning the minority language.

Preservation of minority languages is linked to traditional lifestyles, and often to the preservation of the environment as well. According to a recent study, the Menomini of Minnesota, by using traditional methods to harvest mixed forests, practice the only truly sustainable timber industry in the United States. Such cases suggest an intimate connection between biological and linguistic diversity.

LANGUAGE REVIVAL

Just as plants and animal species can be preserved and recreated by preserving their DNA, the sounds, grammar, and vocabulary of languages can be stored on tape and disk for posterity and even for later resuscitation. Although there is room for question as to whether the recreated language would be the same following a break in its transmission to children, it can be done if the will is there.

REVIVING A DEAD LANGUAGE

Recent attempts to revive the Cornish language have confronted the problem of which variety to adopt. There are three options:

•**Unified Cornish**: Based on the medieval literature from the Middle Cornish period (1200–1500), most of which is in verse, this language was developed in the 1930s. This is rather like reconstructing Elizabethan English from the poetic language of a Shakespearean play. The language is felt to be unsystematic and dauntingly complex.
•**Modern Cornish**: Based on the most recent surviving documents from the eighteenth century. This variety shows some of the characteristic simplification of a dying language.
•**Common Cornish**: A recent compromise between the medieval and modern varieties.

Some enthusiasts are raising their children bilingually in English and a chosen variety of Cornish, which may result in convergence on a new standard. Today around 2,000 people can speak some Cornish. As with Welsh, widespread knowledge of Cornish may depend on its adoption in schools.

Above: *Cornwall, in the extreme southwest of England, is a rugged and remote area which for many centuries preserved a Celtic language and identity which was quite separate from the rest of England.*

The most successful case of revival has been that of Hebrew, driven by the reuniting of the Jewish people in Israel after World War I. The original language of much of the Old Testament, for centuries Hebrew was not spoken on a daily basis, but was kept alive by scholars and through use in worship. From the nineteenth century, Hebrew began to be spoken again in Palestine, in a movement led by Eliezer Ben-Yehuda (1858–1922), whose son became the first native speaker of Modern Hebrew. With the foundation of the state of Israel in 1948, Hebrew was taught in Israeli schools, and immigrants to Israel have since shifted to Hebrew, often at the expense of other languages of Jewish culture such as the Germanic Yiddish and the Romance Ladino.

Hebrew demonstrates that revival of a dead or moribund language is feasible. Recent efforts have sought to revive the moribund Occitan and Gascon in France, and even the extinct Manx and Cornish in Britain. These modest movements may suggest that in Europe, the tide is beginning to turn from centralization to regionalism.

The potential for revival is one motivation for studying endangered languages. Another is the light that each language may throw on the human language faculty. It is ironic that in linguistics the detailed study of a single language currently enjoys less prestige than theoretical pursuits and the study of language as a faculty: this focus may allow languages to disappear unnoticed, thereby making it impossible to answer questions about certain types of language. Languages with the object-subject-verb word order, for example, exist only in the ecologically threatened Amazon region. Much of the crucial documentation work has been done by missionaries engaged in Bible translation, coordinated by the Summer Institute of Linguistics.

Below: A London newspaper printed in Hebrew and English. Modern Hebrew revived by Eliezer Ben-Yehuda (1858–1922) is a successful example of the revival of a dead language. Hebrew is now taught in Israeli schools and also used in worship.

THE REVITALIZATION OF HAWAIIAN

A recent case of revival of a dying language has taken place in Hawaii. Hawaiian is a Polynesian language related to Tahitian and Maori, brought by seafaring settlers around 500 AD. When colonization by western powers began in the nineteenth century, missionaries introduced written Hawaiian, newspapers were established, and some oral literature was written down. Following the annexation of the islands as a state of the U.S.A. in 1898, however, Hawaiian was banned in schools and English rapidly took over, with Hawaiian Creole English developing as the common language of imported plantation workers.

Beginning in the 1960s, awareness that Polynesian language and culture were in danger of being forgotten led to conscious efforts toward revitalization. The local traditions of hula dancing, chanting, and song were revived. Songs in Hawaiian are widely heard in the media (see example below), a reminder to visitors that this is not just another state of the U.S.A. Hawaiian words even permeate the local English, in which words such as *aloha* "goodbye," *mahalo* "thank you," and *keiki* "child" are a mark of island identity even for those who do not speak Hawaiian. In 1978 Hawaiian was again acknowledged as an official language. Local initiatives set up schools where children could learn Hawaiian, with teachers who learned the language as adults from elderly speakers. The *Punana Leo*, "Language nests" provide an immersion programme in which young children learn through Hawaiian.

Unlike Hebrew and Cornish, Hawaiian was in continuous use as a spoken language, although down to barely 2000, mostly elderly, speakers at one point. While the motivation for the revival of Hebrew was strongly religious, in Hawaii the cultural traditions that go with the language, as well as a sense of righting former wrongs, have been instrumental in reversing the language's decline.

A Kona Hema `O Ka Lani (The King At South Kona)—Traditional

A Kona Hema `o ka lani	*At South Kona, the king*
Nânâ iâ Ka`awaloa	*Observes Ka`awaloa*
`Ike i ka la`ia `Ehu	*Knows the peace of `Ehu*
Ehuehu `oe e ka lani	*Majestic are you, o king*
Ka helena a`o Hawai`i	*Going to Hawai`i*
Mâlamalama na moku	*To take care of the districts*
Ahuwale nâ kualono	*In plain view of the mountaintops*
`Ike `ia ka pae `ôpua	*Seen are the cloud banks*
E kukû ana i ke kai	*At mid-tide on the sea*
I ke kai hâwanawana	*On the whispering sea*
`Ôlelo o Kawaihae	*Speaking of Kawaihae*
Hae ana e ka naulu	*Stirred by the sudden shower*
Ka makani hele uluulu	*The wind increases*
Kû ka e'a i ka moana	*The sea rises*
Ka moana o Mâhukona	*The sea of Mahukona*
Ka makani `Âpa`apa`a	*The wind named `Âpa`apa`a*
Le`i mai `o Kohala	*Crowded is Kohala*
I ka nuku na kânaka	*To the mouth with people*
Ha`¯na mai ka puana	*Tell the theme*
O ka lani Kaulilua	*The royal Kaulihua*

Left: *Local traditions such as hula dancing were revived in Hawaii in the 1960s as part of a conscious effort toward revitalization of the Hawaiian language and culture. The strong cultural traditions attached to the Hawaiian language have been instrumental in reversing its decline.*

Language extinction also has an impact on the study of the prehistory of languages and cultures. The question of whether the Tasmanian languages were related to the Papuan, Australian, or any other languages has become controversial, but we may never know the answer because so much of the Tasmanian language and culture were irretrievably lost within a few decades of the British conquest. As the indigenous languages of Taiwan die out, the history and affiliations of the Austronesian family may also be buried with them. As Samuel Johnson wrote: "I am always sorry when any language is lost, for language is the pedigree of nations."

LANGUAGE DIVERSITY IN THE MEDIA

The communications media have often been blamed for the spread of major languages at the expense of local ones. Television is especially guilty as minority language programming is rarely commercially viable. This need not be the case with all technological media, however. Radio programs in Ladin and Romantsch, for example, help to keep these Rhaeto-Romance languages in use for more than merely domestic purposes.

The Internet offers an increasingly affordable and accessible platform for language learning materials, debate on standardization, and promotion of minority language use. The Internet already hosts communications in such minority languages as Galician, Occitan, and Gascon in Europe, and even aboriginal languages of Australia. The World Wide Web has encouraged the use of languages which were previously not widely used in written form. The French-based creoles of Haiti and Mauritius, for example, have seen their status rise through use on the Internet and other media.

Non-governmental organizations concerned with language preservation such as the Foundation for Endangered Languages (www.ogmios.org) and Terralingua: Partnerships for Biological and Linguistic Diversity (www.terralingua.org) also have a strong presence.

Global communications media, which have been instrumental in spreading English and other dominant languages, may yet play a vital part in the preservation of endangered languages. Multimedia technology, able to store digitalized speech, song, and images in any desired combination, is far better suited to this task than the traditional book, while on-line dictionaries and "internet grammars" increasingly complement their print counterparts. If the twenty-first century sees a continued decline in linguistic diversity, the blame will not fall entirely on technology or on the media.

Glossary of terms

Acrophony The use of a pictogram or hieroglyph of an object phonetically to represent the initial syllable or sound of the word that denotes the object.
Affixes One or more sounds or syllables added to a word to modify its signification; a general term including prefixes, infixes, and suffixes.
Alphabet A phonetic writing system which consists of symbols (letters) representing individual consonant and vowel sounds (from the first two Greek letters *alpha, beta*).
Alveolar A sound formed by the tongue touching or near the alveolar ridge, just above and behind the upper front teeth.
Agglutination The formation of words by adding separate constituents, each with a distinct meaning.
Antonyms Words of opposite meaning.
Aspirate A consonant in which breath is released.
Augmentative suffix A suffix indicating bigness.
Bilabials Consonants formed by the use of both lips (English *p, b, m*).
Cartouche An oval or oblong figure used in Egyptian script for the name of a monarch.
Case One of the inflectional forms of a noun, pronoun, or adjective that indicate its grammatical relation to other words, as that of subject, object, attribute, and so on. For example, the six cases in Latin are: nominative (for subject), vocative (for address), accusative (for object), genitive (for possession), dative (for donation or attribution), and ablative (for external causation or removal). Other languages have more cases, especially locatives (denoting spatial relations). *See also* Ergative.
Continuant sounds Sounds which a speaker may prolong, like English *shhhh.*
Creoles New languages formed by children exposed to a pidgin or mixture of languages.
Cuneiform Writing system using wedge-shaped characters (e.g. Sumerian).
Demotic A simplified form of the hieratic writing used by the ancient Egyptians (literally, *of the common people*).
Dentals Consonants formed with the tip of the tongue against the front teeth (English *t, d, s, z*).
Determinatives Elements attached to words to distinguish meanings.
Diacritic A mark placed over, under, or through a letter to denote a modification of its sound value.
Diphthong A speech sound changing continuously from one vowel to another in the same syllable.
Dialects, dialectology Geographical variations within a language, and the study of them.
Diminutive suffix A suffix indicating smallness.
Discontinuous root A word root whose consonants do not occur next to one another (for example in Arabic).
Ejective A consonant produced by expulsion of air under pressure with the glottal passage closed.
Ergative A case system involving special forms for the subjects of transitive verbs.
Fricative A speech sound characterized by a frictional rustling of the emitted breath (English *f, z, th*).
Fusional language A language in which the affixes are merged with roots and may express more than one meaning.
Glottal stop A speech sound produced by closure of the glottis (the space between the vocal chords).
Glyph A carved figure or mark.
Gutturals Sounds formed in the throat.
Hieratic Writing in a simplified form of ancient Egyptian hieroglyphics used by priests.
Hieroglyphs, hieroglyphics A system of writing using mainly pictorial characters.
Homonym A word having the same pronunciation as another, but differing from it in origin, meaning, or spelling.
Homophones, homophony Words which sound alike but have different meanings.
Honorific A form of address conferring honor or respect.
Ideogram, ideograph A picture or symbol used in a writing system to represent a thing or an idea, but not the word or sound for it .
Incorporation A process whereby a word (usually a verb) forms a compound with its object and modifiers but retains its original function in the sentence.
Infix One or more sounds or syllables combined in the body of a word to modify its signification.
Inflections The changes of form which words undergo to mark distinctions of case, gender, number, tense, person, mood, voice.
Isoglosses Lines on a map which represent the dialectal divides between the domain of one word, form or pronunciation and that of another.
Isolates Languages for which no relationship with any other language can be demonstrated.
Isolating language A language wherein grammatical concepts are expressed by separate words which do not divide into smaller units.
Labials Consonants formed by the lips (English *b, p, m*)
Labiodental A sound formed with the lower lip and the upper teeth (English *f, v*).
Labial nasal A sound made by the joint use of the lips and the nasal passage (English *m*).
Labiovelar A sound formed with the lips rounded, narrowed or closed, and with the back of the tongue touching or near the velum (the soft palate).
Language family A set of languages which can be shown to derive from a common ancestor.
Language phylum A larger grouping encompassing several language families which are distantly related.
Language shift When speakers of one language adopt another.
Language typology The study of language types.
Language universals Statements which hold true for all languages.
Lateral velar affricate A rare sound produced at the back of the mouth (like *g*) but with the side of the tongue (like *l*).
Lingua franca A language used for commerce between peoples with different native languages.
Loan words Foreign words adapted and added to the vocabulary of a "borrowing" language.
Logograms, logographs Symbols used by a logographic system.
Logographic script Writing systems consisting of characters which represent words in their entirety rather than as their phonetic components.
Matres lectionis or "the mothers of reading." The consonantal characters of ancient Aramaic script.
Mixed languages Languages derived from two or more ancestors.
Morphemes The individually meaningful constituents of words.
Morphology The study of the structure of words and their components.
Modifier A word or word group which modifies another (for example English *this* and *that* as in *this/that book*).
Nominal prefix A prefix added to a noun.
Orthography A writing system, usually standardized.
Palatal A sound formed with the tongue near or touching the hard palate, in the roof of the mouth (English *y* as in *yield*).
Pharyngeal A sound formed in the pharynx (the part of the alimentary canal between the mouth and the esophagus), as found in Arabic.
Phoneme The smallest unit of speech that in any given language distinguishes one word from another (English *p* in *pin* and *b* in *bin*).
Phonetic, phonetics Of or pertaining to the voice, the science of speech sounds.
Phonetic complement A syllabic symbol which provides a phonetic clue to the correct reading of a logogram.
Phylum A group of languages related more remotely than those of a family.
Pictogram, pictograph A picture or hieroglyph used in a writing system to represent a thing or an idea.
Pidgins Simplified or hybrid forms of a language, used for restricted purposes such as trade between speakers of different languages.
Polyphones, polyphony Single logograms that have acquired two or more word-values.
Polysynthetic language A language in which, by incorporation, whole sentences can be expressed by a single compound word.
Predicate The word or words in a sentence or clause which express what is said of the subject.
Prefix One or more sounds added to the beginning of a word to modify its meaning or to indicate a grammatical change (e.g. *un-* in *unbreakable*).
Pronominal Pronoun-like.
Rebus A mode of expressing words and phrases by pictures of objects whose names resemble those words, or the syllables of which they are composed; or a puzzle made up of such representations.
Reduplication The doubling of a word or syllable.
Retroflex A speech sound produced by raising and bending back the tip of the tongue under the hard palate, as in an American English *r.*
Semantics The science of language meanings.
Stock A language family.
Substrate An underlying language structure, such as the influence of a language A on a language B when speakers of A adopt B.
Suffix One or more sounds or syllables added to the end of a word to modify its meaning or to indicate a grammatical category (e.g. *-s* in *trips*).
Syllabic script A writing system in which words are broken down and recorded syllabically by means of a set of symbols (the syllabary), each of which denotes a spoken syllable.
Syllable One or more speech sounds constituting an uninterrupted unit of utterance and forming either a whole word (*man*) or a division of a word (*A-mer-i-ca*); also, one or more letters representing a spoken syllable.
Syllabogram A symbol representing a syllable.
Synonyms Different words with the same meaning.
Tone languages Languages which use pitch to distinguish words. Lexical tone is used to distinguish words' meanings, grammatical tone is used to distinguish their grammatical functions.
Vowel harmony A rule that a word can contain only a certain type of vowel.

Bibliography

Introduction
Cavalli-Sfora, L.L., *Genes, Peoples and Languages*, North Point Press, NY, 2000.
Comrie, B. (ed.), *The World's Major Languages*, Routledge, London, and Oxford University Press, New York, 1987
Grimes, B. F. (ed.), *Ethnologue* (13th ed.), Summer Institute of Linguistics, Dallas, 1990.
Hawkins, J. A. and Gell-Mann, M. (eds.), *The Evolution of Human Languages* (Santa Fe Institute Studies in the Sciences of Complexity XI), Redwood City, Addison-Wesley, California, 1989
Lieberman, P., *The Biology and Evolution of Language*, Harvard University Press, Cambridge, Mass., 1984
Robins, R. H. and E. M. Uhlenbeck (eds.), *Endangered Languages*, Berg, Oxford 1991
Stringer, C. and Gamble C., *In Search of the Neanderthals*, Thames and Hudson, New York, 1993

Development and Spread of Languages
Asher, R. E. and Moseley, L., *Atlas of the World's Languages*, Routledge, 1994
Dtv-Atlas zur Deutschen Sprache, München, Deutscher Taschenbuch Verlag, 1978
Comrie, B., *Language Universals and Linguistic Typology*, Blackwell (Oxford, 1989)
Jeffers, R. J. and Lehiste, I., *Principles and Methods in Historical Linguistics*, (MIT Press, Cambridge, 1979)

Europe and Eurasia
Abondolo, D. (ed) *The Uralic Languages*, Routledge, London.
Ball, M. (ed.), *The Celtic Languages*, Routledge, London, 1994
Comrie, B., *Languages of the Soviet Union*, Cambridge University Press, 1981
Harris, M. and Vincent N.(eds.), *The Romance Languages*, Routledge, London, 1988
Miller, R. A., *Nihongo: In Defence of Japanese*, Athlone Press, London, 1986
Shibatani, M., *The Languages of Japan*, Cambridge University Press, 1990
Sohn, Ho-Min, *Korean*, Cambridge University Press, 1998

South and Southeast Asia
De Francis, J., *The Chinese Language: Fact and Fantasy*, Honolulu: University of Hawaii Press, Honolulu, 1984
Ramsey, S. R., *Languages of China*, Princeton University Press, 1987

Africa and the Middle East
Arnott, D. W., *The Noun and Verbal System of Fula*, Clarendon Press, Oxford, 1970
Bauer, L., *Introducing Linguistic Morphology*, Edinburgh University Press, 1988
Bleek, W. H., *Comparative Grammar of the Bantu Languages*, Juta, Cape Town, 1869
Doke, C. M., *A Comparative Study in Shona Phonetics*, University of the Witwatersrand

Press, Johannesburg, 1931
Encyclopedia Britannica. Nigeria
Fortune, G., *A Grammar of Shona: Notes from the Department of African Languages*: University of Rhodesia, 1969–94
Gary, J. O. and Gamal-Eldini S., *Cairene Egyptian Colloquial Arabic*, Lingua Descriptive Studies, Vol 6. North-Holland, Amsterdam, 1982
Guthrie, M., *Comparative Bantu* (4 vols), Gregg International Publishers, Farnborough, 1969–90
Hannon, *Shona Dictionary*, Salisbury, Rhodesia
Khalafallah, A. A., *A Descriptive Grammar of Sa'i:di Egyptian Colloquial Arabic*, Mouton, The Hague, 1969
McEvedy, C., *The Penguin Atlas of African History*, Viking-Penguin, London, 1980
McKie, R., *Genes Rock the Fossil Record*, Geographical Magazine, November 1992
Nancarrow, O. T., *A Grammar of Ndebele: Notes from the Department of African Languages*: University of Rhodesia 1969–74
Oxford Encyclopedia of Linguistics: African Languages (Oxford University Press)
Ruhlen, M., *A Guide to the World's Languages, Vol 1*, Stanford, California, 1991
Ruhlen, M., *The Origin of Language*, Wiley, New York, 1994
Spencer, A., *Morphological Theory*, Blackwell, Oxford, 1991
The Gospel in Many Tongues, British and Foreign Bible Society, London, 1965

Pacific
Bellwood, P., *Man's Conquest of the Pacific: The Prehistory of Southeast Asia and Oceania*, Oxford University Press, New York, 1979
Bellwood, P., *Prehistory of the Indo-Malaysian Archipelago*, Academic Press, Orlando, Fla., 1985
Bellwood, P., *The Polynesians: Prehistory of an Island People*, Thames and Hudson, London, 1987
Benedict, P., *Austro-Thai Language and Culture, With a Glossary of Roots*, HRAF Press, New Haven, 1975
Clark, R., "Austronesian Languages" in B. Comrie, (ed.) *The World's Major Languages*, Croom Helm, London, 1987
Dahl, O.C., *Malgache et Maanjaan*, Egede-Instituttet, Oslo, 1951
Duranti, A., *From Grammar to Politics: Linguistic Anthropology in a Western Samoan Village*, University of California Press, Berkeley, 1994
Dutton, T. and Tryon, D.T. (eds.), *Language Contact and Change in the Austronesian World*, Mouton de Gruyter, Berlin, 1994
Foley, W. A., *The Papuan Languages of New Guinea*, Cambridge University Press, Cambridge, 1986
Ochs, E., *Culture and Language Development: Language Acquisition and Language Socialization in a Samoan Village*, Cambridge University Press,

Cambridge–New York, 1988
Pawley, A., 1974, "Austronesian Languages" in *The New Encyclopedia Britannica, Macropaedia* (Vol. 2),15th ed. Encyclopedia Britannica Inc. Chicago
Wurm, S. A. and Shiro Hattori, *Language Atlas of the Pacific Area*, Canberra: Australian Academy of the Humanities, Canberra, 1981–84

Australia
Lonely Planet Australian Phrasebook, Lonely Planet Publications, 1994.
Horton, D. (ed.), *The Encyclopaedia of Aboriginal Australia*, Australian Institute of Aboriginal and Torres Strait Islander Studies, 1993
Thieberger, N. and McGregor, W. (eds.), *Macquarie Aboriginal Words*, The Macquarie Library, (Sydney), 1994

The Americas
Grimes B.F. (ed.), *Ethnologue Index*, 13th ed. Summer Institute of Linguistics, Dallas, Tex., 1996
Coe, M. D., *Breaking the Maya Code*. New York: Thames & Hudson, New York, 1992
Goossen, I. W., *Navajo Made Easier; A Course in Conversational Navajo*, Northland Press, Flagstaff, Ariz. 1979
Greenberg, J. H., *Language in the Americas*, Stanford University Press, Stanford, 1989
Langacker, R. W., *Fundamentals of Linguistic Analysis*, Harcourt Brace Jovanovich, New York, 1972
Pullum, G., *The Great Eskimo Vocabulary Hoax and Other Irreverent Essays on the Study of Language*, University of Chicago Press, Chicago, 1991
Sapir, E. & Swadesh, M., *Nootka Texts: Tales and Ethnological Narratives*, Linguistic Society of America, Philadelphia, 1939
Sapir, E., *The Collected Works of Edward Sapir*, Mouton de Gruyter, Berlin, 1987
Shopen, T., *Languages and their Status*, Winthrop Pub., Inc., Cambridge, Mass, 1979
Wolfart, H. and Carroll, C. & J. F., *Meet Cree: A Guide to the Cree Language*, 2nd ed., University of Alberta Press, Edmonton, 1981

Pidgins and Creoles
Bickerton, D., *Roots of Language*, Karoma, Ann Arbor, 1981
Crowley, T., *From Beach-la-mar to Bislama: The Emergence of a National Language in Vanuatu*, Clarendon Press, Oxford, 1990
Holm, J., *Pidgins and Creoles* (2 volumes), Cambridge University Press, 1989
Keesing, R. M., *Melanesian Pidgin and the Oceanic Substrate*, Stanford University Press, 1988
Mühlhäusler, P., *Pidgin and Creole Linguistics*, Blackwell, Oxford, 1986
Romaine, S., *Pidgin and Creole Languages*, Longman, London, 1988

Romaine, S. *Language, Education and Development: Urban and Rural Tok Pisin in Papua New Guinea*. Oxford University Press, 1992
Wurm, S. A. and Mühlhäusler, P. (eds.), *Handbook of Tok Pisin* (New Guinea Pidgin), Pacific Linguistics, Canberra, 1985

Writing Systems
Antonsen, E.H., "The Runes: The earliest Germanic Writing System," in Senner, pp. 137-158, 1989
Bellamy, J.A., "The Arabic Alphabet," in Senner, pp. 91-102, 1989
Bonfante, G. and Bonfante, L., *The Etruscan Language*, New York, 1983
Bonfante, L., "Etruscan" in Hooker, pp. 321-378, 1990
Bricker, V., *A Grammar of Mayan Inscriptions*, New Orleans, 1986
Chadwick, J., "Linear B," in Hooker, 1990
Cook, B.F., "Greek Inscriptions," in Hooker, pp. 259-319, 1990
Coulmas, F., *The Writing Systems of the World*, Oxford, 1989
Cross, F.M., "The Invention and Development of the Alphabet," in Senner, pp.77-90, 1989
Daniels, P., and Bright, W., *The World's Writing Systems*, Oxford, 1996
Davies, W.V., "Egyptian Hieroglyphs," in Hooker, pp. 75-135, 1990
Diringer, D., *The Alphabet*, 3rd ed, NY, 1968
Driver, G.R., *Semitic Writing*, London, 1976
Fischer, H.G., "The Origin of the Egyptian Hieroglyphs," in Sennner, pp. 59-76, 1989
Gelb, I. J., *A Study of Writing*, Chicago, 1963
Green, M.W., "Early Cuneiform," in Senner, pp. 43-57. 1989
Healey, J.F., "The Early Alphabet," in Hooker, pp. 197-257, 1990
Hooker, J.T. (introduction), *Reading the Past*, Berkeley and Los Angeles, 1990
Jeffery, L. H., *The Local Scripts of Archaic Greece*, Oxford, 1990
Keightley, D.N., "The Origins of Writing in China: Scripts and Cultural Contexts," in Senner, pp. 171-202, 1989
Lehmann, R.P.M., "Ogham: The Ancient Script of the Celts," in Senner, pp. 159-170, 1989
Lounsbury, F.G., "The Ancient Writing of Middle America," in Senner, 1989
Page, R. I., *Runes*, Berkeley and Los Angeles, 1987
Reeves, N., *The Complete Tutankhamun*, London, 1990
Sampson, G., *Writing Systems*, Stanford, 1985
Schmandt-Besserat, D., "Two Precursors of Writing: Plain and Complex Tokens," in Senner, pp. 27-41, 1989
Scott, D., Woodard, R., McCarter P., et al., "Two Ancient Greek Copper Plaques: Schøyen MS 108" in collaboration with David A. Scott, P. Kyle McCarter et al, in *Manuscripts in the Schøyen Collection* (MSC) vol. IV, Jens Braavig (Ed.), Oslo,

Hermes Publications, 2003.
Senner, W. (editor), *The Origins of Writing*, Lincoln, Nebraska, 1989
Stroud, R.S., "The Art of Writing in Ancient Greece," in Senner, 1989
Ventris, M. and Chadwick, J., *Documents in Mycenaean Greek*, 2nd edition, Cambridge, 1973
Wallace, R., "The Origins and Development of the Latin Alphabet," in Senner, pp. 121-135, 1989
Walker, C.B.F., "Cuneiform," in Hooker, pp. 15–73, 1990
Woodard, R., *Greek Writing From Knossos to Homer*, OUP, Oxford, 1997.
Woodard, R. (ed) *The Cambridge Encyclopedia of the World's Ancient Languages.*

Epilogue
Ball M., (ed.), *The Celtic Languages*, Routledge, London, 1995
Fishman, J., *Reversing Language Shift*, Multilingual Matters, Clevedon UK, 1991
Grenoble, L.A. & Whaley, L.J., *Endangered Languages: Current Issues and Future Prospects*, Cambridge, 1997
Nettle, D. & Romaine, S., *Vanishing Voices: the Extinct of the World's Languages*, Oxford University Press, 2000

Index

Page reference in *italics* indicate illustrations/maps and/or their captions. Page references in **bold** indicate sections other than main text.

A
Abaza 51
Abkhaz-Adyghean languages 50–52
Aboriginal languages 13, *20–1*, *110–11*, 110–14, 115,113–14, *122*
 and education 122–3
 and English 123, **123**
 grammar 115, 117–19
 kinship 18, 118–20
 oral culture 112, 120–2
acrophonic principle 171
Adamawan **79**, 80
Adnyamathanha 119
Adyghe 51
affixes 78, 87, 82, 205
 Niger-Congo languages 82–7, **83, 86, 87**
 see also prefixes; suffixes
Afghanistan 44, 45, 47
Africa 30, 74–89, *77*, 154, 156, 172, 76
Afrikaans 42, 158
Afro-Asiatic languages *20–1*, **38**, 74, 78–80, *77*, **78, 79, 81**, *82*
agglutinating languages 47, **48**, 51, **53**, 60
 Altaic languages 47–8
 Austronesian languages 95–6
 Far East languages 53–4

Kiwai languages **104**
 Nakh-Daghestanian languages 51
agreement markers 87–8, **137**
Ainu 18, *18*, 54, *54*
Akkadian 14, 167
akkadograms 178
Albanian 34, **35**, 38, 39, 44, 52; script 193
Aleutian 53
Algic languages 126, **128**
Algonquian languages 13, 24, 26, 126
alphabets *161*, 163
 Etruscan *185*, 187–8, 191, 207
 European (non-Latin) 188, 189, 190, 191–33, *191*
 Greek *183*, *184*, 193, 206–7
 Latin 43, 163, 188, 189, 189, 191, 193, 207
 Korean 55, *203*, 204
Altaic languages *20–1*, 38, **38**, *41*, 46–7, **47**, 49, **49**, *50*, 54, *66*
Americas 54, 126–39
Amerind languages *20–1*, 28, 29, 133
Anatolia 38, 172, 174, 178
Anatolian languages 38, **39**, 178
Angaataha 107
Anglo-Saxon 42; script *188*, 189
antonyms **158**
Arabic 39, 78–80, 95, 176
 script 176, *176*, 177
Aramaic script 174, 176, 177, 186, 193, 207
Arawak 158
Archi 51
Armenian 38, **39**, 44, 50, *192*
Aslian languages 62, *92*
Assamese *59*, 60
Assyro-Babylonian writing system 167, 168
Athabaskan 135
Australia 54, *99*, 100
 see also Aboriginal languages
Austric hypothesis 65, **65**
Austric languages *20–1*, 28
Austro-Asiatic languages *59*, 61, *62*, 68
Austronesian languages 54, *68*, **69**, 92, *92*, *94*, 156, 158, 217
 cognates in 93
 distribution of **94**, *97*
 Melanesia 101–2, *103*
 Polynesia 93–101
auxiliaries **40**
Avar 51, 52
Aymara 140
Azerbaijani 50
Aztec-Tanoan 126, **129**

B
Baba Malay **159**
Babylonian 167
Bai 67
Balkan languages 34, 35, 44
Baltic languages 38, *41*, **43**, 43–4, 45
Baluchi 45, *59*, 60
Bangladesh 58, 60
Bantu languages *76*, *79*, 80, **81**, 83–4, 95
Basque 20, 35, 38, 29, *41*, 44, **45**, 45, *212*
Batak script 198, *199*, 207
Be 62, 69

Belarusian 43
Bella Coola 138–9, **139**
Ben-Yehuda, Eliezer 215
Bengali *59*, 60, 194
Benue-Congo *77*, **79**, 80
Berber *77*, **78**, 138; script 177
Berbice Dutch *155*, 158, 159
Bhutan 60, 71
biconsonantal signs 168, **170**
Bihari *59*, 60
bilingualism 30–1, **30**, 34, 122, 140, 211, 214
bioprogram hypothesis 150, 151
Bislama 105, 146, **146**
Bolgar languages 47
borrowings 29, 30, 31–4, 64
 Aboriginal languages 112, 123, **123**
 Austronesian languages 95, 96
 see also loans
boustrophedon writing direction 206–7
Brahmi script 193–4, 195
Brahui *59*, 60
Brazil *132*, 140
Breton 38, 39, 211, *212*
Britain 42, 106
Broken 105, 114, 115, **146**, *147*
Buginese script 198, *198*
Bulgarian 34, **35**, 431, 191
Buriat 48, **49**
Burma *see* Myanmar
Burmese 61, 67; script 198
Burushaski *20*, 29, *59*, 60

C
Caddoan languages 134
Cambodia 61, 65; script 197, 198
 see also Khmer
Cameroon 30, 80
Canaanite dialect 171
Canada 13, 140, *141*
Cantonese 23, **30**, 34, 62, 68, 69, *70*, 71, 140, 211
Cape York Creole 114–15
Caribbean creoles 150, 151, 154, **155**, 156, **156**, 157, 158
Carthage 177
cartouches 168–9, *169*
case systems 43, 48, 60
 accusative 45
 Balkan languages 34, **35**
 ergative 45, 51, 53, **59**, 71, 98
 Hungarian 46, **46**
 Indo-European 28
 Nakh-Daghestanian languages 51–2
 Sanskrit **60**
 Uralic languages 46
Catalan 40, *212*, 214
Catawba 210
Caucasian languages *20–1*, 28, 38, 44, 45, 50–2, **51**, 53, 193
cave art *12*, *45*, *121*
CCV (consonant+vowel+consonant) symbols 182, 195
Celtic languages 14, 26, 38–9, **39**, *41*, 211; scripts *188*, 189
Central America 34, 126–7, **130**, *130*, 135, 140, 154
 see also Native American languages

Chamalal 51
Champollion, Jean-François **131**, 169
Chari-Nile languages 74, *77*
Chavacano 158, **158**
Chechen 51, *51*, 52, 193
Cherokee script 205, *206*
Chewa *82*
Chimbu languages 100
China 13, 47, 48, 62, 64, 65, *66*, 67, 71
Chinese 19, 24, **53**, *63*, 66, 67–71, *67*, 161
 in America 140, 211
 and borrowing 30, 55, 61
 dialects 23, 68–9, *70*
 grammar 22, 69–70
 writing systems 55, 61, 67, 68, 200–2, *200*, *201*, 207
Chiquihuitlan Mazatec **135**, 138
Chukchi 13, 53, **53**, 54
Chukotko-Kamchatkan languages *20–1*, *48*, 53, *53*
Chuvash 47, 193
Circassian 51
class system *see* noun classes
classification of languages 19–22, 34–5, 53
 Aboriginal 112–13
 Austronesian 92–3
 into family groups 19, *20–1*, 25–9, Native American 132, 133–5, **134**
classifiers *65*, **136, 137**
clay tablets 162, 163, *165*, 166
clay tokens 162–3, *162*
click sounds **76**
code-mixing **30**
cognates **93**
colonization 106, *107*, 113–14, 150–1, 191
compound characters 201
consonant clusters 43
consonant symbols (writing systems) *161* 168, **170**, 171, 172, *173*, 174, 176, 177, *183*, *184*, 185–6, 186
 see also matres lectionis; CCV; CV; CVC; VC symbols
consonantal scripts *161*, **170**, 171, 172, *172*, 174, 177, 197
consonants 22
 Abkhaz-Adyghean languages 51
 Aboriginal 117
 American languages 135
 Arabic 79
 Austronesian languages 95
 ejective 44
 Japanese 54
 retroflex 58
 Slavic languages 43–4
 soft 44
contact between languages 29–34
continuants 138–9
Copper Island Aleut 26, 53
Coptic script *190*, 191 207
Cornish 39, *212*, **214**
Costa Rican Creole 150, 151
Cree script 205, *207*
Creole languages 18, 22, 26, 112, 150–1
 Aboriginal 114–15
 European language based 143, 144,

152–3, 154, *155,* 156—8
grammar 26, 150, 151, 154, **156**, *157,* 159
origins 150, 151
semi-creoles 156, 158
vocabulary 26, 150, 151, 154, **156, 157, 158**
Crete 44, 178, 179, 186
Croatian 43
Crowley, Terry 114, 146
cuneiform scripts *163, 165,* 166, 168, 172, 178, 206
cursive scripts 169, *169,* 176, 178
CV (consonant+vowel) symbols 167, 172, *173,* 174, 179, 182, 195, *195,* 196, *197,* 199
CVC (consonant+vowel+consonant) symbols 167
Cypriot script 182, *182,* 185, 207
Cypro-Minoan scripts 182
Cyrillic script 40, 43, 44, 48, 51, 52, 191, *191, 193,* 207
Czech 43

D

Dalmatian 40
Damara 78
Danish 42
Dargwa 51, *51,* 52
dead languages 14–15, 18, 50, 210–11, 215, 217
demotic script, Egyptian 169, *169,* 191, 206
Dené-Caucasian hypothesis 52, **52**
determinatives 165–6, 167, 178, 201, 205
Devanagari script **60**, 194, *194,* 195–6, 197
dialects 22–3, 24–5
diacritic vowel points 174, 176, 177, 195, *198, 199*
diminutive suffixes 86, **86**
Ditinaht **136**
diversity of languages 12–15, 18–22, 210, 217
Diyari 112, 122
Dravidian languages *20–1,* 22, **38**, 58, **58**, *59,* 60–1
dual pronouns 102, 154
Dutch 22, 23, 25, 42, 108
and Creole languages 152–3, 154, 158
Dyirbal 13, 14, 211
Dzongkha 60, 71

E

Easter Island *91, 94,* 99
education 31
and Aboriginal languages 122–3
and Tok Pisin 149–50
Egyptian **78**, 167–9, 191; scripts 167–9, **168**, *169,* **170**, 206, 207
ejective consonants 44
Elamite 163, 167
Enga 100, *103*
English 19, 34
African-American 158
in the Americas 140, *141*
in Australia 122, 123, **123**
and Creole languages 152–3, 154, **154,** *155,* 159
and French 25, 29–30, *29,* 31

and German 25
in Hong Kong **30**, 34, 70
in India 60
an Indo-European language 25, **26**,42
loan words 31, 34
in Melanesia 107, 147
and Pidgin languages 145–6, 148–9, 149–50
in Singapore **71**
ergative languages 45, 51, 53, 71, 99–100
Eskimo-Aleut languages *20–1,* 26, 28, 53, **53, 128,** 133, **136,** 139
Estonian 35, **41,** 45–6
Estrangela script *177*
Ethiopic script 172, *173*
Etruscans *186,* 187
Eurasia 38–55, *48–9*
Europe 38–46, *41,* 178–93
European languages 35, *41*
in the Americas 140, *141*
and Creole languages 143, 144, *147,* 152–3, 154, 156–8
minority 39, 43, *212–3,* 217
see also Indo-European languages
Evans, Sir Arthur 178, 179, *181*
evolution of languages 11–12
extinction of languages 14–15, 18, 210–1, 217

F

families, language *see* classification of languages; *individual language groups*
Far East languages 48, 52–5
Faroese 43, *212*
Fijian 94, 98, *101*
Finnish 35, *41,* 42, 45, 46
Finno-Ugric languages 45–6 **46**, *48*
franglais 31
French 18, 39, 107
in Africa 30
in the Americas 140, *141*
and borrowing 31
and Creole languages *152–3,* 156, **156**
and English 25, 29–30, *29,* 31
Germanic substrate 34
noun classes 83
Frisian 42, *212*
Fulani 80, 81, 84–6, **86**
fusional languages **53**
futharks *188,* 189

G

Gaelic 34, 39, **136,** 140, *212*
gairaigo 55
Galician 40, *212,* 217
Gascon 45, *212,* 217
genders **40,** 84
genetic groups and languages 18, 29, 74, **75**
Georgian 50–1; script *192,* 193
German 22–4, 28, 40, **41,** 42, **42**
in the Americas 140
and English 23, 25
in Melanesia 107
noun classes 84
Germanic languages *25,* 26–8, 34, 38, **39,** 41, 42–3, **42**; scripts 189, *189*
Glagolitic script 191, 193

glottal stop 85, 95, 172
glyphs *see* hieroglyphic scripts; petroglyphs
Gothic 26–8, 42, 189; scripts *26,* 189
grammar 12–13, 22
Aboriginal languages **115,** 117–19
African languages 81–8
Altaic languages 47, **48**
Austronesian languages 95–6, 98–9
Caucasian languages 51–2
dying languages 211
Far East languages 53–4, **55**
Indo-European languages 39, **40, 42,** 43, 45
Melanesian languages 102, **104, 106**
Native American languages **136–7,** 134–5
Pidgin and Creole languages 26, 148, 150, 151, **156, 157,** 158, 159
Southeast Asian languages 58, **65**
Uralic languages 46, **46**
see also word-order
Greek 34, **35, 39**
ancient 28, 38, 44, 169
scripts 178, **180,** *181,* 182
Greenlandic **136**
Guaraní 131, **137**
Gujarati *59,* 60, 194
Gur *79,* 80
Gurmukhi script 194

H

Haitian *155,* 156, 217
Hakka dialect 65, **67,** 69
Hamtai 107
Han'gul script 55, *203,* 204
Haruai 100
Hattic 178
Hausa 74, 81
Hawaiian 95, **216**
Hebrew 14, 78, 174, 215; scripts 174, *175,* 176, 177
hieratic script, Egyptian 169
hieroglyphic scripts 178
Egyptian 167–9, **168,** *169,* 171, 206
Luvian 178, 207
Mayan *131,* 204–5, *205*
Hindi 18, *59,* 60, 195
hira-gana script 55, *202,* 204
Hiri Motu 105–6, **106, 146,** 149
Hittite 38, 178; scripts 178
Hixkaryana **137**
Hmong 61, *63,* 65; script 65
Hmong-Mien languages 24, *63,* 64–5, *69*
Hokan-Siouan languages 126, 129, 130
Hokkien **159**
homophones 148, 165, 167, 201
Hong Kong **30,** 34, 68, 69, *70,* 71, 140
honorifics 55, **55**
hui yi characters 202
Huichol 135
Hungarian 22, **26,** 35, *37,* **41,** 45, 46, 211
Hutterite sect 140

I

Iatmul 104
Icelandic 43
Ijo 158
inalienable possession **95,** 96

Incas 131
India 30, 35, 44, 58, *59,* 60, 61, 71, 95, 156, 196
Indic languages 22, 44, **44,** 45, 58–61, **58,** *59*; writing systems 61, 193–9
Indo-European languages 18–19, *20–1,* *25,* 35, 38–45, **38, 39,** *41,* **42, 43,** *49,* 50, *50,* 58
relationships between 25–6, *25,* **26, 39** and writing systems 178, 188
Indo-Iranian languages 39, 44, **44,** 58, *59*
Indonesia 92, *92,* 95, 156
inflectional languages 43, **53**
inflections 22, 26, **40**; *see also* case systems
Ingush 51, **51**
Internet 217
Inuit 53, **53**
Inuktittut 53
Iranian languages 44, **44,** 45, *59,* 60
Irian Jaya 106
Iroquoian 134, 137, **137**
Isle de France creole 156
isoglosses 24, **24**
isolating languages **53,** 58, 61, 69–70
Istro-Rumanian *212*
Italian 26, 39, **40,** *41,* 140
Italic languages 26, 39, **40,** 188

J

Jacaltec **136**
Jacobite script 177, *177*
Jamaican 154, 159
Japanese 19, 26, 47, 48, 54–5, 98
and Chinese 30, 61
scripts 202, *202,* 204
Javanese *92,* 99; script 198, *199*
Jiwarli 118, 119

K

Kabardian 51
Kalmyk 48
Kam-Sui languages 62, *63,* 64
kanji logograms 55, *202,* 204
Kannada *59*; script 195, *195*
Karanga dialect 82, 86
Karen languages 71
Kartvelian languages **38,** 45, 50–1, *50*
kata-kana script 55, *202,* 204
Kavi script 198
Kazakh 47
Kerek 530
Ket *49,* 52–3, **52**
Khalkha 48
Kharoshthi script 193, 194
Khmer 61, *63,* 198; script *197*
Khoekhoe 78
Khoisan languages *20–1,* 74, *76, 77,* 78
Khordofanian *77,* **79,** 80
Khutsuri script 193
Kickapoo 126, 127
kinship terms 25–6, **26,** 28
Aboriginal languages 118–20
African languages 89, **89**
Kiwai languages **104**
Korean 47, 48, 49, 54—5, 61
scripts 55, *203,* 204
Koryak 53
Kosovo, Serbia 44

Index

Kriol 115, 117, **146**
Kru English 151
Kufic script 176, *176*
Kunwinyku 117
Kurdish 45
Kutenai 134
Kwa languages **79**, 80, **81**

L

Ladin 23, *212*, 217
Lahu 71
Lak 51, 52
Lakhota Sioux 126, *126*
Lao *63*, 64; script *197*, 198
Lapita culture 93
Lapps 46
Latin 12, 14, 26, 28, 38, 39–40, 46, 188
Latvian 42, 43
Laz 50
Lemnian Stone 187–8
Lezgian 51, 52
Li 62, **66**, 69
ligatures 195, 196
Lihyanic script 172
Linear A script 179, **180**, *180*, 185
Linear B script **43**, 44, 179, *180*, *181*, 185, 207
lingua francas 60, 74, 146, 151, 174
  mission 104, *105*
Lisu 71
Lithuanian 42, 43, 140
loan words 31–4, 55, 58, 62, 188
  see also borrowings
logograms 165–6, 166, 167, 168, 178, 179, 204, 205
  Chinese 201–2, 204
  Egyptian 167, *170*
  Persian *166*, 167
  Sumerian 165–6, 167
Luvian 178, 179; script 178, 207
Lycian script *190*, 191

M

Macanese 159
Macedonian *212*
Madagascar 92, 93, 95, 101
Maisin 102, **102**
Malacca *149*, 157, 159
Malagasy 95, 96, 98
Malay 71, 92, *92*, **93**, 159
Malayalam *59*, 60, 195
Malaysia 62, 92, *92*, 95, 96, 156, 157
Manchu 48–50, 54
Mandarin 13, **53**, 61, **67**, 68–9, 70–1, 89
Mandé **79**, 80
Manipuri 71
Manx 14, 39, *212*
Maori 96, 98
Marathi *59*, 60
Mari 46
matres lectionis 174, 186
Mauritian Creole 151, **157**, 159, 217
Mayali 120
Mayan hieroglyphs **131**, 204–5, *205*
Mayan languages 126, **130**, *130*
Mazatec **138**
Melanesian pidgin 104–5, 107, 145–6,
Menomini 214

Meriam Mer 114
Mesopotamia 14, 162–7, *163*, 174
Mexico 126, 127, *130*
Miao 9, 64, 65, *66*
Min dialects 68, 69, 71
Mingrelian 50
Minoan civilization 44, 178, **180**
minority languages 31, 39, 43, 48, 62,
  64, *66*, 210, *212*, 214, 217
missionaries 104, 112, 145, 191
mixed languages 26, 52, 102, 151, **154**
Mkhedruli script 193
Moabite 174
modifiers 64, 87–8
Mohawk 134, **137**
Moldavian 40
Mon 61–2, *63*
Mon-Khmer languages 61–2, **62**, *63*, *66*
Mongolian 47, 48, **48**, 49, 54, 193
  scripts *203*, 204, 207
monoconsonantal signs 168, **170**
monolingualism 31, 211
moribund languages 14, 107, 210–1, 215
morphology *see* word-structure
Mosan languages **128**, 135, **136**, 138
Motu 98, 104, 105, **106**
Mozambique 80, 81
multilingualism 30–1, 102, 104, 110
Munda languages 58, *59*, 61, **62**
Mura-Pirahã 135
Myanmar (Burma) 62, *64*, 71
Mycenaeans 179, **180**, 181

N

Na-Dené languages 20–1, 28, 52, **128**,
  133, 135, **136**, 139
Nabatean Aramaic script 176, 179
Nabateans 176, *177*
Nahki script 176
Nahuatl 126
Nakh-Daghestanian languages 50, 51–2
Naskhi script 176
Native American languages 14, 126–31,
  128–9, *132*
  grammar 134–5, **136–7**
  origins 133
  vocabulary 138–40, **139**
  writing systems 204–5
Navajo 135, **136**
Ndau dialect 81
Ndebele **76**, *80*, 81, **83**, 84, 85, 87, 89, **89**
Ndjuka 154
Negerhollands creole *155*, 158
Nepali *59*, 60
Nestorian script 177, *177*
New Caledonia 99, 102, 106
New Guinea 13, *20*, 92, 93, 99, 102,
  103, 105, 106, 107, *107*
New Hebrides 104, 106–7, 146
Newari *59*, 60, 71
Niger-Congo languages 20–1, 74, *77*, 79,
  80–81
  grammar 81–8, **83**, **85**, **86**, **87**
  vocabulary 85, **89**
Nilo-Saharan languages 20–1, 74, 76
Nivkh 38, *49*, 52, 53
non-Pama-Nyungan languages *110*,
  112–13, 117, 118
North America 13, 34, 52, 126–7, *127*,

128–9, 140, 205
  see also Native American languages
Norse 34, 43
Norwegian 26, 27, **41**, 42, 85
Nostratic hypothesis 38, **38**, 74
noun classes 83–6, **83**, **85**, 87
noun classifiers 58, **65**
noun phrases 87–8
nouns 22
  Arabic 80
  Classical Mongolian **48**
  Mosan languages 135
  Slavic languages 43
  Tagalog **96**
numerals 25, 26, **26**, 27, *166*
Nuuchahnulth 13, 134, 135, 139–40, **139**

O

Occitan 39–40, *212*, 217
Oceania 93, 99
Ogham script *188*, 189
Oirat 48
Old Persian 167
Old Church Slavonic 26, 191; script *190*
open syllables 54, 95
Oriya script 194–5, *194*
Oroqen 48
Oscan alphabet *187*, 188, 190
Ossetic 45, 50
OSV (object-subject-verb) word-order
  19, 215
Oto-Manguean languages 126, **130**, 138
OVS (object-verb-subject) word-order
  19, **137**

P

Pacific Region 92–107, *94*, 150, 154
Pakistan 44, 45, 58, *59*, 60
palatized consonants 44, *202*
Palenquero *155*, 157, 159
Pama-Nyungan languages *110*, 112,
  114, 115
Papia Kristang *147*, 156, 157
Papiamentu 157, 159
Papua New Guinea 30, 99, 100–1, 104,
  107, 146, 149
Papuan languages 20–1, 98, 101,
  102–4, **103**, *103*
Pashto 45, *59*, 60
Pennsylvania Dutch 140
Penutian languages 126, **129**, **130**
Persian 44, 45; script *166*, 167
Peru 131, 140
petroglyphs *137*
Phaistos Disk 179, *179*
pharyngeals 78
Philippines 93, **96**, *97*, 98, **98**, 99, 158
Phoenician script 171, 174, *175*, 177,
  185, 186, 207
phonemes 100, **106**; *see also* sounds
phonetic complement 165, 168
phonetic scripts 163, 165, 171, *172*
phonetic symbols 165, 178
phonology *see* sounds
pictographic scripts 163, *163*, 165, 169,
  171, 174, 178–9, 200
Pidgin languages 22, 144–6, **144**, **146**,
  147, *152–3*

Aboriginal 112, 114–15
Melanesian 104–5, 107, 145–6, 148
  see also Creole languages; Hiro Motu;
    Tok Pisin
Pitcairn Island *147*, **145**
Police Motu 105, **106**
Polo, Marco 95, *95*
Polynesia 92, 93, *94*, 95–9
polyphony 165, 167
polysynthesis **53**, 54, 134–5
Porome **105**
Portuguese 19, 40, 140, *141*
  and Creole languages 151, *152–3*,
    154, 156–7, 158, 159
possession **95**, 96
predicates **96**
prefixes
  Aboriginal languages 112, 117
  American languages **136**
  Japanese 54
  Niger-Congo languages **79**, *79*, 83–4,
    83, **84**, **85**
pronominal suffixes 96
pronouns 25, 28, 34
  Aboriginal languages 117, 119
  American languages 133
  Austronesian first person 96
  Baba Malay **159**
  dual 102, 117, 154
  male and female 89
  Pidgin languages 148
Proto-Canaanite script 171–2, 174, 207
proto-languages 9, 26–9, **65**, 93, **93**,
  112–13, 133
Proto-Siniatic script 171, *171*
Punic script 177
Punjabi *59*, 60
Pyrenees 38, 45

Q

Québec 26, 10, *141*
Quechuan languages 131, *132*, 140

R

Rapanui 99
rebus principle **131**, 165, 201, 204
reconstructions *see* proto-languages
reduplication 22, 96, 158
religion and language 23, 61, 95, 176,
  189, 191
retroflex consonants 58, 117
revival of languages 14, 211, **216**, 217
Rhaeto-Romance languages 23, 39, 217
romaji script *202*, 204
Romance languages 23, *25*, 39–40, **40**,
  39, 41
Romanian 26, 34, **35**, 39, 40
Romantsch 23, *212*, 217
Romany *44*, 45
rongorongo script 99, *100*
roots, word 28, 78–80, 135, 168
Rosetta Stone *168*, 169
Rotokas 100, **106**
runic scripts *188*, 189
Russenorsk 144
Russian 18, 24, **26**, 43, 44, 53, 140
  script *see* Cyrillic script
Ryukyuan 54

S

Saami **41**, 46
Safaitic script 172
Saharan languages 74, *77*
Salish languages **138**, 134
Samaritan script 174, *175*
Samoa 193, 98, 146
Samoan *94*, 96
Samoyedic languages 46, **46**, 48
Sanskrit *25*, 26, 28, 38, 45, 60, **60**, 195
   loan words 61
Santali *59*, 61
Sapir, Edward *127*, 135, 210
Saramaccan 154
Scots Gaelic 39, *212*
secondary affixes 86, *87*
Sejong, King 55, 204
Selvon, Samuel 154
semantic tags 201, 205
semantics 139, **148**
Semitic languages *77*, **78**, 168, 171,
   172, 174, 176
   writing systems 80, **170**, 193
Sepik **102**, 104, 149
Sequoya (a Cherokee) *161*, 205
Serbian 43, 191
Serbo-Croatian 42
serial verbs 154
Shan 62, *63*
Shanghainese 68, *70*
She 64–5, 67
shift, language 30, 34, 49, 62, 210–11, 214
Shona 80–1, 81–3, 86, **87**, 89, **89**
Siberia 38, 45, 46, 47, 48, 52, *52*
sign languages 22, **121**, 189
Sindhi *59*, 60
Singapore **71**, 159
Sinhalese *59*, 61; script 195, *196*
Sinicization 65
Sinitic languages *63*, **67**; *see also* Chinese
Sino-Tibetan languages *20–1*, 28, 52,
   59, 62, 67–71, **67**, 68
slave trade 144, *144*, 150, 151, *152–3*, *155*
Slavic alphabet *see* Cyrillic
Slavic languages 26, 38, 39, *41*, 42, 43–5
Slovakia 43, 46, 193
Slovenian 43
social groups
   Aborigines 119–20
   Austronesia 99
Solomon Islands 99, 100, 102, 104, 106,
   107, 145, *145*, 146
Solomons Pijin 105, **146**
Songhai 74, *77*
songs
   Aboriginal 112, 120–1
   Sega **157**
Sorbian, Upper and Lower 43, *212*
sounds *11*, 29; *see also* tone
   Aboriginal languages 117
   Arabic 78
   click in African languages **76**
   Melanesian languages 100
   Native American languages 135
   retroflex 58, 117
   Rotokas **106**
South America 126, 131, *132*, 135, **137**, 140
   see also Native American languages

South Arabian script 172, 174
South Asia 45, 58—61, *59*
Southeast Asia 24, 26, 34, 58, 61–5, *63*,
   67, 69
SOV (subject-object-verb) word-order
   19, 156
   Austronesian languages 98
   Eurasian languages 22, 47, 48, 49,
     54–5, 55
   Melanesian languages 100, 102
   Native American languages **136**
   South Asian languages 58, *59*
   Southeast Asian languages 71
Spanish 39
   in the Americas 34, 127, 131, 140, *141*
   and Creole languages *152–3*, *155*, 157–8
spatial relationships 46, **46**, 51–2
Sranan 154, *155*
Sri Lanka 58, 61, 156, 195
stories, Aboriginal 112, **119**, 120–2
styluses 162, 166, *167*
substrates 34, 151
suffixes
   Aboriginal languages 112, **115**, 117, 118
   American languages 134, **136**
   Austronesian pronominal 96
   Balkan definite article 34, *35*
   Hungarian spatial relationship 46
   Nakh-Daghestanian languages 51–2
   Niger-Congo languages 84–5, **85**
   Uralic vowel harmony 46
Sumerian 14, 167; script 163, *163, 164*,
   165–7, 176, 206
Summer Institute of Linguistics 100,
   104, 107, 215
supplemental characters 186–7
Surinam 154, *155*
Susuami 107
Svan 50
SVO (subject-verb-object) word-order
   19, **40**, 98, 102, **137**, 151
   Southeast Asia languages 61, 64–7, 71
Swahili 15, 74, 80, 81, *82*
Swedish 42, **42**
Switzerland 23, 25, 30
syllabaries
   Cypriot 182, *182*, 185–6
   Ethiopic 172, *173*, 174
   Indic languages 195–6, 198
   Japanese 55, *202*, 204
   Linear B 179
   Native American 204–5, *206*
   Persian *166*, 167
syllables 165; open 54, 97
syllabograms 165, 167, 178, 179
Syriac script 177, *177*

T

Tabassaran 51, 52
taboos, word 18, 101
Tagalog **93**, **96**, *97*, 98, 158
Tai-Kadai languages 62–4, *63*, **64**, 65, *66*
Taiwan 54, 68, *68*, 92, 93, 217
Tajik 45
Tamil 58, 59–60, *59*, 60, 61, **71**; script 195
Tanzania 15, 81
Tasmanian languages 112, 113–14, 217
Tay Boy *147*

Telugu *59*, 60; script 195
Tepehua 127
Thai 61, 62, *63*, 64, **65**; script 64, 198, *198*
Thamudic script 172
Tiberian script 176
Tibetan *57*, 67, **67**, 71, 198; script 61, 196
   196, 197, 198
Tibeto-Burman languages 58, *59*, 60, *63*,
   66, 67, 71
Tifinagh script 177, *178*
Tillamook 134
Tocharian 38, **39**
Tok Pisin 105, 106, 107, 144, **146**, 148–150
tone; *see also* sounds
   American languages 135, **135**, 138, **138**
   Baltic languages 43
   Chinese 19, 70–1
   Chiquihuitlan Mazatec 138
   Niger-Congo languages 81–3
   Southeast Asian languages 34, 58, 61,
     62, 64, 65
   Swedish 42
   and writing systems 198
Torres Strait 99, 105, 112, 114, 115, **146**
Totonac languages 129
trade languages 104, 144, 146
Trans-New Guinea Phylum **103**
transitive verbs **45**
triconsonantal signs 168, **170**
Tsakhur 51
Tsez 51–2
Tungusic languages 47, **47**, 48–9, *49*, 50
Turkic languages 45, **46**, *48*, 50, *61*, 204;
   runic script 204
Turkish *41*, 44
typology 19, **53**

U

Ubykh 18, **50**, 51
Udi 52
Udyghe 48
Ugarit 171, 182
Ugaritic script 171–2, *172*
Uighur 47, **49**; script 49, 204
Ukrainian 43, 191
Umbrian alphabet *187*, 188
Ural-Altaic 28
Uralic languages **41**, 45–6, **46**
Urdu *59*, 60
Uruk, Sumeria 162, *163*
USA 140; *see also* North America

V

V (vowel) symbols 167, 179, 182, 195,
   195, 196, 199
Vanuatu 99, 100, 102, 105, 107, 146, 150
VC (vowel+consonant) symbols 167, 168
verbs 19, 22, 78–9
   Aboriginal languages 117–18, **118**
   Arabic 78–9
   Balkan languages 34
   Bantu 82, 87
   Basque 45
   Creole languages 151, 154
   English and Latin compared 12
   Kiwai languages **104**
   Mosan languages 135
   Slavic languages 43

   see also case systems; OSV; OVS;
     SOV; SVO; VOS; VSO word-order
Vietnamese **53**, 61, *63*
vocabulary 13, 22, 25, 28
   Aboriginal languages 18, 118
   Austronesian languages 95, 99
   Creole languages 150, 154, *155*, **156**,
     157, 158, **158**
   dying languages 211
   Native American languages 13,
     133–4, 139, **139**
   see also borrowings; loan words
VOS (verb-object-subject) word-order
   19, 98
vowel harmony 46, 47, 49–50
vowel points, diacritic 174, 176, 177,
   195, *198*, *199*
vowel symbols (writing systems) **161**,
   167, 168, 177, *183*, 189, 195
   see also CCV; V; CVC; V; VC symbols
   Abkhaz-Adyghean languages 51
   Afro-Asiatic vowel changes 78
   American languages 135, 138
   Austronesian languages 95
VSO (verb-subject-object) word-order
   19, **23**, 39, 98, **136**, **137**

W

Wakashan languages 13, **128**
Welsh 38, *38*, 39, **136**, 211, *212*
West Semitic languages 171, 174
whistled speech *138*
word-endings *see* suffixes
word-order 13, 19, **19**, 22,
   Aboriginal languages 112, 117
   Germanic languages **42**
   Native American languages **136–7**
   see also OSV; OVS; SOV; SVO; VOS; VSO
     word-order
word-structure **53**
   Egyptian 168
   incorporation 53–4
   Native American languages 134–5
   see also agglutinating languages;
     isolating languages
word roots 28, 78–80, 135, 168

X

Xhosa 81
xi-sheng characters 202

Y

Yahi 210
Yakut 47
Yao 62, *66*, 69
Yaqui 126
Yeniseyan languages 52, *52*
Yi languages 67, 71
Yiddish 42, 140
Yimas 104
Yue dialect *67*, 69
Yukaghir 46, **46**, *49*, 52; writing *47*
Yupik 53

Z

Zezuru dialect 80, 81
Zhuang 62, *63*, *64*
Zulu **76**, 80, 81

Consultant Editors

Bernard Comrie is Director of the Department of Linguistics of the Max Planck Institute for Evolutionary Anthropology, Leipzig. He is also Honorary Professor of Linguistics at the University of Leipzig and part-time Distinguished Professor of Linguistics at the University of California, Santa Barbara. He is author of *Language Universals and Linguistic Typology* (Oxford/Chicago, 1981, 1989), *Languages of the Soviet Union* (Cambridge, 1981), *Tense* (Cambridge, 1985), and *The Russian Language in the Twentieth Century* (with Gerald Stone and Maria Polinsky, Oxford, 1996). He is editor of *The World's Major Languages* (Oxford/New York, 1987), *The Slavonic Languages* (with Greville G. Corbett, London, 1993), *Causatives and Transitivity* (with Maria Polinsky, Amsterdam, 1993), and *Approaches to the Typology of Word Classes* (with Petra Vogel, Berlin, 2000), and managing editor of the journal *Studies in Language*.

Stephen Matthews studied modern languages at Cambridge University and subsequently gained a Ph.D. in linguistics at the University of Southern California. He is Associate Professor in Linguistics at the University of Hong Kong persuing research on Chinese dialects and southeast Asian languages, language contact, and bilingualism. He has served as president of the Linguistic Society of Hong Kong and coauthored *Cantonese: A Comprehensive Grammar* with his wife Virginia Yip.

Maria Polinsky received her Ph.D. in Linguistics at the Institute for Linguistics, Russian Academy of Sciences. She is currently Professor of Linguistics at the University of California, San Diego. She co-edited *Causatives and Transitivity* (Amsterdam, John Benjamins, 1993) and *Explanation in Linguistic Theory* (Stanford, CSLI, 2003), wrote *The grammar of Niue* (Moscow, Nauka, 1992), and co-authored *The Russian language in the Twentieth century* (with B. Comrie and G. Stone; Oxford, OUP, 1996). She has published extensively on some of the little-described languages of the world (Chukchi, Kinyarwanda, Tsez, Malagasy). Her articles have appeared in a number of journals including *Folia Linguistica*, *Studies in Language*, and *Theoretical Linguistics*.

Contributors

Peter K. Austin is Hans and Lisbet Rausing Professor at London's School of Oriental and African Studies, where he has special responsibility for research on endangered languages. He is past President of the Australian Linguistic Society. He is author of seven bilingual dictionaries and co-author of the first fully hypertext bilingual dictionary on the Internet. He is also currently working on Sasak and Samawa, Austronesian languages of eastern Indonesia, in an international collaborative project with scholars in Indonesia, Japan, Germany, and Australia. His theoretical research is in morphosyntax and typology.

Owen Nancarrow lectures in Linguistics at the University of Hong Kong. Previously he taught in the Department of African Languages at the University of Rhodesia, pursuing research on Ndebele and other Bantu languages.

Geoff P. Smith lectures in English and Applied Linguistics at the English Centre at the University of Hong Kong. Previously he worked at the Papua New Guinea Institute of Technology, pursuing Ph.D. research on Tok Pisin. His research interests include language contact and change, and the acquisition of lexical tone. He is author of *Growing up with Tok Pisin: Contact, creolization, and change in Papua New Guinea's national language* (Battlebridge, London, 2002).

John Stonham is Senior Lecturer in Linguistics at the University of Newcastle upon Tyne. He received his Ph.D. from Stanford University and has taught at the universities of Maryland, Ottawa, and Hong Kong. He specialises in phonology, morphology, and the structure of native American languages such as Nuuchahnulth, as well as Sinhala and Cantonese. His books include *Combinatorial Morphology*, *Linguistic Theory and Complex Words*, and *A Nuuchahnulth Dictionary*.

Roger Woodard is Andrew V.V.Raymond Professor of the Classics at the University of Buffalo (The State University of New York). He is author of several works, including *Greek Writing from Knossos to Homer* (Oxford University Press, 1997), and editor of the *Cambridge Encyclopedia of the World's Ancient Languages* (Cambridge University Press, 2003).

Acknowledgments

Key: a above; b below; c center; l left; r right

Image Bank 2-3, 6, 7 & 9; Karl Ammann/Ace 10; Image Select/Ann Ronan 12-13; Fortean Picture Library 14; L Le Plante/Panos 15; C M Dixon 17; Japan National Tourist Organisation 18; Jay Freis/Image Bank 22; La Belle Aurore 23; from the collection of George Stern, courtesy of Michael Nicholson 25; AKG Photo 26; ET Archive 29; Image Bank 31; ET Archive 34; AA Picture Library 37 & 38; Mansell Collection 39 & 40; Pictor 42; C M Dixon 43; Peter Barker/Panos 44; Jon Spaull/Axiom 51a & J C Tordai/Panos 51b; Chris Rennie/Art Directors 52; Topham Picturepoint 54; Alexander Kuznetsov/Art Directors & Trip 55; Pictor 57; John Readon/Rex Features 58b, from the collection of George Stern, courtesy of Michael Nicholson 60; Andrew Conway/Ace 61a & Image Bank 61b; Moira Clinch 62; AnneRippy/Image Bank 64 ; Image Bank 65; Alain Le Garsmeur/Panos 67; Nigel Hicks/Ace 69; Alain Le Garsmeur/Panos 70; Pictor 73; Adrian Boot/Retna 76; Sean Sprague/ Panos 79; Topham Picturepoint 80; Trygve Bolstad/Panos 82; Powerstock 85, Betty Press/Panos 86; Jeremy Hartley/ Panos 88ab; M Coyne/Image Bank 91;Ben Simmons/Ace 98; David Horwell 100; Jeff Gutekunst 101; Geoff Smith 104; La Belle Aurore 109; AKG Photo 112; Topham/Fotomas 113; Penny Tweedie/Panos 114; Linda Freeman 116-117r; Pictor 119; John Miles/Panos 121; Retna 124&125; P & M Walton/Ace 125; Ben Glass/Orion Pictures 126; Peter Newark Pictures 137; Fotopic/Ace 138; Northwind Picture Archives 139; Solvang Conference & Visitors Center, USA 141; Ben Simmons/Ace 143; Tim Motion 144; ET Archive 145a & Pictor 145b; Geoff Smith 150; G A Rossi/Image Bank 151; Mansell Collection 154; Antiquarian Images 156; Guido Rossi/Image Bank 158; Andrew Driver/Ace 159; Peter Newark Pictures 161; Oriental Institute, Chicago 162; Visual Arts Library 164a & Spectrum 164b; ET Archive 165b, 166b, 168ab, 169b & b & C M Dixon 169a; Hulton-Getty 172; C M Dixon 175, 176, 177, 179 & 181; ET Archive 184; Lesley & Roy Adkins 185; Italian State Tourist Board 186; ET Archive 189; C M Dixon 192; Neil Cooper/Panos 193 & 194; ET Archive 201; Japan National Tourist Org 202; Ann Ronan at Image Select 205; The Times/Rex Features 209; Richard Brook/Ace 210; Rafael Macia/ Ace 211; TRIP/A.M. Bazalik 212; Pictor 214; TRIP/H. Rogers 215; TRIP/A. Tovy 217.

All other photographs are the copyright of Quarto Inc.

Every effort has been made to acknowledge copyright holders. Quarto would like to apologize should any omissions have been made.

Quarto would like to credit the following for allowing us to reproduce or adapt copyright material:
p94 table adapted from Clark, R. "Austronesian Languages" in Bright, W., (ed.) *Encyclopedia of Languages and Linguistics*, vol. 1, Oxford University Press, New York, 1992; p170 mono- bi- and triconsonantal figures reproduced from Hooker, J. T., *Reading the Past: Ancient Writing from Cuneiform to the Alphabet*, University of California, Berkeley, 1990. Copyright © 1990 Trustees of the British Museum; p180 (left) reproduced from *Recueil des inscriptions en lineaire A*, vol 5, pXXII, Ecole Française d'Athenes; p183 adapted from p244, J. Hooker, *Reading the Past*, University of California Press, 1990; p200 (top) adapted from a table in *The Origins of Writing*, edited by Wayne M. Senner, by permission of the University of Nebraska Press, copyright © 1989 by the University of Nebraska Press; p200 (bottom) adapted from Cambell, G., *Compendium of the World's Languages*, Routledge, 1991; p205 adapted from Coe, Michael D., *Breaking the Code*, Thames and Hudson, 1992.